Comparing Learning Outcomes

Comparing Learning Outcomes provides an insider's look at the policy and practical issues in conducting and using the information from international assessments of education and is a key resource for researchers and policy makers in education.

This book covers a variety of important topics related to international comparative assesssment, including:

- history of international assessment, the factors contributing to its growth and the impacts of such growth
- what it means to assess different domains
- how information from international assessments has been used by policy makers in different countries
- technical considerations in analysing and using assessment data.

Reflecting the increasing involvement of policy makers in the field of international education assessment, *Comparing Learning Outcomes* brings together the research and experience of professionals in twelve countries who are part of a long-standing collaborative OECD project that gathers cross-national, comparative information on education for use by governments.

Jay H. Moskowitz is Vice-President and Director of the Education and Human Development Program at the American Institutes for Research where **Maria Stephens** is Research Analyst.

Comparing Learning Outcomes

International assessments and education policy

Edited by
Jay H. Moskowitz
Maria Stephens

American Institutes for Research

 RoutledgeFalmer
Taylor & Francis Group

LONDON AND NEW YORK

First published 2004 by RoutledgeFalmer

11 New Fetter Lane, London EC4P 4EE

Simultaneously published in the USA and Canada
by RoutledgeFalmer
29 West 35th Street, New York, NY 10001

RoutledgeFalmer is an imprint of the Taylor & Francis Group

Typeset in Sabon by Hardlines Ltd, Charlbury, Oxford
Printed and bound in Great Britain by Antony Rowe Ltd,
Chippenham, Wiltshire

British Library Cataloging in Publication Data
A catalogue record for this book is available
from the British Library

Library of Congress Cataloging in Publication Data
  Comparing learning outcomes : international assessment
  and education policy / [edited by] Jay H. Moskowitz and
  Maria Stephens.

p. cm.

Includes bibliographical references.

ISBN 0-415-30419-9 (hard : alk. paper)

1. Educational evaluation–Cross-cultural studies.
2. Academic achievement–Evaluation–Cross-cultural studies.
3. Educational indicators–Cross-cultural studies.
4. Education and state–Cross-cultural studies. I. Moskowitz,
Jay H., 1946– II. Stephens, Maria, 1972-
LB2822.75.C64 2004
379.1'58–dc22
2003021709

ISBN 0-415-30419-9

Contents

List of illustrations

List of tables

List of boxes

List of acronyms and abbreviations

ALL   Adult Literacy and Lifeskills (Study)
BIB   Balanced incomplete block
CivEd   Civic Education (Study)
CMEC   Council of Ministers of Education, Canada
COMPED   Computers in Education (Study)
CRESST   Centre for Research on Evaluation, Standards
           and Student Testing
DeSeCo   Definition and Selection of Competencies
           (Project)
EAG   *Education at a Glance*
EPA   Education Policy Analysis
ETS   Educational Testing Service
FIMS   First International Mathematics Study
FRS   Functional Reading Study
IALS   International Adult Literacy Study
ICT   Information communication technology
IAEP   International Assessment of Educational Progress
IEA   International Association for the Evaluation of
           Educational Achievement
IMST   Innovations in Mathematics and Science
           Teaching (Project)
INES   International Indicators of Education Systems
           (Project)
IRT   Item response theory
ISCED   International Standard Classification of
           Education
LSUDA   Literacy Skills Used in Daily Activities
NAEP   National Assessment of Educational Progress
NALS   National Adult Literacy Survey
NCES   National Centre for Education Statistics
NEMP   National Education Monitoring Progamme

OECD	Organisation for Economic Co-operation and Development
PCEIP	Pan-Canadian Education Indicators Programme
PIRLS	Progress in Reading Literacy Study
PISA	Programme for International Student Assessment
RLS	Reading Literacy Study
SAIP	School Achievement Indicators Programme
SES	Socio-economic status
SIALS	Second International Adult Literacy Study
SIB	Statistical index bias
SIMS	Second International Mathematics Study
SISS	Second International Science Study
SITES	Second International Technology in Education Study
SOLO	Structure of observed learning outcomes (taxonomy)
TIMSS	Trends in International Mathematics and Science Study (formerly Third International Mathematics and Science Study)
UNESCO	United Nations Educational, Scientific and Cultural Organisation
YALS	Young Adult Literacy Survey

Contributors

Roel J. Bosker University of Groningen, Netherlands

Guillermo Gil National Institute of Educational Evaluation and Quality, Spain

Douglas Hodgkinson Council of Ministers of Education, Canada

Helga Jungwirth Interuniversity Institute of Interdisciplinary Research and Continuing Education, Austria

Eckhard Klieme German Institute of International Educational Research

Konrad Krainer Interuniversity Institute of Interdisciplinary Research and Continuing Education, Austria

Dominique Lafontaine University of Liège, Belgium

Kimmo Leimu University of Jyväskylä, Finland

Steve May Ministry of Education, New Zealand

Jay H. Moskowitz American Institutes for Research, United States

T. Scott Murray Statistics Canada

Eugene H. Owen National Centre for Education Statistics, United States

Jules L. Peschar University of Groningen, Netherlands

Friedrich Plank (retired) Federal Ministry of Education, Austria

Tom A.B. Snijders University of Groningen, Netherlands

Arnold A.J. Spee (retired) Ministry of Education, Culture and Science, Netherlands

Helga Stadler Interuniversity Institute of Interdisciplinary Research and Continuing Education, Austria

Maria Stephens American Institutes for Research, United States

Anita Wester National Education Agency (Skolverket), Sweden

Lynne Whitney Ministry of Education, New Zealand

Acknowledgements

We would like to express our gratitude to our colleagues in the OECD INES Project, past and present, whose collective intellectual contributions have made the project the successful endeavour that it is today and the starting point for this volume. In particular we thank Eugene H. Owen of the US National Center for Education Statistics (NCES) for his vision and leadership of INES Network A, in measuring learning outcomes, for nearly a decade. We also thank him and Valeno Plisko White, also of NCES, for their support for the production of this volume. From the OECD we would like to acknowledge Andreas Schleicher, Head of the Indicators and Analysis Division of the Education Directorate, for his tireless efforts and invaluable leadership in overseeing the implementation of PISA. Special thanks are due to the authors and sponsors of chapters for their contributions and their patience in seeing this book to fruition, and to many INES Network A members for their comments and support throughout the process. Finally we would like to thank those individuals at American Institutes for Research who assisted in preparing the book: Ellie Abrams for copy editing, Sterlina D. Harper for preparing the manuscript and Tracy Gray for her editorial contributions.

Jay H. Moskowitz
Maria Stephens

Introduction

Over the past ten years there has been a tremendous growth in countries' use of and participation in international assessments to obtain information on student performance and adult skills. Although many factors have contributed to this rise, one of the primary factors is the increasing interest of policy makers to have information on what students and citizens know and can do and to use such information to make improvements in education and training systems, which is widely acknowledged as ever more vital for competing in the global economy. This volume reviews key features in the development of international assessment and reflects on some of important conceptual, technical and practical issues related to assessment in the future. The volume documents the shift in international assessment from a field that focuses primarily on research to one that includes a policy perspective as well.

The ten chapters were produced as a collaborative effort by a group of countries that have been working together for over ten years in an OECD project that collects and publishes cross-national comparative information on education for use by governments: Network A of the Indicators of Education Systems (INES) Project. INES Network A focuses on reporting, generating and improving the collection of information on the knowledge and skills of students and adults in OECD countries. Their efforts to develop a strategy for collecting information on student performance resulted in the implementation of the Programme for International Student Assessment (PISA), and the group continues to conduct development work to improve the utility of assessment data. This volume marks a turning point in its work, with the successful implementation of PISA, and it covers the rise of international assessments, assessment practice in traditional and non-traditional domains, recent policy uses of information from assessment and indicator programmes and, importantly, technical issues in using, analysing and presenting information from assessments in meaningful ways to inform educational policy.

The first chapter provides an overview of the major developments in international educational assessments since their inception over forty years ago. The chapter documents a marked increase in the number of assessment programmes, in the number of countries participating in them and in their visibility to policy makers and the public, and describes the substantive, methodological and procedural advances that helped to foster this rise. The first chapter sets the context of the topics and issues that are raised in subsequent chapters.

Whereas Chapter 1 provides a broad overview, Chapters 2–5 focus on how assessment is conducted for particular domains. Chapters 2–3 detail important developments in the way reading skills have been defined and tested over the years – Chapter 2 in relation to students' abilities and Chapter 3 in relation to adults' skills. Chapters 4–5, rather, focus on developments in domains that, until recently, have not been addressed in large-scale educational assessment. Chapter 4 focuses on an assessment of students' ability to regulate their own learning; Chapter 5 on approaches to assessing problem solving.

Moving from approaches to conducting assessment to approaches to using data, Chapters 6–7 provide concrete examples of how information from such assessment programmes has been used to answer research questions and inform policy and practice in individual countries. Chapter 6 includes two authors' reflections on their countries' involvement in indicator programmes. Chapter 7 is more data-oriented and presents the results from analyses of TIMSS 1995 data in five countries that undertook to answer a variety of questions of particular national interest.

Having examined what skills are measured and some examples of how information has been used, Chapters 8–10 reflect on some of the technical considerations that researchers and policy makers encounter in the field of international educational assessment. Chapter 8 takes on issues of cross-national comparability and validity. Chapter 9 discusses the role of multi-level modelling in data analysis. Finally, Chapter 10 brings the volume full circle, describing some of the limitations of country comparisons and offering possible new methods for presenting information from international studies in ways that will allow the educational research community, policy makers and the public to make more meaningful use of the information gained in these important studies.

Chapter 1

Toward education improvement

The future of international assessment

Eugene Owen, Maria Stephens,
Jay Moskowitz and Guillermo Gil

Comparative international assessment is rising at this moment because of a growing interest among public administrators responsible for education to have information that can contribute to improving the quality of education. There are great new projects in the process of being established, broader and more stable than those in the past, and that benefit from the prior experience and worldwide infrastructure of researchers and institutions that have been created as a direct result of previous comparative educational assessments.

(Gil 1999)

The previous decade clearly demonstrates the usefulness of education assessment data for policy purposes, their importance politically and the public's interest in and appetite for such information. The successful expansion of comparative assessments was due, in part, to timing. The major political issues faced in developed countries during the 1990s – economic crises, education and youth employment – were paralleled by responses from the education sector to establish higher and more clearly articulated standards. Many countries sought to implement systemic reform and turned to education statistics and assessment to evaluate students' cognitive and affective outcomes.

With the past a prelude to the future, it is safe to assume that international comparisons of student outcomes and adult skills will continue well into the future. Reflecting briefly on the history of international assessments in education – and most specifically on the lessons of the 1990s – this chapter looks at the future of assessment, describing some of the opportunities afforded by methodological innovations, technology and expanding policy interests. It also reflects on some of the challenges and issues associated with these efforts. This chapter sets the context for the subsequent chapters, which first focus on specific domains (Chapters 2–5), then provide examples of how international assessment data have been used in national contexts (Chapters 6–7) and finally discuss issues related to considering, presenting and using assessment results (Chapters 8–10).

A brief look back

According to legend, international assessments of educational achievement started more than four decades ago when C. Arnold Anderson of the University of Chicago mused at an international meeting about the possibility of an international study to compare national education systems using empirical data on students' achievement on common test items (Husén and Tuijnman 1994). With the support and interest of other experts in the field, such as Robert Thorndike, Benjamin Bloom and Torsten Husén, a feasibility study was undertaken to explore the possibility of conducting international assessments that would be sufficiently scientifically rigorous to produce meaningful results. The feasibility study assessed samples of 13-year-old students in twelve countries on their mathematics, science, reading comprehension, geography and non-verbal reasoning, using existing test items translated into the eight languages of the participating countries (Foshay 1962).

Although this important study illustrated both the methodological and the organisational difficulties that international comparative studies can present, it demonstrated that such studies were indeed feasible with further development (Foshay 1962). The International Association for the Evaluation of Educational Achievement (IEA) was officially established in 1961. (For a more detailed history of the beginnings of IEA and the pre-1960s contributions of Ralph Tyler and his early explorations of educational evaluation see Husén and Tuijnman 1994.)

Over the years IEA implemented numerous international assessments of education aimed at providing data that would be useful for ascertaining the effectiveness of educational systems (see Table 1.1) and for identifying factors related to student achievement. For a variety of reasons, including technical limitations on certain in-depth analyses, a basic approach used for reporting the results from these studies was to rank countries using national average scores, or selected sub-scores (e.g. boys versus girls), on assessments in a host of different subject areas.

Although the information from these early assessments was actually quite extensive, outside the research community the focus on the 'horse race' among nations became a primary characteristic of assessment, fuelled in great measure by the media coverage of these studies. As researchers close to the early IEA projects have noted (Noah 1987), however, the seizing of the media upon the national scores and the horse race mentality was against the wishes of the researcher community and the practice was regularly decried by the IEA spokespersons.

The popularity of international assessments continued to grow over time and took another leap in the 1980s. Four individual studies (on mathematics, science, written composition and classroom environment) were conducted before the first half of the decade was over. The results from at

Table 1.1 International assessments of learning outcomes, 1960 to the present

Name	No. of countries	Population	Data collection	Domain(s)
Feasibility Study	12	LS	1960	Mathematics, science, reading, comprehension, geography and non-verbal reasoning
First International Mathematics Study (FIMS)	13	LS, US	1964	Mathematics
Six Subject Survey	10–19[a]	P, LS, US	1971	Science, reading comprehension, literature, civic education and English and French as foreign languages
Classroom Environment Study[b]	10	P, LS	1981	Mathematics, science and history
Second International Mathematics Study (SIMS)	20	LS, US	1982–3	Mathematics
Second International Science Study (SISS)	24	P, LS, US	1983–4	Science
International Study of Achievement in Written Composition[c]	14	P, LS, US	1984–5	Writing
International Assessment of Educational Progress (IAEP '88)	6	LS	1988	Mathematics and science
International Assessment of Educational Progress (IAEP '91)	9–20[a]	P, LS	1991	Mathematics, science and geography (optional)
Reading Literacy Study	32	P, LS, US	1990–1	Reading literacy
International Adult Literacy Survey (IALS)	12	A	1994–5 1996	Prose, document and quantitative literacy
Second International Adult Literacy Survey (SIALS)	8		1997–8	
Third International Mathematics and Science Study (TIMSS 1995)	45	P, LS, US	1994–5	Mathematics and science

Table 1.1 concluded

Study				
Third International Mathematics and Science Study Repeat (TIMSS 1999)	41	LS	1999	
Trends in International Mathematics and Science Study (TIMSS 2003)	53	P, LS	2003–	
Civic Education Study	28		1999	Civics (facts and using knowledge)
Programme for International Student Assessment (PISA)	32 (2000), 33 (2003)	US	2000, 2003, 2006–	Reading literacy, mathematical literacy, scientific literacy and cross-curricular competences
PISA Plus	11 (2001)		2001, 2004–	
Adult Literacy and Lifeskills (ALL) Survey	14	A	2003/5	Prose/document literacy, numeracy, analytical reasoning and ICT familiarity
Progress in Reading Literacy Study (PIRLS)	35	P	2001, 2006–	Reading literacy
Second Information Technology in Education Study (SITES) Module 3	—	P, LS, US	2004	Information technology skills

Notes
a Depending on subject.
b Descriptive investigation about classroom processes and instructional practices to identify factors relevant to learning.
c Aimed at contributing to conceptualisation of writing mastery and description of instructional practices related to written composition. P Primary. LS Lower secondary. US Upper secondary. A Adult. Since the 1970s the IEA has also conducted a pre-primary study and two initiatives to survey computer use and access (COMPED, Computers in Education study, and SITES, Second Information Technology in Education Study). However, because these are not assessments of achievement or skills (rather they are descriptive studies relying solely on self-report or qualitative measures), they are not included in this inventory. Italics in the second column indicate the anticipated number of countries to participate as of June 2003.

Sources
Anderson et al. (1989), Beaton et al. (1996a, b), Burnstein (1992), Campbell et al. (2001), Carrol (1975), Comber and Keeves (1973), Elley (1992, 1994), Foshay (1962), Garden and Robitaille (1989), Gorman et al. (1988), Husén (1967), IEA (1988), Keeves (1992a, b), Keeves and Rosier (1992), Lapointe, Askew et al. (1992), Lapointe, Mead et al. (1989), Lapointe, Mead et al. (1992), Lazer (1992), Lewis and Massad (1975), Martin et al. (1996), Mullis et al. (1996), Mullis et al. (2001), OECD (2001), Olmsted and Weikart (1989), Postlethwaite and Wiley (1992), Purves (1973, 1992), Thorndike (1973), Torney et al. (1976), Torney-Purta et al. (2001), Travres and Westbury (1989), Walker (1976).

least the mathematics assessment gained widespread notice, leading in the United States to the publication of *A Nation at Risk* (National Commission on Educational Excellence 1983), the well-known education call-to-arms.

It was not until the 1990s that the education community saw a true explosion in international education assessment and the development of methodologies that further validated the reliability of results from these comparative studies. In the 1990s there were:

- Two administrations of IEA's Trends in International Mathematics and Science Study (TIMSS),[1] which in 1995 was the largest study of student achievement undertaken to date.
- The IEA Reading Literacy Study (RLS), conducted in 1990–1 in thirty-two countries.
- Three waves of data collection for the International Adult Literacy Survey (IALS) in a total of twenty countries between 1994 and 1998.[2]
- The IEA Civic Education Study (CivEd), expanding upon previous studies of civic education with the integration of both qualitative and quantitative methodologies (i.e. in-depth case studies to document the context of civic education and surveys and assessments for empirical data on students' attitudes and skills) in twenty-eight participating countries.

In addition, during this period, planning began for the activities that are now being implemented, including the Adult Literacy and Lifeskills (ALL) Study[3] and the Organisation for Economic Co-operation and Development's (OECD) Programme for International Student Assessment (PISA). Each of these studies arose from a desire for more policy-oriented information about the work force's (or soon-to-be work force's) competences for the twenty-first century and is characterised by a broad conceptualisation of what knowledge and skills should be assessed and by their explicit goals to involve policy makers in planning and implementation. The IEA's Progress in Reading Literacy Study (PIRLS), which examines the reading literacy skills of 9-year-old students, also took shape during this time.

International education assessment in the 1990s

Perhaps the most marked characteristic of assessment in the 1990s was the dramatic increase in the number and range of countries participating in international assessments. Forty-five countries participated in the TIMSS 1995 assessment of eighth-grade students – more than twice as many as participated in the earlier mathematics and science studies. A number of countries participated in the TIMSS 1995 assessments of fourth-grade and end-of-secondary school students, as well. What was remarkable was that countries from all over the world and from widely ranging levels of economic development participated in TIMSS 1995 and 1999, supplementing the list of mainly Western developed countries that had historically been the primary (though not exclusive) participants in such endeavours.[4] For instance, eighteen non-OECD countries participated in TIMSS 1995. By TIMSS 1999 twenty-three non-OECD countries had joined, and thirty-four non-OECD countries are participating in TIMSS 2003, in which for the first time Arabic is among the largest language blocs in the study. This phenomenon is not limited to the TIMSS programme: many non-OECD countries participated in CivEd, PIRLS and PISA.

Assessment in the 1990s was also characterised by the capitalisation on unparalleled advances in statistical methodology and quality control procedures. For instance, TIMSS and IALS used modern psychometric techniques such as Item Response Theory (IRT) and complex matrix sampling, which permitted the development of more robust assessments covering a wider range of testing material than in previous studies and which improved the comparability of results and depth of analysis across countries (Rasch 1980; Adams and Gonzalez 1996). The quality, depth and accuracy of results from international assessment have also been enhanced by multivariate analysis techniques and scale creation (Keeves 1992c), multi-level modelling based on hierarchical linear modelling (see Chapter 8) (Bryk and Raudenbush 1992; Kreft 1995) and structural equation modelling with LISREL® analysis (Hayduk 1987; Joreskog and Sorbom 1993; Munk 1992). Motivated both by a desire to use new psychometric approaches and by an even stronger need to be included in cross-national assessments and to publish comparative results, countries have shown eager willingness to adopt often 'foreign' statistical methods.

Comparability of assessments was further validated by the enhancement of quality control procedures and the investiture of external quality control monitors in the international assessment process. Previously, lack of uniform test administration and other difficulties at the national level created problems in obtaining quality data and sufficient response rates. With the use of these new procedures, countries persisted in improving the national implementation and administration of international assessments, though there admittedly remains room for improvement in this area (Gil 1999). Over the years resource estimation for personnel, materials and operations improved greatly, such that precise predictions of both international and national costs could be made at a project's outset (Loxley 1992).

With new players and new procedures came new forms of reporting. Before the 1990s results from educational studies were primarily fairly technical, research-focused narratives (e.g. see references). However, the publication of the results from international assessments in indicator format, such as in OECD's premier indicator report *Education at a Glance* (EAG), brought assessment results to a wider audience, extending beyond the education research communities. From 1992 through the present, OECD has drawn upon studies from IEA as well as its own research and, in the early days, from the International Assessment of Educational Progress (IAEP) (administered by the Educational Testing Service, ETS, in the United States) to develop a series of policy-relevant indicators. Over the years these indicators have included mean performance of countries, distribution of achievement scores within countries and variation in student achievement associated with differences among students and among schools. Although the information in EAG was from previously published sources, OECD presented the information within a policy context and used an indicator approach to present the results. Successive issues of EAG have become progressively more innovative and more focused on the policy implications of the analyses (e.g. OECD 1992, 2001). For example, the publication of the companion volume *Education Policy Analysis* (EPA) is an extension of key EAG indicators (e.g. OECD 1997).

Taking their cue from policy makers' and educators' desire for comparative information, the media provided extensive coverage of educational failures and successes. For example, the US press often examined differences in education finance and in teacher qualifications and salaries among schools and systems in relation to student outcomes. The results of assessments, made public via the media, became a force in the political debate and public discussion on education. These results were used by some to legitimise their actions or by opposition groups as a basis on which to consolidate their criticisms and advocate particular educational reforms (Gil 1999).

During the 1990s the development of an international system for education indicators, such as the OECD's International Indicators of Education Systems (INES) Project (Bottani 1990), supported the development of national indicator systems and the growing practice of national assessment (Mullis and Owen 1994). In fact a survey conducted by the National Ministry of Education in France (1995a) documented that, in the early 1990s, the number of countries conducting national assessments had increased from previous years, as had the number of subjects and grade levels being assessed and the frequency of assessment. For instance, New Zealand, Portugal and Sweden introduced national assessment programmes in this decade, and several programmes introduced or revamped in the 1980s (e.g. those in Spain and the United Kingdom) took further hold in their respective education communities. Also, many countries began compiling and publishing results from international assessments, national assessments and other sources of education data in indicator reports relevant to their specific national contexts (e.g. Canadian Education Statistics Council 1996; National Ministry of Education 1995b).

Together, these developments enabled the international assessment community to continue to grow and move to an ever more broad use of the results for informing and impacting educational improvement. This is perhaps the most significant evolution of international assessments to date.

Factors contributing to the growth of international education assessments

A variety of factors account for the marked expansion of international assessments. The primary reason is simply that the comparative information gained from such assessments came to be of prime importance to policy makers. As evidenced by Article 4 of the *World Declaration on Education* in 1990, there was widespread recognition that information on the 'actual learning' of students, or outcomes, to supplement traditionally gathered information on the inputs to education was of vital importance to understanding and improving education systems (UNESCO 1990). Furthermore, the increasingly pervasive belief that an economy's health would be determined by the capacity of its citizens to compete in a global environment underscored for many policy makers that assessments of education would have to include information that compared their students with those in other countries. Hence international assessments received widespread support.

This was further heightened by the adoption in many countries of systems of accountability, or standards, the encapsulating catch phrase for attempts in many countries to raise the quality of education. Standards provided the narrative descriptions of what educators and policy makers thought students should be able to do, while assessments served as the tool to measure how well the standards were being achieved. International assessments were viewed as a natural extension of the accountability and standards movement in that they provided policy makers with information on how well students were progressing toward the standards set by the highest-performing students in the world.

Finally, although researchers have played a vital role in the administration, development and execution of international studies, beginning with TIMSS and even more with PISA, national Ministry personnel also have become active participants in international assessments and are involved in day-to-day decisions about the content, policies and directions of the studies. This shift from a primarily research-oriented motivation to a more policy-oriented motivation, and the corollary increased inclusion of policy makers in the planning and implementation of comparative studies, further fed and shaped their growth in the 1990s.

Impact of international education assessment in the 1990s

The results of international assessments of education have been put to many uses and have had positive impacts in several countries. In some countries where there is no national assessment (e.g. the Czech Republic, Switzerland) international assessments play an important role in providing the only available macro-level data on student outcomes. Moreover, in countries with more decentralised systems, where there is no clear definition of educational objectives or established curriculum at the national level (e.g. Spain), it is even more necessary to have as a point of reference data from other countries that may have similar contexts (Husén and Tuijnman 1994, cited in Gil 1999). As noted earlier, international assessments have spawned increased attention to the development of national assessment and indicator systems (Mullis and Owen 1994).

International assessments have had an impact on the research community, as well, providing forums for experts from different countries to work together for the continual improvement of conceptual frameworks for the cognitive domains being assessed and for the development of innovative methodologies to assess these domains. For example, the history of international assessment in reading shows a transformation of the domain from a focus on comprehension and a view of literacy as a dichotomous state (literate versus illiterate) to a focus on reading as an interactive activity between readers and a variety of different texts and purposes in which a wider range of skills and processes are identified along a continuum of ability (see Chapter 4). In a number of countries participation in international assessments promotes the training and professional development of local education researchers, which in turn benefit the overall assessment through the contributions of experts from different backgrounds, education and origins.

The impact of the information gained from assessments has been of major importance as well. Comparative information has been used to stimulate debate among policy makers and to assist them in determining priorities. As one example, the Flemish community of Belgium drew upon the results of the Second International Adult Literacy Survey (SIALS) to inform the development of national goals for secondary school students (L. Van de Poele, personal communication, 15 March 1998). Furthermore, by illuminating relative strengths and weaknesses, international assessments also have been useful in informing policy makers on difficult questions related to the allocation of resources. For instance, as a result of the Second International Mathematics Study (SIMS), the mathematics study prior to TIMSS 1995, New Zealand increased the number of mathematics advisers in secondary schools (D. Philips, personal communication, 4 March 1998). Similarly, results from the fourth-grade population of TIMSS 1995 prompted officials in Sweden to allocate more resources to teacher training for primary school mathematics and science (B. Fredander, personal communication, 4 March 1998).

Assessment results also have triggered changes in curriculum. In Finland policy makers reported that international assessments have considerable influence on curriculum development (K. Leimu, personal communication, 16 March 1998), and in the Netherlands results have spawned the establishment of study centres dedicated to particular curricular areas (e.g. the Dutch language: F. van der Schoot, personal communication, 19 February 1998).

Finally, policy makers and the education and research communities have found international assessments useful because many topics cannot be studied within the confines of a single education system. More specifically, because certain variables (e.g. class size and number of instructional hours) are relatively uniform within a system, studying the influence of those variables on outcomes is difficult because they cannot be modified within the system for experimental purposes. Thus international assessments offer a 'world laboratory' where one can compare the effects of multiple variables and their combinations, thereby supporting a variety of education research purposes. One such example of a research agenda within an international assessment programme is found in TIMSS 1995, which was complemented by a video study that examined teaching practices in the three participating countries: Germany, Japan and the United States. (For more information see Stigler *et al.* 1999.) In the United States results from the TIMSS 1995 assessments and background questionnaires, coupled with information learned in the video study, were compiled into a resource kit for practitioners on how to interpret the results and how to apply the lessons of TIMSS to their own practice. (A more extensive video study was conducted with TIMSS 1999.)

In summary, in the 1990s the international assessment community witnessed a dramatic growth in participation in comparative education studies due in part to countries' growing concern about economic competitiveness, their adoption of standards movements and a general shift in interest to outputs, not just inputs, of education. This growth was supported by advances in statistical methodologies and the inclusion of policy makers in planning and implementation and was evidenced in the widespread media attention to and use of the results to review and set education policy. We can only expect that interest in international assessments of education will remain strong as the education community and the public continue to learn to use comparative data to support educational improvement. The next section focuses on the opportunities for and challenges to assessment in the near future.

Looking forward

International assessment will continue as a viable tool for informing education practice and policy well into the future. PISA is assessing reading, mathematical and scientific literacy, as well as selected cross-curricular competences, on a three-year cycle, with two data collections having already occurred (2000 and 2003) and another upcoming in 2006. TIMSS was also repeated in 2003 (from its four-year cycle), and organisers and countries are discussing a 2007 administration. The ALL study also is collecting data in 2003, with a second wave planned for 2005. PIRLS had a data collection in 2001 and plans a second collection for 2006. Meanwhile, in the OECD context, countries have begun talks on what a data strategy –

for collecting information on both student and adult populations – might look like for the next decade.

While some future developments are fairly easy to speculate upon (as they are extensions of existing programmes), other developments are not as apparent. The next section of the chapter describes some of the issues – both exciting and challenging – that the assessment community is likely to encounter in the coming years.

Probable developments in international education assessments

In the past decade, education reform literature emphasised the setting of high standards (e.g. O'Day and Smith 1993), and assessments at both the national and international levels provided benchmarks that might be set in the future. An important component of the standard-setting literature, however, was the emphasis on standards for all students. The context of assessment in the 1990s was standards; the key issue for the first decade of the 2000s is equity. As the education community takes on the challenge created by high standards – namely providing support for those students most in need of extra assistance to reach high standards and preventing drop-outs and failure – one possibility for the future is that education systems will use the information gained from national and international assessments to set performance targets for their students and monitor that all students are progressing towards those targets. Some countries (e.g. England and Wales, the United States) are already doing this.

It is also foreseeable that future studies will construct ever more sophisticated tests that take advantage, to the extent that it is financially feasible, of multiple item types and formats. For example, whereas the IEA RLS of 1990–1 included 10–25 per cent constructed-response (versus multiple-choice) items, PIRLS 2001 included over 50 per cent constructed-response items, representing approximately 65 per cent of the score points. In the PISA 2000 reading literacy assessment, nearly 50 per cent of the items required constructed responses (see Chapter 2 and OECD 1999).

In another example, PIRLS developed a study to explore children's literacy with electronic texts, which study designers note are rapidly becoming more prevalent in children's everyday experience and which may turn out to tap different reading processes from print-based texts and sources (Campbell *et al.* 2001). At this time the initiative has been limited to gathering background information on students' use of computers and the Internet and their attitudes toward texts presented in this way, but in the future a direct assessment is desired.

The assessment community also has begun to address important questions related to the role of technology in this decade. Many countries have expressed an interest in utilising the computer as a tool for the delivery of assessment, creating a challenge for the assessment community to explore the feasibility of doing so in a large-scale, multinational setting with limited financial resources. In PIRLS, developers have already proposed that one of the test booklets be administered via the computer, which may happen in the 2006 administration.

Of interest to many countries is one of the most exciting opportunities afforded by technology as a delivery mechanism: technology as an integral part of the design and functioning of the assessment. For instance, the use of computer simulations that are adaptive and interactive – and presumably more authentic and able to gather more precise and meaningful information – is likely to be an area of growing interest. From Germany, which administered a computer-delivered assessment of students' problem-solving abilities as a national option in PISA 2000 (see Chapter 5), interesting results emerged indicating that the use of the computer allows the skills being tested to be isolated from general intelligence, in a way not found in similar paper-and-pencil examinations.

Another issue related to technology is how students' skills with technology may be assessed in the future. Information communication technology (ICT) is fast becoming a key component of curricula in many countries and integrated across it in others, but there is little information about appropriate methods for assessing the proficiency of students with ICT or on assessing ICT's impacts on their performance overall. One review (unpublished) conducted for the INES project concluded that while although there are sufficient examples of self-report instruments or basic skills assessments (e.g. on using word-processing or spreadsheet technologies) at both the national and international level, there seem to be fewer well-developed examples of assessments of how students learn with technology or when technology is an integral part of the assessment. However, development work is underway for an assessment of students' ICT literacy in PISA 2006, which could become the first major cross-national assessment of this domain. The draft framework for this assessment calls for students to work on a variety of tasks in a simulated web environment via standardised laptop computers (Kirsch *et al.* 2003). There also have been discussions about including a student performance assessment as a third module of the IEA Second International Technology in Education Study (SITES), though further development and implementation remain dependent on securing additional funding. Both these examples illustrate the expense and novelty of working in this area.

Co-ordination among language, regional or cultural groups is another trend likely to expand in the coming years. In PISA 2000 several German-speaking countries co-ordinated their translation efforts and worked together to produce a German-language version of the assessment, which was adapted for national variations within the different German-speaking countries and communities. It is likely that we will see an increase in regional analyses or comparisons among countries with similar cultural backgrounds or social contexts. We have seen an example of this in recent years as several Latin American countries have begun working together to develop a regional indicators system and have even administered a regional assessment of the reading and mathematics skills of third- and fourth-grade students in eleven countries (Cassasus *et al.* 1998). The OECD's World Education Indicators project is assisting countries (linked with one another by their level of economic development) to participate in and to develop a system of education indicators. At the initial stages of inquiry, the Organisation of Ibero-American States, the Arab Gulf Council and the Organisation of Southeast Asian Ministers of Education each have shown interest in the field of assessment, initiating studies to compare education systems and promoting increased capacity for research and evaluation. Finally, it will be interesting to see if the participation of Brazil and China in PISA has an impact in their respective regions in subsequent cycles.

It is also likely that we will continue to see a rise in targeted research efforts to supplement international assessments. Both TIMSS 1995 and TIMSS 1999, for instance, included video-tape studies of teaching practice. Following the widespread interest in and utility of the first video study, which examined mathematics teaching in Germany, Japan and the United States, the second video study examined mathematics teaching in seven countries (Hiebert *et al.* 2003) and science teaching in five countries. The success of and interest in these studies indicate that the more in-depth, qualitative information which can be gained through ethnographies, video studies and case studies could be an important component of international assessments in the future. Such efforts can provide detailed information about teaching practices, quality of life in schools, school leadership, programme offerings, parent and student levels of satisfaction and levels of parental involvement that cannot adequately be measured with context questionnaires. Of course, the interest in such studies will continue to be balanced by cost considerations and concerns about overloading any one assessment programme with too many components.

National options in international assessment are perhaps, then, the more likely option for supplementary activities, which indeed are growing in importance. For example, the problem-solving assessment in Germany referred to earlier in the chapter was implemented as a national option in PISA 2000. In its national implementation Canada oversampled students to allow for breakdowns in analyses at the provincial/territorial level as well as a longitudinal follow-up study. Several countries (e.g. Austria and Ireland) incorporated a reading speed component to study the possible effects of the amount of text in the assessment on results. In future rounds of assessment, countries may want to consider the integration of qualitative methodologies or the addition of national options – as some countries (notably Canada and Germany) are already doing with PISA – to maximise the utility of international assessments for their own specific contexts.

Issues and challenges

Although there are many foreseeable opportunities for assessment, the assessment community should be prepared for several issues and challenges that may have to be addressed.

Answering the 'limits of testing' proponents

Almost since their inception, international assessments of educational achievement have been challenged on a variety of grounds. One particular challenge has been the implicit assumption that the student achievement scores reported in such studies can, in fact, be attributed to their educational experiences and, thus, represent a valid assessment of the comparative effectiveness of national educational systems. Critics of international assessments contend that the nature (i.e. collaborative) of international assessments produces results that are irrelevant to national interests. This vocal minority challenges, for example, the comparability of the student populations being tested and the relevance of the frameworks used to guide test development, as well as whether the tests are measuring the domains they claim to measure and the degree to which cultural differences (e.g. students' motivation for or comfort with the test) may bias results. Moreover, there is uncertainty in this group about the extent to which a student's (or a country's) performance can be generalised beyond the items on the test. In some cases, critics call for the development of new methods of assessment; in other cases, the need for international assessment is questioned more broadly. (See Chapter 8 for a comprehensive examination of issues in comparability. See Chapter 10 for a critique of how to make international comparisons more meaningful.)

As the field moves forward, a critical mass of developed countries have been participating in both international and national education assessments for almost two decades. The level of financial investment in such activities has been massive, and critics of assessment, such as those mentioned above, have been vocal. By the end of this decade, countries will have trend data and results from multiple cycles of several international assessments. Because of this, convincing governments of the continued need for and utility of international assessments may be challenging. Also, there is the concern that it may be found that, in assessment after assessment, countries' relative standing remain constant – forcing the assessment community to examine more closely what may account for constancy. Finally, although policy decisions are made based on assessment results, it may take a long time for those decisions to impact the education system. The reflection of those decisions in changed assessment results may take even longer. This may give sceptics of international assessment an opportunity to then hold sway over the public and policy makers, questioning the need for large-scale programmes.

One of the challenges for the assessment community is in assisting their governments in developing assessment agendas that balance international and national activities, determining the optimal or necessary linkages among assessments (e.g. between subject matters or ages or grade levels) and usefully presenting and learning from the stories that emerge from their endeavours. In the United States study sponsors are putting forth efforts to ensure that the education community and the public understand the differences and similarities across studies by, for example, commissioning papers analysing the major national and international programmes together (e.g. Nohara 2001, which describes the relationship among the respective frameworks for TIMSS 1999, PISA 2000 and the National Assessment of Educational Progress, NAEP). For members of the assessment community, the future is as much about thoughtful strategic planning and education for policy makers and the public as about maintaining and furthering the measurement technology that answers the arguments of the critics.

Grappling with ideological shifts

Another important set of challenges comes from the shift in emphasis from focusing primarily on the curriculum to incorporating new and broader domains into assessment programmes. For example, whereas the TIMSS mathematics assessments are organised around curricular areas, such as geometry and algebra in mathematics, PISA's mathematics literacy assessment focuses on 'big ideas,' such as space and shape (OECD 1999). Many in the education community support this change because they believe it will capture a more general range of what students know, which is more applicable to what students will be required to do in work and life. However, others in the community will continue to criticise the shift because assessment content may then move outside and beyond what students are actually taught in school, thereby putting an education system's high, or even predictable, results on assessments at risk. Moreover, some may consider it difficult to implement changes to the education system based on results that are presented outside a strict curricular framework.

Again, this underscores the need for the assessment community to expend additional efforts to educate the public and policy makers to understand assessment data and how they can be used. It will also require that the assessment community continue to support and look for supplementary, targeted research efforts, as described in an earlier section, to provide the type of in-depth explanatory information that policy makers and the public crave.

One activity that is helping the public to understand the results of international assessments (and national assessments, for that matter) is public disclosure of test items and answers. As the assessment community asks the public to believe accounts of student performance (positive or negative), to make judgements between critics' and proponents' positions on testing and possibly to support policy changes based on the results of assessment, assessment developers feel pressure to provide information about test construction and design as detailed as the items and scoring procedures themselves. Although public disclosure has historically been more a facet of examination versus assessment programmes, the rise in public disclosure coupled with the current tone of discussions among international assessment participants indicates that disclosure of at least some test items is important in many countries looking to disseminate information that will be useful at the school and classroom level. However, as assessment programmes have become more sophisticated and trend-oriented (such as TIMSS, PISA and PIRLS) the confidentiality of items that must be used in multiple rounds of assessment – items that were developed laboriously and to fit the assessment frameworks over time – is a singular priority. The current compromise has been to keep at least 50 per cent of the items confidential.

Developing valid measures in non-traditional domains

Another challenge for the assessment community is to continue the tradition of sound measurement. As cognitive theory advances and more is learned about knowledge acquisition and the development of twenty-first-century skills, the assessment community will rely on psychometricians to help find ways to measure such skills. In particular, the assessment of some domains (e.g. communication or teamwork) that appeal to policy makers, educators and the public as important twenty-first-century competences presents challenges to finding appropriate, valid means of measuring them.

This latter concern has a great deal of relevance for the current development of measures of cross-curricular competences and other domains in which assessments are being pioneered (see Chapters 4–5). For example, early in the planning for the ALL study it was anticipated that there would be an assessment of teamwork. Although the ALL study does include a teamwork component, it is, at this point, limited to a self-report questionnaire on attitudes and experiences, because additional study is required to develop a direct measure. The findings of the Definition and Selection of Competencies (DeSeCo) project will be a vital input to the planning of future assessments of students and adults that look beyond traditional literacy measures. DeSeCo, which aimed to provide solid theoretical and conceptual foundations for a broad range of competences that will be important for citizens of OECD countries to possess, identified three broad categories of competences – acting autonomously, using tools interactively and functioning in socially heterogeneous groups – around which further development work for assessment and indicators could centre (Rychen and Salganik 2003).

Looking into and beyond the social context

For many years, studies of educational achievement have indicated that socio-economic status (SES) is important in explaining student achievement, and that low-SES children are often among the lowest-performing students and high-SES children are among the highest. This leads to the perception among the public that it is often the uncontrollable variables (such as SES) that explain all the differences in student performance. While SES is undoubtedly an important explanatory variable, it is important to move beyond this fact in the future and to explore it in more depth to find explanations that may be more policy-malleable. For instance, income-adjusted studies and multivariate analyses will be important means for policy makers in the future of making adjustments to education systems that are meaningful to all students. As is discussed in more detail in Chapter 9, researchers can ask and answer various questions. How do the achievement levels of low or high-SES students compare across countries? Do some countries have greater (or less) variation in achievement among low or high-SES students? For example, one interesting finding from PISA 2000 was that students' engagement in reading appeared to moderate the impact of parents' SES on their children's reading literacy performance (Kirsch *et al*. 2002). Additional analyses such as these may prove similarly enlightening in the future.

Summary

International assessments have gained notable importance by providing policy makers, researchers and the education community with valuable information about student performance. They offer an external and relative point of reference that contributes to the objective evaluation of education systems' efficiency and effectiveness. Since the groundbreaking body of work in this field in the 1960s up to the present, there has been tremendous growth in participation in these studies, in the scope of the studies and in the technical expertise to implement and administer these ever more massive assessment programmes. Despite a long list of accomplishments, achieving unequivocal comparability of populations and domains, exploring new domains that reflect the requirements of present-day society and presenting results in such a way that scientific rigour and understanding by the general public and practitioners are married continue to challenge the international assessment community as it moves forward.

Notes

1 This chapter refers to the TIMSS programme by its new appellation, Trends in International Mathematics and Science Study. The 1995 and 1999 administrations were formerly referred to as the Third International Mathematics and Science Study and the TIMSS Repeat.

2 The second wave of data collection is sometimes referred to as IALS one-and-a-half, and the third wave is sometimes referred to as SIALS, the Second International Adult Literacy Survey.
3 Formerly, ALL was known as the International Life Skills Survey (ILSS).
4 For example, Israel was a participant in early IEA studies.

References

Adams R.J., and Gonzalez E.J., 1996. The TIMSS test design. In Martin and Kelley (eds) *Third International Mathematics and Science Study (TIMSS) Technical Report* I. *Design and Development* (Chestnut Hills MA: International Study Center, Lynch School of Education, Boston College).

Anderson L.W., Ryan D.W. and Shapiro B.J. (eds), 1989. *The IEA Classroom Environment Study* (Oxford: Pergamon Press).

Beaton A.E., Martin M.O., Mullis I.V.S., Gonzalez E.J., Smith T.A. and Kelly D.L., 1996a. *Mathematics Achievement in the Middle School Years. IEA's Third International Mathematics and Science Study* (Chestnut Hills MA: International Study Center, Lynch School of Education, Boston College).

Beaton A.E., Martin M.O., Mullis I.V.S., Gonzalez E.J., Smith T.A. and Kelly D.L., 1996b. *Science Achievement in the Middle School Years. IEA's Third International Mathematics and Science Study* (Chestnut Hills MA: International Study Center, Lynch School of Education, Boston College).

Bottani N., 1990. The OECD international education indicators. *Assessment in Education*, 1 (3), 335–50.

Bryk A.S. and Raudenbush S.W., 1992. *Hierarchical Linear Models. Applications and Data Analysis Methods* (London: Sage).

Burnstein L. (ed.), 1992. *The IEA Study of Mathematics* III. *Student Growth and Class Processes* (Oxford: Pergamon Press).

Campbell J.R., Kelly D.L., Mullis I.V.S., Martin M.O. and Sainsbury M., 2001. *Framework and Specifications for PIRLS Assessment 2001* (2nd edn, Chestnut Hills MA: International Study Center, Lynch School of Education, Boston College).

Canadian Education Statistics Council, 1996. *Education Indicators in Canada* (Toronto: Canadian Education Statistics Council).

Carrol J.B., 1975. *The Teaching of French as a Foreign Language in Eight Countries* (Stockholm: Almquist & Wiksell; New York: Wiley).

Cassasus J., Froemed J.E., Palafox J.C. and Cusato S., 1998. *First International Comparative Study of Language, Mathematics, and Associated Factors in Third or Fourth Grade* (Santiago: UNESCO).

Comber L.C. and Keeves J.P., 1973. *Science Education in Nineteen Countries. An Empirical Study* (Stockholm: Almquist & Wiksell; New York: Wiley).

Elley W., 1992. *How in the World do Children Read?* (The Hague: IEA).

Elley W., 1994. *The IEA Study of Reading Literacy. Achievement and Instruction in Thirty-two School Systems* (Oxford: Pergamon Press).

Foshay A.W. (ed.), 1962. *Educational Achievement of Thirteen-year-olds in Twelve Countries. Results of an International Research Project 1959–1961* (Hamburg: UNESCO Institute of Education).

Garden R.A. and Robitaille D.F. (eds), 1989. *The IEA Study of Mathematics* II. *Context and Outcomes of Student Mathematics* (Oxford: Pergamon Press).

Gil G., 1999. *Basic Concepts and Current Reality of the International Comparative Evaluation of Student Educational Results.* Translated, unpublished paper. Madrid: National Institute of Evaluation, Ministry of Education.

Gorman T.P., Purves A. and Degenhart R. (eds), 1988. *The IEA Study of Written Composition* I. *The International Writing Tasks and Scoring Scales* (Oxford: Pergamon Press).

Hayduk L.A., 1987. *Structural Equation Modeling with LISREL. Essentials and Advances* (Baltimore MD: Johns Hopkins University Press).

Hiebert J., Gallimore R., Garnier M., Bogard Givvin, K., Hollingsworth H., Jacobs J., Chui A.M.Y., Wearne D., Smith M., Kersting N., Manaster A., Tseng E., Etterbeek W., Manaster C., Gonzales P. and Stigler J., 2003. *Teaching Mathematics in Seven Countries. First Results from the TIMSS 1999 Video Study.* NCES 2003–013 (Washington DC: National Center for Education Statistics, US Department of Education).

Husén T. (ed.), 1967. *International Study of Achievement in Mathematics. A Comparison of Twelve Countries* I–II (Stockholm: Almquist & Wiksell; New York: Wiley).

Husén T. and Tuijnman A.C., 1994. Monitoring standards in education: why and how it came about. In Tuijnman and Postlethwaite (eds). *Monitoring the Standards of Education. Papers in Honor of John P. Keeves* (Oxford: Pergamon Press).

IEA, 1988. *Preliminary Science Results in Seventeen Countries* (Oxford: Pergamon Press).

Joreskog K.G. and Sorbom D., 1993. *LISREL 8. Structural Equation Modeling with SIMPLIC Command Language* (Chicago: Scientific Software International).

Keeves J.P., 1992a. *The IEA Science Study* III. *Changes in Science Education and Achievement 1970–1974* (The Hague: IEA).

Keeves J.P., 1992b. *Learning Science in a Changing World. Cross-national Studies of Science Achievement 1970–1974* (The Hague: IEA).

Keeves J.P., 1992c. Scaling achievement test scores. In Keeves (ed.) *Methodology and Measurement in International Educational Surveys* (The Hague: IEA).

Keeves J.P. and Rosier, M. (eds), 1992. *The IEA Study of Science* I. *Science Education and Curriculum in Twenty-three Countries* (Oxford: Pergamon Press).

Kirsch I., De Jong J., Lafontaine D., McQueen J., Mendelovits J. and Monseur C., 2002. *Reading for Change. Performance and Engagement across Countries* (Paris: OECD).

Kirsch I.S., Kozma R., Lee C-H., Reeff J-P., Régnier C., Spee A.A.J. and Van Joolingen W., 2003. The PISA Framework for assessing ICT literacy. Report of the ICT Expert Panel. Unpublished report to OECD, April.

Kreft L.G.G. (ed.), 1995. Hierarchical linear models: problems and prospects. *Journal of Educational and Behavioral Statistics*, 20, 2.

Lapointe A.E., Askew J.M. and Mead N.A., 1992. *Learning Science* (Princeton NJ: Educational Testing Service).

Lapointe A.E., Mead N.A. and Askew J.M., 1992. *Learning Mathematics* (Princeton NJ: Educational Testing Service).

Lapointe A.E., Mead N.A. and Phillips G.W., 1989. *A World of Differences. An International Assessment of Mathematics and Science* (Princeon NJ: Educational Testing Service).

Lazer S., 1992. *Learning about the World* (Princeton NJ: Educational Testing Service).

Lewis E.G. and Massad C.E., 1975. *The Teaching of English as a Foreign Language in Ten Countries* (Stockholm: Almquist & Wiksell; New York: Wiley).

Loxley W., 1992. Managing international survey research. *Prospects*, 23 (3), 289–96.

Martin M.O., Mullis I.V.S., Beaton A.E., Gonzalez E.J., Smith T.A. and Kelly D.L., 1996. *Science Achievement in the Primary School Years. IEA's Third International Mathematics and Science Study* (Chestnut Hills MA: International Study Center, Lynch School of Education, Boston College).

Mullis I.V.S. and Owen E.H., 1994. The monitoring of cognitive outcomes. In Tuijnman and Postlethwaite (eds) *Monitoring the Standards of Education. Papers in Honor of John P. Keeves* (Oxford: Pergamon Press).

Mullis I.V.S., Martin M.O., Beaton A.E., Gonzalez E.J., Kelly D.L. and Smith T.A., 1996. *Mathematics Achievement in the Primary School Years. IEA's Third International Mathematics and Science Study* (Chestnut Hills MA: International Study Center, Lynch School of Education, Boston College).

Mullis I.V.S., Martin M.O., Smith T.A., Garden R.A., Gregory K.D., Gonzalez E.J., Chrostowski S.J. and O'Connor K.M., 2001. *Trends in International Mathematics and Science. Assessment Frameworks and Specifications* (Chestnut Hills MA: International Study Center, Lynch School of Education, Boston College).

Munk I.M.E., 1992. Linear structural equation models. In Keeves (ed.) *Methodology and Measurement in International Educational Surveys* (The Hague: IEA).

National Commission on Educational Excellence, 1983. *A Nation at Risk. The Imperative for Educational Reform* (Washington DC: National Commission on Educational Excellence).

National Ministry of Education, 1995a. An evaluation of national assessments. Presented at Network A meeting, Volterra, Italy, March.

National Ministry of Education, 1995b. *L'État de l'école* (Paris: Ministry of National Education).

Noah H.J., 1987. Reflections on the IEA. *Comparative Education Review*, 31, 137–49.

Nohara D., 2001. A comparison of the National Assessment of Educational Progress (NAEP), the Third International Mathematics and Science Study Repeat (TIMSS-R), and the Programme for International Student Assessment (PISA). Working Paper 2001–07 (Washington DC: National Center for Education Statistics, US Department of Education).

O'Day J.A. and Smith M.S., 1993. Systemic reform educational opportunity. In Fuhrman (ed.) *Designing Coherent Education Policy. Improving the System* (San Francisco: Jossey Bass).

OECD, 1992. *Education at a Glance* (Paris: OECD).

OECD, 1997. *Education Policy Analysis* (Paris: OECD).

OECD, 1999. *Measuring Student Knowledge and Skills*. A New Framework for Assessment (Paris: OECD).

OECD, 2001. *Knowledge and Skills for Life. First Results from PISA* (Paris: OECD).

OECD, 2001. *Education at a Glance* (Paris: OECD).

Olmsted P.P. and Weikart D.P. (eds), 1989. *How Nations serve Young Children. Profiles of Child Care and Education in Fourteen Countries* (Ypsilanti NY: High Scope).

Postlethwaite T.N. and Wiley D.E., 1992. *The IEA Study of Science* II. *Science Achievement in Twenty-three Countries* (Oxford: Pergamon Press).

Purves A.C., 1973. *Literature Education in Ten Countries. An Empirical Study* (Stockholm: Almquist & Wiksell; New York: Wiley).

Purves A.C. (ed.), 1992. *The IEA Study of Written Composition* II. *Education and Performance in Fourteen Countries* (Oxford: Pergamon Press).

Rasch G., 1980, *Probabilistic Models for some Intelligence and Attainment Tests* (Chicago: University of Chicago).

Rychen D.S. and Salganik L.H. (eds), 2003. *Key Competencies for a Successful Life and a Well-functioning Society* (Berne: Hogrefe & Huber).

Stigler J.W., Gonzales P., Kawanaka T., Knoll S. and Serrano A., 1999. *The TIMSS Videotape Classroom Study. Methods and Findings from an Exploratory Research Project on Eighth-grade Mathematics Instruction in Germany, Japan, and the United States.* Research and Development Report (Washington DC: National Center for Education Statistics, US Department of Education).

Thorndike R.L., 1973. *Reading Comprehension in Fifteen Countries. An Empirical Study* (Stockholm: Almquist & Wiksell; New York: Wiley).

Torney J.V., Oppenheim A.N. and Farnen R.F., 1976. *Civic Education in Ten Countries* (Stockholm: Almquist & Wiksell; New York: Wiley).

Torney-Purta J., Lehmann R., Oswald H. and Shultz W., 2001. *Citizenship and Education in Twenty-eight Countries. Civic Knowledge and Engagement at Age Fourteen* (Amsterdam: IEA).

Travres K.J. and Westbury I. (eds), 1989. *The IEA Study of Mathematics* I. *Analysis of Math Curricula* (Oxford: Pergamon Press).

UNESCO, 1990. *World Declaration on Education for All. Meeting Basic Learning Needs.* Statement adopted by the World Conference on Education for All, March, Jomtien, Thailand.

Walker D.A., 1976. *The IEA Six Subject Survey: An Empirical Study of Education in Twenty-one Countries* (Stockholm: Almquist & Wiksell; New York: Wiley).

Chapter 2

From comprehension to literacy

Thirty years of reading assessment

Dominique Lafontaine

In the introduction of a book dedicated to the Reading Comprehension Study of the IEA Six Subject Study (1973), Robert Thorndike pointed out that it is both simpler and more complex to elaborate appropriate assessment material for reading than for other subject matters.

> In the field of reading, there seems to be much more consensus as to the objectives of the instruction.... There would be general agreement that children should be able to get meaning efficiently from written material of various styles and content areas. On the other hand, the preparation of genuinely equivalent tests in reading, where the essence of the task involves very intimately the language of a particular country, would seem to present very serious difficulties.
>
> (Thorndike 1973, p. 14)

In a few words this quotation outlines the framework within which international reading assessments would gradually advance in the years to come. In comparison with other disciplines such as mathematics or science, in the assessment of reading, the link with the curriculum remains rather loose while links to the cultural and linguistic stakes of present-day societies prevail. This chapter illustrates that, even though comparative assessments have undergone considerable changes over time, their key challenge remains unchanged: to achieve comparability by drawing nearer to equivalence, a goal that some consider mythical. This chapter examines the locus of major developments that marked assessments during the three decades that elapsed between the founding study (IEA Six Subject Study in 1971) and contemporary studies such as PISA, PIRLS and ALL.[1] The features of these studies are summarised in Table 2.1.

Reading and literature as separate subjects to literacy in a broad sense

In the IEA Six Subject Study two separate studies related to reading were conducted: (1) reading comprehension and (2) comprehension and interpretation of literary texts (literature education). While 10-year-olds were assessed exclusively on reading comprehension, 14-year-olds were assessed on both comprehension and literature. The dividing line between those two studies fits the outline of those categories that later studies would refer to as aspects (PISA) or processes (PIRLS) in their respective frameworks. The study of comprehension focused on cognitive aspects whereas the literature study was more open to aesthetic and affective aspects, as well as to reflexive or critical dimensions, of reading. The IEA study of reading comprehension was founded on the implicit model of a reader who gets meaning from the text and restores it correctly. The IEA literary study reflected the 'response to literature' movement, which defined response as 'the ongoing interaction between the individual and the work, an interaction that may continue long after the individual has finished reading' (Purves 1973, p. 36). Basically, the domains collectively covered by the two early IEA studies are not very different from what PISA or PIRLS are currently assessing within the single domain of reading literacy.

With regard to the actual scope of the reading domain assessed, one could establish two distinct groups: (1) the two early IEA studies, PISA and PIRLS, because they assess a relatively broad range of aspects, and (2) the IEA RLS and IALS because they have a narrower definition of the field of investigation.

The IEA RLS in 1991 and IALS in 1994 were the first international reading assessments to make extensive reference to the concept of 'literacy'. While the IEA Six Subject Study was predominantly underpinned by references to school and curriculum, the IEA RLS study drew on the concept of functional literacy (with intentional reference to the issue of illiteracy[2]) and adopted a definition of 'reading literacy' that aimed to reconcile the societal importance of reading (e.g. to meet economic needs) with its more traditionally valued importance to education or personal goals: 'Reading literacy is the ability to understand and use those written language forms that are required by society and/or valued by the individual' (Elley 1994, p. 5). The new focus on the concept of literacy in IEA RLS (see Table 2.2) coincided with the massive emergence of documents, or non-continuous texts (e.g. maps, graphs, tables and forms), as stimuli in the assessment tasks, which did not occur in the previous assessments. Such texts were thought to reflect what individuals should be able to read in order to cope with society. Perhaps as a consequence of referring to the concept of literacy, which always implies the notion of basic skills or a minimum threshold, the IEA RLS wound up focusing on comprehension and use of reading, without considering the more critical or reflexive aspects of reading.

Table 2.1 Main features of international reading and literacy assessments

Study	Scope	Population	Organisation	Skills/Processes	Reporting scales	Design	Item format
Six Subject Study (1971) / IEA	Reading comprehension	10–11 years 14–15 years Last grade of upper secondary education	No sub-domains specified; all texts are continuous (narrative and expository)	Reading comprehension Reading speed/vocabulary	–	No booklet rotation	100% multiple choice
RLS (1991) / IEA	Reading literacy	9–10 years 14–15 years	Narrative prose Expository prose Documents	Verbatim Paraphrase Main idea Inference Locate and process	Narrative Expository Document	No booklet rotation	75% to 90% multiple-choice items; some 'closed' open-ended items
IALS (1994) / OECD and Statistics Canada	Literacy	Adults	Prose literacy Document literacy Quantitative literacy	–	Prose Document Quantitative	Complex matrix sampling	100% open-ended

Table 2.1 concluded

PISA (2000, 2003) / OECD	Reading literacy	15 years	Continuous texts Non-continuous texts	Retrieve information Develop broad understanding Develop an interpretation Reflect on content Reflect on form	Retrieving information Interpreting text Reflecting and evaluating Continuous Non-continuous	Complex matrix sampling	55% multiple-choice items, 45% open-ended items with constructed response
PIRLS (2001) / IEA	Reading literacy	9–10 years	Reading for literary purposes Reading to acquire and use information	Focus and retrieve explicitly stated information / Make straightforward inferences/Draw and justify complex inferences and interpretations/ Examine and evaluate content, language and textual elements	Reading for literary purposes Reading to acquire and use information (i.e. by purposes)	Complex matrix sampling	30% multiple-choice items; 70% open-ended items with constructed response

Table 2.2 Definitions of reading or literacy in international assessments

Survey	Definition
IEA (1971)	Reading comprehension (without a more precise definition)
IEA RLS (1991)	Reading literacy is the ability to understand and use those written language forms that are required by society and/or valued by the individual
IALS (1994)	Using printed and written information to function in society, to achieve one's goals, and to develop one's knowledge and potential
PISA (2000, 2003)	Understanding, using and reflecting on written texts, in order to achieve one's goals, to develop one's knowledge and potential and to participate in society
PIRLS (2001)	Reading literacy is the ability to understand and use those written language forms required by society and/or valued by the individual. Young readers can construct meaning from a variety of texts. They read to learn, to participate in communities of readers and for enjoyment

The definition of literacy adopted in IALS (only 'literacy', not 'reading literacy' in this case) was close to that of the IEA RLS, even though the focus was more on functional aspects of reading than on comprehension – not surprisingly, because the study targeted adults. Literacy in IALS was defined as follows: 'Using printed and written information to function in society, to achieve one's goals, and to develop one's knowledge and potential' (Murray *et al.* 1998, p. 17). The intent of the test developers was to break with the simplistic vision of literacy which traditionally contrasts those who possess reading skills and those who do not (i.e. the so-called 'literate' and the 'illiterate'). Test developers stressed the multidimensional aspect of reading by defining three separate domains of literacy: prose literacy, document literacy and quantitative literacy.

PISA and PIRLS appear to have initiated a new tradition in the field of international reading assessments. Prior to the design and development of the test stimuli and items themselves, a detailed framework is developed, including comprehensive explanations and relevant theoretical references regarding domain organisation choices, methods of assessment, reporting scales and interpretive schemes (OECD 1999; Campbell *et al.* 2001). It is likely that previous studies used similar working documents for internal use. However, the wide release of such framework documents, first among participating countries and experts and ultimately among the public, as in PISA and PIRLS, exposes these documents to extensive discussion and undeniably leads to increased effort in planning test construction. Current and future studies will be far more theoretically driven than the previous ones, in which a more empirical approach prevailed.

The definitions of reading literacy adopted by PISA and PIRLS clearly reflect a greater awareness of recent developments in basic research on reading (e.g. referring to an interactive concept of reading). For instance, in PISA, reading literacy is 'understanding, using and reflecting on written texts, in order to achieve one's goals, to develop one's knowledge and potential and to participate in society' (OECD 1999, p. 20). Besides comprehension and use, the focus is on the reader's capacity to reflect, which plays an active part in constructing meaning. Reading is now envisaged as an interactive process between a text, a reader and a context. To achieve his or her reading purposes, a reader implements strategies and draws on previous knowledge to construct meaning and respond to the text. Using the same line of thinking, PIRLS adopted the following definition in its framework: 'Reading literacy is the ability to understand and use those written language forms required by society and/or valued by the individual. Young readers can construct meaning from a variety of texts. They read to learn, to participate in communities of readers and for enjoyment' (Campbell *et al.* 2001). Continuity with the 1991 IEA RLS is evident, although one noticeable difference stands out. Reference to those theories that regard reading as an interactive process of meaning construction is prominent in PIRLS, and those theories are given concrete expression in the assessment of more elaborate processes (e.g. 'to draw and justify complex inferences and interpretations' or 'to examine and evaluate content, language, and textual elements'). These ambitious definitions are far from the narrow, functional concept of literacy. Both recent assessments give definitions of 'reading literacy' that are aligned with what the early IEA researchers ascribed to 'literary' education or culture.[3] Not all students were assessed in cultural literacy at that time, as is the case in PISA or in PIRLS today. The assessment of literature in the 1971 IEA study targeted a more selective sample of students in academic tracks and, more generally, still attending school. (At that time, higher proportions of students had already left school at age 15, which PISA now targets as an age in which school enrolment is still nearly universal in OECD countries.) At present, however, all the students in PISA or PIRLS are exposed to the full range of the assessment framework. The concept of reading as an interactive process is underpinned both by a theoretical reference, which sees comprehension as the outcome of a construction process and of an interaction between the text material and the reader's previous knowledge, and a pragmatic reference to the requirements of society, which are constantly on the rise.

Domain organisation and characteristics of the reading tasks

Documentation of the conceptual development process by functional expert groups or steering committees has not always been as transparent or widely disseminated as is the current practice. As evidence of this, for the earlier assessments, the reader often would need to refer to the introductions of reports to retrace the main lines of domain organisation and task characteristics.[4]

Types of text

The one consistent feature in terms of domain organisation across the various studies is the omnipresent reference to type of text or to a variety of written material that should be included in assessment. In the 1971 assessment of reading comprehension Thorndike (1973) wrote that 'written material of various styles and content areas' was used as stimulus material for the assessment (e.g. expository texts, literary texts, prose or poetry). However, the inclusion of such various materials was no more than a safeguard aimed at ensuring some diversity of stimulus material. In fact no specific balance was *a priori* required for the construction of the tasks. In the IEA RLS, as in IALS, the first element of organisation is the 'domain', which relates to broad categories of written material: narrative prose, expository prose and documents for the IEA RLS and prose literacy, document literacy and quantitative literacy for IALS. In PISA and PIRLS, the type and format of written material also is an essential organising concept, although it plays out slightly differently. In PISA, a distinction is made between continuous and non-continuous texts, which is further broken down into specific typologies (in accordance with theoretical work on text typology). Subsequently, a proportion of units and/or items was established beforehand for every type of text included in the framework, and the test developers were instructed to remain faithful to the given ratio as much as possible. While there is no reference to text typology in PIRLS, one of the two main lines of its organisation is the 'purpose of reading', which outlines divisions similar to those based on the type of text. Under 'reading for literary experience' and 'reading to acquire and use information', one could easily identify the main types of text listed above, even if the authors specify that the 'purposes for reading do not align strictly with types of texts' (Campbell *et al.* 2001). As in PISA, a previously determined proportion of tasks relate to each of the specified purposes of reading. All surveys since the IEA RLS have reported or considered reporting results on separate scales according to the types of text. Although the PISA 2000 international report (OECD 2001) reported results on three scales according to the 'aspect' dimension, in the thematic report dedicated to reading literacy, results also were reported on two scales according to text format (Kirsch *et al.* 2002).

Skills, abilities, processes or aspects

We have seen that the first main line of domain organisation basically focuses on the nature of the texts and stimuli (one pole in the text–reader–context threesome). It appears logical, then, that the second main line should pertain to the nature of the abilities assessed. Which aspects, processes and abilities related to reading will the assessment cover? Although the terminology and concepts used to encapsulate this dimension may have varied over time, all assessments have considered an explicit domain organisation based on the reader's abilities.

As noted earlier, in 1971 IEA made this distinction by organising two separate studies for reading comprehension and for literary interpretation. However, their principles of organisation differed. For the study of reading comprehension, Thorndike (1973) stated, 'It was decided to focus upon the cognitive content of the passage and to forgo most efforts to get any appraisal of style, feeling, tone or literary techniques' (p. 19). Once this principle was set, the discussion on which skills to assess evolved towards the options of assessing (1) reading comprehension, (2) reading speed and (3) knowledge of the vocabulary. The existence of mental processes in reading comprehension is not mentioned in the rationale for the assessment, although a careful scrutiny of the items enables one to see that these items do require mobilisation of processes or aspects that differ in nature and in complexity (e.g. some reading tasks require identifying the main idea of a passage, others require drawing inferences). The 1971 comprehension study reflects the state of advancement of research in reading theory at the time, bearing the imprint of a behaviourist concept. The study was centred on prerequisites and skills associated with reading comprehension (vocabulary and speed), although comprehension itself was still a sort of 'black box' or unexplored continent. Indeed, that study precedes the tremendous development of cognitive models in reading from the 1980s (Barr *et al.* 1990), which sought to determine what actually lay inside the black box. In the late 1960s widely diversified assessment items intuitively captured a variety of processes, but the theoretical references needed to plan this diversity beforehand did not exist at the time.

Conversely, the 1971 IEA literary study was founded on a very elaborate rationale. The design of the assessment was based on a cross-classification grid in which four categories of content intersected (literary texts, contextual information, terminology and theory of literature and information related to mythology). In addition, there were ten different behaviours ranging from 'applying knowledge of specific literary texts' and 'developing a coherent preference pattern ...' to 'responding to the text ...' and 'applying a cultural reference...'. This cross-classification grid seems to originate in theoretical references peculiar to the domain of literary criticism and in taxonomies. At the time, the theoretical framework of literary criticism was well structured, and Rosenblatt's first research on the transactional theory of literary work, which is a seminal work, dates back to 1938.

The 1991 IEA RLS was a decisive turning point in reading assessment. Elley's (1994) report indicates that the issue of skills (or mental processes) had not been discussed initially.[5] The issue of skills did not stand out either in the development stages of the assessment or during the process of defining the domain. However, the issue was clearly at stake when the final assessment material had to be described. At that point, the specification of the mental processes involved added up to the previously defined domains, which pertained to the types of text (narrative, expository or documents). The way in which those mental processes are determined seems to owe a great deal to intuition and empirical approaches. No direct reference to a theory was presented. The study's steering committee classified the items by processes and submitted this classification to the review of a panel of volunteer judges from different countries. The processes differed, depending on the type of text. For narrative and expository texts, a distinction was made between 'verbatim' response and 'paraphrase' and between questions about the main idea and those requiring inference.[6] For documents two different aspects were defined: locating information and locating and processing information. In comparison with the 1971 studies, intuition had gained in accuracy, even though it does not appear to actually have guided the test developers in designing the assessment. Arguably, one could theorise that the need to classify the items by mental processes clearly arose when the option of presenting mean international results on IRT[7] scales[8] came about.

With IALS, the link between theoretical models and assessment was firmly established, and this link was reciprocal. While the assessments were underpinned by the findings of theoretical research, data collected within the framework of the assessment, in turn, supported further basic research (e.g. on the factors that account for the difficulty in reading tasks). Kirsch and Mosenthal's (1995) work based on the Young Adult Literacy Study (YALS) and the IEA RLS, in particular with a view to modelling factors that account for the relative difficulty in reading tasks, would eventually be reinvested in IALS and in other studies.[9] In this way, although PISA covers a broader domain of literacy than did IALS, the relation of IALS to PISA is evident theoretically. The process variables, which Kirsch *et al.* (1998) isolated as highly relevant predictors of task difficulty (i.e. type of match, plausibility of distractors and type of information), actually became 'micro-aspects' in the PISA reading literacy framework, yet it is clear that the same set of references is at play.

PISA is illustrative of the outcome of this long history, which began with *ex post facto* intuition or empirical classification and resulted in developing frameworks that define at a high level of detail how domains will be assessed. The framework for reading literacy in PISA outlines five macro-aspects[10] to be assessed: broad understanding of a text, retrieving information, developing an interpretation, reflecting on the content of a text and reflecting on the form of a text. The proportion of items for each macro-aspect is determined prior to test development, and each item is classified according to the macro-aspect and according to the micro-aspect it mobilises. These two criteria determine what is referred to as the 'question intent'. For example, a given item may be classified as a 'retrieving information: synonymous match' item. The need to specify each item in this way and to provide for a given numerical balance between the different categories is closely linked with the issue of IRT scaling, in particular with the prospective number and nature of interpretative scales on which results are to be reported. It would indeed be unfortunate to find out at a later stage that a key dimension was not represented in a sufficient number of items or that the items covering that particular dimension did not vary in range of difficulty to allow the dimension to be reported on a separate scale. One can argue that the emergence of IRT scaling forced a transition from intuition or empirical approach to test development to a more theoretical approach and the technically more complex quest for an appropriate balance among items.

Design of the assessment and reporting scale

The use of IRT analyses (Rasch 1980) in large-scale comparative assessments can be regarded as one of the major breakthroughs in the last twenty years in comparative assessment. As described earlier, the use of IRT scales contributed to the introduction of a stage of theoretical conceptualisation prior to the design of the assessments. Moreover, such techniques make using complex matrix sampling with rotating test booklets possible. With such a design, more items can be used in the assessment and thus more abilities can be assessed without increasing the burden upon examinees. The various items are distributed in booklets that have a common section (e.g. twenty-five items out of sixty) and a variable section. The 'anchor item' technique makes comparing the scores of students who did not respond to identical sets of items possible.

The principle of IRT scaling models makes characterising the difficulty of an item and the level of proficiency of an individual on a common scale possible. An individual who obtains a score with value n on a given scale has a probability (which is higher than a set threshold, or 'response probability', usually set at 50 per cent or 80 per cent) of performing a task correctly if its level of difficulty is lower than n. Conversely, the same respondent's probability of correctly performing a task for which the level of difficulty is higher than n will lie below the set threshold. As Kirsch et al. (1998) noted, 'Item response theory (IRT) scaling provides a way to focus both on people and tasks together' (p. 105). IRT scaling makes it possible to go beyond the strictly normative perspective, which merely consists of ranking individuals (or countries, in international assessments) from the highest to the lowest performance. Before the introduction of IRT scaling there was only room for a qualitative analysis once the ranking was over. Because IRT models are used, the information is refined and becomes increasingly diagnostic. Not only does a country become aware of whether its performance ranks higher or lower than that of another country, but it can also know what proficiency levels are reached by its students. In a certain way these models succeed rather elegantly in combining a normative approach (which remains at the core of any comparative study) with the diagnostic refinement of a criterion-based approach, because the latter cannot be implemented as such within the framework of an international assessment.

Item format

Item format was certainly one of the issues that proved to be of concern to researchers involved in international assessments. Should assessments use open-ended or multiple-choice items, closed or constructed-response items? To simplify, one could say that the advantage of closed and multiple-choice items is that they can be rated (scored) quickly and are reliable and cost-effective. At the same time, they are inadequate for the evaluation of a number of aspects of the domain (critical reflection, notably). Open-ended and constructed-response items are judged to be more authentic and are indispensable for assessing certain aspects of domains, but they also require developing standard marking guides, which are necessarily expensive to implement because of the training required to achieve comparability across different raters (e.g. high inter-rater reliability). Furthermore if an item calls for an elaborate response, the assessment of reading proficiency may merge with the writing skills of the student. Successive assessments handled this highly controversial issue in various ways.[11]

For the initial major international reading assessment in 1971 all efforts were centred on the priority of demonstrating that such a comparative survey was feasible, and therefore the proposed item format remained rather cautious. 'The reading comprehension test was to be of the conventional type in which a passage is presented to the pupil together with multiple-choice questions based on that passage' (Thorndike 1973, p. 20). For the literature study, alternative formats including both multiple-choice items and open-ended questions were used for the field trial, with a view to measuring the impact of item format on performance and improving distractors (i.e. the incorrect choices in multiple-choice items). The results of the field trial showed that 'multiple-choice items *per se* do not measure anything different from what is measured by open-ended questions on the same topic'; thus the assessment eventually confined itself to using multiple-choice items only (Purves 1973, p. 67). This choice, motivated by cautiousness, was consistent with the reading model that inspired the assessments. Indeed, for every question asked there was but one correct answer. This was unambiguously echoed by the way the instructions to the students were worded; therefore, from the theoretical standpoint, nothing spoke against proposing only multiple-choice items.

In 1991 the IEA RLS repeated those choices with very few deviations. Some national representatives may have asked for more open-ended or constucted-response items, but the steering committee chose to proceed cautiously. To support its position, the steering committee referred to a study (Elley and Mangubhai 1992) in which apparently similar results were obtained with two different item formats.[12] As a consequence, the assessments consisted of a majority of multiple-choice items (from 75 per cent to 90 per cent, depending on the population); 10–20 per cent of the items were open-ended questions, to which the answer was a single word, a figure or a few words (i.e. items that do not give rise to any rating difficulties). Two constructed-response items also were included as an international option at each level, and the results of this option were analysed in Kapinus and Atash (1995).

With IALS a different and bold challenge was undertaken: all the items were open-ended questions. This choice was motivated more by psychological considerations than by psychometric or theoretical reasons. 'All of the literacy tasks were open-ended rather than multiple-choice, because it was thought that adults would be more interested in performing such tasks' (Murray *et al.* 1994, p. 19).

In PISA and PIRLS, multiple-choice items, simple open-ended questions (i.e. one rater is sufficient for marking or simple marking) and open ended questions with constructed responses (e.g. several raters are required, or multiple marking) are used. However, the distribution of item types differs somewhat in the two studies. In PIRLS, approximately one-third of the items are multiple-choice items, compared with over half (55 per cent) in PISA. In both cases, the choice of item type did not rest solely on psychological reasons or 'face validity' (i.e. to make the tasks more authentic), but was guided by theoretical motives. Because some of the aspects or processes assessed in PISA and PIRLS assume that the reader will bring his or her previous knowledge to the task at hand, several correct responses can be envisaged. Casting such questions, which draw on the reader's creativity to some extent, in a multiple-choice format is awkward. At the same time, constructed-response items should not be used exclusively to assess the more complex processes or aspects. If such items are used exclusively, the variables (item format and processes) would merge together, giving rise to serious difficulties in interpreting the data. As a result, there are additional constraints in developing an assessment framework, which combines a number of criteria that must carefully be balanced.

The transition from assessments in which multiple-choice questions prevail to those in which the respondent must write out his or her answers raises additional issues. Questions arise as to the effect of item format on student motivation, on boys versus girls and in combination with the context of test administration (i.e. the cultural context in the broad sense of the term and the specific context of a given classroom). Research is necessary to shed more light on such issues, which have not been resolved entirely by previous studies. Analyses of PISA 2000 data show, for instance, that there is an interaction between item format and gender. Items that require a long response are easier for girls and short-answer and multiple-choice items are easier for boys.

When a high proportion of constructed-response items becomes one of the cornerstones of a large-scale assessment programme, not surprisingly, there are concomitant requirements and constraints, including high costs, the need for strict monitoring of inter-rater reliability both within and across countries[13] and the need to develop standard marking guides. The latter should include both general principles for rating and a sufficient number of example responses and should avoid placing raters in situations of cognitive overload. Another method being explored is double-digit coding, which was used in TIMSS and is being implemented for coding the mathematics literacy items in PISA 2003. The principle of double-digit coding is to try to capture, by means of a second coding operation, the path followed by the student and the existence of representations, partial or erroneous concepts and efficient or inadequate approaches in his or her reasoning. This extends beyond grading the quality or correctness of the response with a higher or lower mark. Double-digit coding enriches and makes the information gained from assessment even more relevant, particularly for teachers.

Cultural and linguistic equivalence and comparability

The issue of comparability recurs like a leitmotiv in reading and literacy assessments. In reading, more than in other curricular areas, task and passage difficulty are directly linked with the written material, which can be altered during the course of a translation process. Students' unequal familiarity with certain types of text or content across cultures and contexts is also a controversial issue. Examining the procedures used to optimise the comparability of data offers valuable information.

In all comparative reading assessments since 1971 participating countries have been invited to contribute to the process of compiling assessment material to ensure representation from diversified linguistic and cultural backgrounds. This process was based on the principle that such material should be as 'universal' as possible to avoid biases because of gender, ethnicity or linguistic peculiarities. In all the international assessments to date, the national project managers and their relevant national expert committees also were invited to react to the stimulus material proposed for the assessment and to judge if it could give rise to any particular problems in national contexts. Evaluating whether this call for national contributions actually had a noticeable outcome is difficult because sufficient data are not available to assess the impact. In the IEA RLS twenty countries submitted material for the assessment, although the exact origins of the material selected for the final test instruments are not known. In IALS approximately half the units originated from North America and the other half from the European participants. Because more countries are involved in PISA, the diversity of origins of texts is greater. However, texts that originate from English-speaking countries are still in the majority. Forty per cent of the units and 37 per cent of the items in the PISA 2000 reading literacy assessment came from the twenty-six non-English-speaking countries, which represent seven different languages. Whatever one's position may be on this issue, English-speaking predominance remains a feature of the test construction process.

Moreover, in every reading assessment except PISA, proposed texts were submitted in English even if the original language of the texts was not English. In PISA, the units could be submitted in English or French, although the French-speaking countries were the only ones to submit their material in French. The implications are best illustrated through an example. If a Swedish text is retained for the assessment and presented to a French-speaking student, it will have undergone two consecutive translations before the student reads it (from Swedish to English and English to French). In the absence of additional quality control or supplementary verification procedures (at the first stage of translation), one could legitimately challenge the quality of the resulting text, as well as its equivalence to the initial text.

The mechanism designed by ALL to ensure greater diversity in the origins of the texts and documents is quite innovative. Several networks of countries, grouped according to their linguistic or cultural kinship, were invited to interact to produce test material and marking guides in their language of origin (e.g. French, German, Spanish, Portuguese). The material was translated and submitted for arbitration by the international centre (ETS) only after this cross-national consultation.

Beyond the question of cultural diversity, what control procedures have been established to ensure optimal equivalence of the reading material? The following discussion is restricted to a brief outline of the major characteristics of these procedures, because a comprehensive description would be too detailed for the purposes of this chapter.

Thorndike's (1973) report on the 1971 reading comprehension study did not indicate particular concern about translation procedures. The steering committee was rather optimistic and seemed to rely on common sense, stating that 'it was felt that with some care, the test could be maintained as nearly enough the same task from one language to another to make the cross-national comparisons interesting and fruitful' (p. 15).

The experts in charge of the sister study on literature education were less optimistic, or more circumspect, and considered several stages of quality control for translation. The national co-ordinators appointed professional translators to verify the translation of passages, assessment items and questionnaire items and to perform a back translation (i.e. to independently translate the translated material back to the source language for comparison with the original). The translations and back translations were then returned to the chairman of the steering committee, who had them verified by colleagues from the language departments of the University of Illinois. The chairman claimed 'in several cases, minor revisions were made between the pre-test and the final forms, but in general, the translations were accurate and literarily appropriate' (Purves 1973, p. 75).

The IEA RLS supplied a set of guidelines for the translation of test material, which had to be undertaken by the national project managers. The guidelines recommended that two independent, bilingual persons should make two translations and that a back translation of each should be forwarded to the international co-ordinator with a report on the translation procedure. Post hoc statistical checks were carried out to see whether there were any systematic differences because of different versions. More precisely, researchers checked the correlation of the mean item difficulty index of each country with the international mean item difficulty index and with the mean difficulty index in the English-speaking countries because English was the source language for that assessment.

The IALS study can be regarded as an important milestone with regard to translation, not because it launched any major innovations in the field of verification procedures but rather because it provided translation guidelines and because 'each country's test booklets were carefully reviewed for errors of adaptation. Countries were required to correct all the errors found' (Murray *et al.* 1998, p. 77). This procedure was not binding, and countries did not always correct the errors pointed out to them, often believing they 'knew better'. In the end, translation and a number of methodological aspects were reportedly the cause of France's withdrawal from the study after having collected data but prior to the release of results. This event triggered an intense reflection process around all aspects relevant to ensuring data comparability, both among IALS supporters and among detractors. It could be said that this 'think-tank effect' was of great benefit to the international assessments to come.

For example, the PISA procedures[14] indicate that the verification of translation equivalence has acquired the dimension of one of the project's nerve centres, with the quality requirements related to translation becoming highly constraining. Because of an original feature specific to the OECD, which has two official languages, the test material is available in two different source languages,[15] and countries should use both versions in the translation process (i.e. double translation). Professional translators who are briefed on the precise guidelines to be followed verify the double translation. A resource expert arbitrates discussions. All national adaptations are closely verified. Finally, a cultural revision panel arbitrates all issues related to equivalence. In summary, the sieve is much finer, the verification procedures are more stringent and there is every reason to believe that, as far as translation equivalence is concerned, nothing will ever be as it used to be. A document issued by the IEA, *Technical*

Standards for IEA Studies (Martin *et al*. 1999), similarly sets very strict quality control standards for translations: double translation followed by a reconciling or merging procedure, quality control of the translations to be performed by the international project centre, strict observance of well defined adaptation rules and, above all, monitoring whether the countries actually follow all the recommendations. Notwithstanding the vastness of the mechanism set up for PISA, reluctant observations are still voiced and criticisms are levelled at several aspects of the new procedures, leading us to surmise that the issue has not yet been resolved to the full satisfaction of all parties.[16] The verification of translation equivalence and task or item difficulty equivalence from one language to another remains a major, sensitive and time-consuming concern for international centres in charge of reading assessments. Of interest, as there are two source versions of the PISA material, one in French and one in English, some features of the stimuli and their impact on item difficulty can be compared. It appears that the French version of the stimuli proved to be significantly longer than the English version (on average, 18.4 per cent more characters in the French version). After controlling for group-by-language interaction, the technical report cautiously concludes that 'although the burden added to the reading tasks in countries using the longer version does not seem to be substantial, the hypothesis that it has some effect on the students' performance cannot be discarded' (OECD 2002).

Beyond face criticism, objections also are raised against the premise on which international comparisons in reading assessments implicitly rest. It is surmised that assessments measure the same latent feature everywhere, no matter what the language, the culture or the country, and that the processes of reading literacy are universal and can therefore be accessed through a comparative analysis. However, not everybody sees it that way. In 2002 a European project examined the possibility of evaluating the skills and abilities of 14–15-year-old students by means of administering original test instruments, which were not translated but judged by experts to feature equivalent task difficulty levels (Bonnet *et al*. 2001). The key challenge in such an approach obviously lies in that last step. Is it possible to agree on sets of objective criteria that account for text/item difficulty across different stimuli, and is that easier or more difficult than ensuring the production of equivalent translations of the same stimuli?

Main challenges for the future

This history of thirty years of reading assessment highlights some of the main lines along which international assessments have developed. In thirty years, however, a key challenge of assessments of reading remains. The point is to assess reading by means of achieving the comparability of the data collected and producing performance indicators, which acquire credit and value in the eyes of policy makers in education across countries. This has not been universally achieved yet, and resistance to comparative assessment is still fierce in some countries. Nevertheless, the responses and technical solutions proposed to successfully take on this challenge have undergone significant changes since the 1970s:

- The concepts of reading comprehension and, at a later stage, reading literacy have expanded considerably, in parallel with the progress achieved in cognitive research on reading processes.
- The initial process of drawing up a theoretical framework has considerably developed under the twofold influence of theoretical models (e.g. cognitive aspects, text typologies, research on task difficulty predictors) and psychometric models (e.g. IRT scaling). The empirical approach, which characterised earlier studies, gradually gave way to a well structured, planned approach whereby the models drive framework and test development.
- The use of identical test booklets for all subjects assessed was replaced with booklet rotations and anchor tests. At the same time, the proportion of multiple-choice items decreased and the use of open-ended questions with constructed response increased, necessitating the development of marking guides that aim to ensure the most objective rating possible for that type of more complex response.
- The emergence of IRT scaling revolutionised methods of presenting survey results, allowing reporting on several scales and discussion in terms of proficiency levels.
- The set of issues relevant to cultural equivalence and quality control for translations has become increasingly sensitive, resulting in the establishment of complex, constraining mechanisms for ensuring good management and monitoring the quality and equivalence of translations.

These different aspects of reading assessments are linked together to form a system. They do not develop independently, and it is awkward to predict with some degree of accuracy what new orientations are likely to guide reading literacy assessments in coming years. Clearly the emergence of theoretical and psychometric models is a powerful factor of change. However, as Kirsch noted in his introduction to the technical report on IALS (Murray *et al.* 1998), to ensure the quality of all aspects of assessment remains a crucial need and generates progress by itself. 'In retrospect, more attention should have been paid to other [other than psychometric] design elements … ; it is now necessary to refine the other data quality-related aspects of the study in future survey cycles' (pp. 15, 22).

In this respect, the qualitative improvement launched by PISA in the field of quality control of translations will have to be maintained and even intensified. Notwithstanding the efforts made, some countries seem to not be fully reassured by the procedures implemented or fully supportive thereof.

On the other hand, the method suggested by ALL (i.e. networking with countries that feature similar languages or cultures and developing more diversified test material, based on a somewhat broader consensus than a purely national one) appears to be quite promising.

Furthermore, the increasing prevalence of assessments based on open-ended items requiring constructed responses versus assessments based on multiple-choice items undoubtedly makes the process of marking and reliability a major issue for the future. In this perspective, the 1999 PISA field trial contained a high proportion of constructed-response items, in compliance with the wish expressed by the Board of Participating Countries. A control procedure was implemented for inter-rater reliability, with mixed results. In spite of the considerable efforts that have been made to produce reliable marking guides and to train raters in the countries, improvements are still needed. 'The coding process is more or less reliable and the countries are more or less reliable' (ACER 1999, p. 180). At this point, the issue of coding had raised enough questions to incite the consortium in charge of the PISA project to take two key decisions for the main test: to maintain multiple marking and to introduce cross-country coding procedures. 'The field trial showed the methodological need to include a reliability study during the main study. It also showed between-country variability, and suggesting that during the main study, a cross-country reliability study will be necessary' (ACER 1999, p. 180). The results of the inter-country reliability are encouraging (OECD 2002). In 91.5 per cent of the cases, on average, there was agreement between the international verifier and all or the majority (three out of four) of the national markers. In twenty-three of thirty countries the agreement was greater than 90 per cent. In four of the remaining countries the rate of 'too lenient' cases was 5 per cent or more, while in the three other ones the case of 'too lenient' and 'too harsh' cases was limited and balanced. Even if PISA clearly gave evidence that some open-ended items can be marked as reliably as multiple-choice items, the weak reliability registered in at least some countries speaks for keeping the standards for quality at the highest level.

Finally, in this third millennium, the need to incorporate an assessment of proficiency in reading electronic texts, documents and messages into the scope of reading literacy can no longer be avoided. PISA took the well considered decision to postpone that aspect for future administrations. PIRLS envisages undertaking a research study and testing a sub-sample of students using an electronic medium (i.e. by presenting one of the PIRLS test booklets in electronic format) and assessing students' ability to use the Internet. INES Network A is investigating the possibility of developing an assessment of students' information and communication technology literacy within the framework PISA 2006. The question arises as to whether aspects such as reading texts presented in electronic format, surfing on the Internet or joint processing of information packages presented as text and images will become an integral part of reading literacy, of computer literacy or of other literacies that have yet to be discussed. The future is uncertain, but, no matter what the outcome, relevant discussion will undoubtedly give rise to an extensive process of restructuring the whole concept of reading literacy in a world where the electronic medium gradually takes over from hard copies.

Leu (2002, pp. 314–15) has identified several features of these 'new literacies':

> they are increasingly dependent on the ability to critically evaluate information.... The extensive information networks of ICT requires new forms of strategic knowledge to exploit them effectively [and] ... they are highly social. The technologies of literacy change too quickly and are too extensive for us to be literate in them all. Each of us, however, will know something useful to others.

One can see that several of these features (e.g. critical reading) have already began to be incorporated in the more recent assessments under the twofold influence of reading theory and new technologies. The next challenge could be to succeed in designing a literacy assessment that incorporates the increasing social and collaborative characteristic of information conveyed by networks of ICT. Such an incorporation would at the same time result in assimilating one of the major components of cognitive psychology, the social and interactive nature of knowledge rooted in the theories of Vygotsky and Bruner and more recently developed by Perkins (1993), under the concepts of 'distributed intelligence' and 'person-plus'. Following Perkins (1993), one should no longer conceive intelligence or cognition as located in one's individual mind, the concept has to be extended to external resources (such as books and information networks) and other individuals. This change of focus could be applied to the concept of literacy: in the future, the most literate will probably be the ones who will be able most efficiently to use the information distributed around them and to work collaboratively with the others through the Internet and other forthcoming technologies.

Notes

1 In 1971 IEA launched an extensive programme of comparative studies in six different subjects (reading comprehension, literature, civics, science and English and French as foreign languages). The OECD's PISA is organised in several cycles and assesses reading literacy, mathematical literacy and scientific literacy. PIRLS is an IEA study that assesses the reading literacy of 9-year-old students. The ALL survey follows IALS/ SIALS, which assessed adult literacy. The adult literacy studies are conducted by Statistics Canada under the auspices of the OECD and with support from the US National Centre for Education Statistics.

2 'The ability to read is denied to one in four of the earth's adult population.... Furthermore, in an increasingly complex, information-ridden world, demands on literacy continue to rise in all nations. Illiterates are at serious disadvantage in most countries today' (Elley *et al.* 1994, p. 1).

3 The definitions adopted by PISA and PIRLS are closer to what some would refer to as 'cultural, advanced or high literacy' (Harris and Hodges 1995). The PIRLS framework (Campbell *et al.* 2001) includes a comparison of the PIRLS and PISA frameworks and specifications.

4 The frameworks for the different studies being disseminated in a variety of ways and the involvement of the author in the studies being uneven should prompt a certain degree of caution. One cannot rule out that, in an attempt to achieve a historical reconstitution of the surveys' preparatory phases, some elements may have been overlooked.

5 That is at least the impression one gets when reading the summary report. However, one should not rule out that this aspect may have been subject to extensive discussion within the steering committee or among the national representatives.

6 Verbatim items are items for which the correct response is a literal match with content stated in the text. For paraphrase items, the correct response is a synonymous match or rewording of content stated in the text. To draw an inference, the reader must go beyond the text and explain elements that the text merely implies.

7 The operating principle of those scales is described later in the chapter.

8 It seems that this last option was taken on in hindsight, because it is not fully integrated with the presentation of results. It is paradoxical that IRT scaling is mentioned in Elley's (1994) introduction rather than in the chapter devoted to international differences in achievement levels.

9 'We believe that, using the paradigm described in this chapter, designers have a better understanding of factors that can be manipulated to affect difficulty along a scale in the future' (Kirsch and Mosenthal 1995, p. 179).

10 They cannot really be defined as 'processes' as such because several processes of a different nature can be mobilised to perform a single reading task. For example, if the point is to identify the main idea of a text, this main idea may be quoted in the text and the respondent will simply need to locate it, while in other cases it may be necessary to draw a simple or even a complex inference.

11 This seemingly technical question raises the far more fundamental issue of the link with school practices and the possible effect of an assessment that uses methods that do not conform to the typical methods of the school or the methods that decision makers in education would like to see the teachers follow.

12 Everything depends on the criteria by which one chooses to measure similarity. Other studies (Kapinus and Atash 1995) resulted in diverging or, at any rate, more qualified answers to the same question.

13 Inter-rater reliability studies were done after the fact in IALS and as part of quality control procedures in PISA. The results of the inter-country reliability study for PISA are described in the *PISA 2000 Technical Report* (OECD 2002).

14 This is described by ACER (1999). The issue of translation and cultural appropriateness of the test material is extensively discussed in the PISA 2000 Technical Report (Adams and Wu 2002).

15 Multiple experts verify the comparability of the two source versions.

16 The harshness of this issue in France and Belgium is typically illustrated by the debate between Romainville (2002) and Lafontaine and Demeuse (2002).

References

ACER, 1999. *Report on the Implementation of the PISA Translation Procedures.* DEELSA/PISA/BPC(99)16. Presented at PISA Board of Participating Countries meeting, Paris, 4–5 October.

Adams R. and Wu M. (eds), 2002. *PISA 2000 Technical Report* (Paris: OECD).

Barr R., Kamil M.L., Mosenthal P. and Pearson P.D. (eds), 1990. *Handbook of Reading Research* II (New York: Longman).

Bonnet G., Braxmeyer N., Horner S., Lappalainen H.P., Levasseur J., Nardi E., Remond M., Vrignaud P. and White J., 2001. *The Use of National Reading Tests for International Comparisons. Ways of Overcoming Cultural Bias* (Paris: Ministère de l'Education nationale, Direction de la programmation et du développement).

Campbell J.R., Kelly D.L., Mullis I.V.S., Martin M.O. and Sainsbury M., 2001. *Framework and Specifications for the PIRLS Assessment of Reading Literacy* (2nd edn, Chestnut Hill MA: International Study Center, Lynch School of Education, Boston College).

Elley W.B., 1994. *The IEA Study of Reading Literacy. Achievement and Instruction in Thirty-two School Systems* (Oxford: Pergamon Press).

Elley W.B. and Mangubhai F., 1992. Multiple-choice and open-ended items in reading tests. *Studies in Educational Evaluation*, 18 (2), 191–9.

Harris T.L. and Hodges R.E. (eds), 1995. *The Literacy Dictionary. The Vocabulary of Reading and Writing* (Newark DE: International Reading Association).

Kapinus B. and Atash N., 1995. Exploring the possibilities of constructed-response items. In Binkley, Rust and Winglee (eds) *Methodological Issues in Comparative Educational Studies. The Case of the IEA Reading Literacy Study* (Washington DC: National Center for Education Statistics, US Department of Education), pp. 105–33.

Kirsch I.S. and Mosenthal P. B., 1995. Interpreting the IEA reading literacy scales. In Binkley, Rust and Winglee (eds) *Methodological Issues in Comparative Educational Studies. The Case of the IEA Reading Literacy Study* (Washington DC: National Center for Education Statistics, US Department of Education), pp. 135–92.

Kirsch I.S., Mosenthal P.B. and Jungeblut A., 1998. The measurement of adult literacy. In Murray, Kirsch and Jenkins (eds) *Adult Literacy in OECD Countries. Technical Report on the First International Adult Literacy Survey* (Washington DC: National Center for Education Statistics, US Department of Education), pp. 105–34.

Kirsch I.S., De Jong J., Lafontaine D., McQueen J., Mendelovits J. and Monseur C., 2002. *Reading for a Change. Achievement and Engagement across Countries* (Paris: OECD).

Lafontaine D. and Demeuse M., 2002. Le bon (critique), la brute (médiatique) et les truands (anglo-saxons). *Revue nouvelle*, 3–4 (115), 100–8.

Leu D.J., 2002. The new literacies: research on reading instruction with the Internet. In Farstrup and Samuels (eds) *What Research has to Say about Reading Instruction* (Newark DE: International Reading Association), pp. 310–37.

Martin M.O., Rust K. and Adams R.J. (eds), 1999. *Technical Standards for IEA Studies* (Delft NL: Eburon).

Murray T.S., Kirsch I.S. and Jenkins L.B., 1998. *Adult Literacy in OECD Countries. Technical Report on the First International Adult Literacy Survey* (Washington DC: National Center for Education Statistics, US Department of Education).

OECD, 1999. *Measuring Student Knowledge and Skills. A New Framework for Assessment* (Paris: OECD).

OECD, 2001. *Knowledge and Skills for Life. First Results from PISA 2000* (Paris: OECD).

OECD, 2002. *PISA 2000 Technical Report* (Paris: OECD).

Perkins D.N., 1993. Person-plus: a distributed view of thinking and learning. In Salomon (ed.) *Distributed Cognitions. Psychological and Educational Considerations* (New York: Cambridge University Press), pp. 88–110.

Perkins D.N., 1995. L'individu-plus : une vision distribuée de la pensée et de l'apprentissage. *Revue française de pédagogie*, 111, 57–71.

Purves A.C., 1973. *Literature Education in Ten Countries. International Studies in Evaluation* II (Stockholm: Almquist & Wiksell).

Rasch G., 1980. *Probabilistic Models for some Intelligence and Attainment Tests* (Chicago: University of Chicago Press).

Romainville M., 2002. Du bon usage de PISA. *Revue nouvelle*, 3–4 (115), 86–100.

Rosenblatt L.M., 1938. *Literature as exploration* (New York: Modern Language Association).

Thorndike R.L., 1973. *International Studies in Evaluation* III. *Reading Comprehension Education in Fifteen Countries* (Stockholm: Almquist & Wiksell).

Acknowledgement

This chapter was prepared with the financial support of the New Zealand Ministry of Education.

Chapter 3

The assessment of adult literacy
History and prospects

T. Scott Murray

One of the defining features of public policy in OECD countries during the twentieth century was the massive public investment in public education. This investment was driven in large part by a belief that human capital is of central importance to the economic and social success of both individuals and national economies. Further, the relative importance of skills to economic success is believed to be increasing as we move towards integrated, knowledge-intensive global markets.

Traditionally, governments and labour economists have relied on inexpensive proxy measures of skill, such as educational attainment, to inform public policy. However, beginning in the late 1970s and 1980s, governments in North America began to field direct assessments of adult literacy, launching a trend that eventually led to the conduct of the world's first international comparative assessment of adult skill, IALS. Using a unique blend of educational assessment technology and household survey research, these studies – both the national and international examples – proved to be operationally demanding, technically complex and extraordinarily expensive. The following question, therefore, arises. Why have countries felt compelled to invest scarce research resources in direct measures – most recently in the ALL study – when data on educational attainment are widely available at low cost?

This chapter attempts to answer the question first by documenting the evolution of assessment of adult literacy skill at the population level. Current approaches embody many scientific and practical advances and, like any emerging methodology, have their share of weaknesses. This chapter also identifies improvements and issues for future cycles of data collection. Such incremental improvement is crucial if the gains realised in IALS are to be incorporated permanently into the system of international and national statistics and indicators.

What are IALS and ALL?

IALS is an international comparative assessment of adult literacy skill which represented the state of the art at the time of its administration (in 1994 and subsequent years). Managed by Statistics Canada on behalf of participating countries, and in collaboration with the OECD, IALS employed a statistically representative sample of adults aged 16 to 65 years to provide a profile of literacy skill in three domains: prose, document and quantitative literacy. Prose literacy is the knowledge and skills needed to understand and use information from texts, including editorials, news stories, poems and fiction. Document literacy is the knowledge and skills required to locate and use information in various formats, including job applications, payroll forms, transport timetables, maps, tables and graphics. Quantitative literacy is the knowledge and skills required to apply arithmetic operations, either alone or sequentially, to numbers embedded in printed materials, such as balancing a cheque book, figuring out a gratuity, completing an order form or determining the amount of interest on a loan from an advertisement.

Conducted in respondents' homes by experienced interviewers, each selected adult was obliged to respond to a thirty-minute questionnaire designed to collect a broad range of demographic and socio-economic variables. Once the questionnaire was completed respondents were asked to complete a task booklet containing six simple tasks.

Respondents who completed two or more tasks correctly were given a much larger set of tasks, drawn from a pool of 114 items, in a separate test booklet. The duration of the assessment averaged one hour. Assessment items were drawn to represent a broad range of difficulty and everyday domains. Theoretical item difficulty was based upon the insights of Kirsch and Mosenthal (1990) regarding attributes of text and task (see Chapter 2). Using advanced psychometric and statistical technology, actual item difficulty and proficiency estimates were derived for all respondents to the background questionnaire (Yamamoto and Kirsch 1998).

The intellectual successor to IALS is the ALL Study, being fielded by Statistics Canada in collaboration with the OECD and with support from the US National Center for Education Statistics. ALL has the same basic objectives as IALS. It is being administered as a household survey in 2003 and 2005 and will collect information on prose literacy, document literacy, numeracy and the analytical reasoning dimension of problem solving, as well as background information on familiarity with and use of ICT. In particular, by measuring prose and document literacy on identical scales and populations nine years after IALS, ALL should also improve understanding of the rate at which skill distributions evolve and what social and economic factors seem to underlie change.

Adult literacy: a measurement history

To appreciate the strengths of the IALS/ALL approach to measurement it is important to understand the weaknesses of earlier attempts. Prior to the advent of direct assessment of adult populations, policy makers relied on a variety of proxy measures that were believed to be highly correlated with reading proficiency. For example, in the Middle Ages signing one's name was thought to be a reliable indicator of reading proficiency because the two skills were almost perfectly correlated.

As learning and access to education became increasingly democratic in modern times, education attainment was taken to be a reliable indicator of reading ability. Thus the United Nations Educational Scientific and Cultural Organisation's (UNESCO) definition attributed illiteracy to less than four years of formal education, functional literacy to four to eight years of formal education, and full literacy to nine or more years of formal education. Similarly, the Human Development Index, which forms the key point of comparison in the UN Development Programme's annual *Human Development Report*, includes a component defined by the percentage of the adult population having completed a certain level of education.

However, the assumption of the reliability of these proxies became increasingly difficult to maintain. Although large percentages of the population in most OECD countries complete secondary education, evidence continues to mount that a significant fraction of individuals lack the literacy skills necessary to cope with everyday reading demands. This is attributable to three factors: that educational quality is highly variable over time and from individual to individual, that reading skills can be learned outside the formal education system and that a range of economic and social forces lead to non-trivial rates of skill attrition in many populations.

Faced with this reality, a few countries experimented with alternative approaches to measurement, often in the context of their national census, but these approaches provided even less reliable estimates of the stock of skill (Statistics Canada 1991). A few of these studies even experimented with the direct assessment of adult reading competence but they tended to cover a very narrow range of proficiency at the bottom end of the literacy skill continuum (Murray 1994).

By the early 1970s policy makers in North America were calling for more reliable measures of adult literacy proficiency, measures that could be provided only by the direct assessment of entire adult populations (i.e. representing the range of skill). Such assessment depended, in turn, on advances in several scientific domains, which emerged only in the late 1970s. Thus IALS and now ALL did not appear out of nowhere, but rather represent a packaging of advances in several domains as enumerated in the next sections.

Advances in the theory of adult reading

Reading assessment has been around a long time, a fact evidenced by a copy of a Nineteenth Dynasty student papyrus, reprinted in the foreword of *Reading the Future: A Portrait of Literacy in Canada* (Statistics Canada, Human Resources Development Canada and National Literacy Secretariat

1996), in which corrections have been added at the top by the student's master. Written by a student scribe, the contents consist of short passages concerned with everyday matters, descriptive pieces with difficult words, formal letters and moral instructions.

Some readers may be surprised to learn that systematic attempts to assess the literacy skills of populations rather than individuals is a relatively recent phenomenon. In an extensive review of literacy work in the United States, Stedman and Kaestle (1987) describe four ways of 'estimating' adult literacy outside the classroom setting: (1) using school attainment as a proxy, (2) administering direct measurement tests, (3) comparing a population's reading grade level with that required to read common materials, and (4) investigating job literacy requirements. Jones (1998) characterises three different approaches to direct measurement: (1) item models, which make no attempt to generalise beyond the actual assessment items themselves, (2) competence models, which assume that general performance is perfectly correlated with performance on the items selected for inclusion in the assessment, and (3) skill models, which rely on explicit theories of item difficulty to support generalisation beyond the items selected for inclusion in the test. IALS built upon the success and insights of four North American studies, described below, that embodied skill models.

The Functional Reading Study

In the early 1970s ETS fielded the Functional Reading Study (FRS) (Murphy 1973, 1975), a component of which attempted to measure the reading ability of adults. To do this, the FRS used a range of 'real life' adult texts and tasks selected to cover the range of difficulty encountered by adults in their daily lives. Thus in many ways the FRS pioneered the measurement approach used in IALS and ALL but failed to generalise performance or item difficulty beyond the level of individual items. This failure occurred because the scientific tools to do so (IRT to place both items and individuals on a common scale and a model of cognitive processing to lay bare the determinants of text and task difficulty) had not yet been developed.

The Young Adult Literacy Study

Fielded in 1985 by ETS for the US Department of Education, YALS was designed to profile the literacy skills of young people 21–25 years old (Kirsch and Jungeblut 1986). YALS was the first study to attempt to incorporate an early variant of Kirsch and Mosenthal's theory of adult reading difficulty (1990). This theory, subsequently refined and validated by the empirical data, identified the features of text and task that make adult reading tasks more or less difficult. That the theory makes item difficulty predictable opened the door to (1) the design of efficient assessments, in which the difficulty of items could be distributed to match the range of ability observed in a heterogeneous population and (2) the generalisation of findings beyond the sample of items or individuals who participated in the assessments, a critical element for making public policy related to education and human development.

The Survey of Literacy Skills Used in Daily Activities

In 1989 Statistics Canada administered a large-scale assessment of adult reading skill in Canada. Modelled after YALS, the survey of Literacy Skills Used in Daily Activities (LSUDA) not only succeeded in profiling the reading skills of an entire adult population, but did so in both English and French (Statistics Canada 1991). Further, analysis revealed that the cut points between performance levels were practically identical to those generated for the National Adult Literacy Survey (NALS) in the United States, leading Kirsch and the author to propose a methodological study to determine whether the observed linguistic invariance held up across a broader group of language and culture (Statistics Canada 1992).

The National Adult Literacy Survey

NALS was conducted in 1990 by ETS for the US Department of Education (Kirsch *et al.* 1993) to profile the skills of the US adult population. NALS was the first assessment to use the full technology that was eventually employed in the IALS study, including a balanced incomplete block (BIB) design, IRT scaling, conditioning, plausible values, proficiency levels and model-based imputation to minimise bias associated with having insufficient cognitive data for some respondents. Because of the large sample size, NALS also provided an incredibly rich database for exploring the social and economic causes and consequences associated with various levels of literacy. For this reason, the IALS scales were explicitly linked with the NALS scales to better understand how these relationships vary from country to country.

Advances in the design of large-scale assessments

IALS, ALL and their antecedents (YALS, LSUDA and NALS) represent a unique fusion of educational assessment with household survey research. Compared with school-based assessments, however, testing time is at an absolute premium because adults are generally unwilling to endure lengthy tests. In IALS the total interview length was engineered to ninety minutes, with one hour reserved for the actual assessment. To extract maximal information value from the time that was available, a BIB design was employed. In other words, no individual respondent took the entire pool of 114 assessment items. First, literacy tasks were assigned to blocks, each of which was designed to contain items from all three scales and to cover the range of difficulty. Seven test booklets, each containing three blocks, were then assembled so that each item was completed by a nationally representative sample of adults in each country. Finally, block order was varied systematically to avoid problems with placement.

BIB designs have advantages and disadvantages. Although they provide maximal coverage of both the ability and the difficulty distribution, this coverage comes at a cost. Such designs do not yield sufficient information to support statistically reliable estimates of individual scores. IALS provides only statistically reliable estimates for population subgroups. BIB designs also create a problem of missing data – specifically, performance must be imputed for those items that were not taken. While the statistical technology to do this imputation is readily available, it does add a level of complexity not present in other studies.

The main, perhaps less obvious, advantages of BIB assessment designs are related to the size of the item pool. Because the item pool can be relatively large with such a design, one can achieve better coverage of the intended domain, from the easiest to the most difficult tasks. In addition, the large item pool allows the inclusion of a much broader range of materials and task types than would be the case with an individual assessment of similar duration. This fact reduces the probability that any given sub-population will be disadvantaged by a lack of familiarity with a particular item. This probability is further reduced because, unlike classical test theory, which treats each test item as equally informative, the statistical technology used in IALS to estimate proficiency draws its information value from the pattern of correct and incorrect responses. In practical terms, the system discounts the impact of items that are randomly correct or incorrect.

A second layer of complexity is added by the need to impute proficiency for those individuals for whom sufficient cognitive data is unavailable. Respondents could refuse to start the assessment, could fail the core tasks or could fail to attempt enough tasks to feed the two-parameter logistic regression models used to estimate proficiency. Obviously, a good deal of this missing data is the result of the respondent having relatively poor skills. To minimise the bias that would otherwise be introduced by excluding these individuals, ETS used the results of a principal components of variance analysis to develop a set of statistical models to impute their proficiency scores.

Advances in psychometrics

The psychometric techniques employed to scale and link the IALS assessment data with the scales from the US NALS data and to produce proficiency estimates are well documented in the study's technical report (Murray *et al.* 1998). As noted by Bock (1997), the IRT scaling that sits at the heart of the IALS psychometric apparatus is not new, but rather has roots that can be traced back to nineteenth-century developments in mathematics and psychology, including the work of Binet and Thurstone on theories of intelligence and standardised individual assessments. Most of the IRT technology that was applied in IALS was developed by the Educational Testing Service for use in the United States' NAEP. This includes the use of estimated latent distributions to strengthen respondents' IRT scale scores by Bayes estimation, in which group membership is taken into account (Little and Rubin 1987; Mislevy *et al.* 1992). IRT makes it possible to summarise the performance of a sample of respondents on common scales, even if they have taken different assessment items. Provided that the relative difficulty of items and tasks can be predicted (as is the case with the Kirsch–Mosenthal theory of adult reading), the regularity in response patterns can be used to characterise both respondents and items in terms of a common scale. A common scale for both items and respondents makes it possible to compare distributions of performance in a population or subpopulations and to estimate the relationship between proficiency and background variables. The fundamental assumption built into the IALS (and ALL) design is that proficiency is related in a regular way to item difficulty, a way that is invariant across language, culture and subculture. Used in the context of an international comparative assessment, the IRT item characteristics curve provides an exquisitely sensitive instrument for detecting the extent to which this assumption holds. Examination of models' fit for the IALS data, using likelihood ratio chi-square statistics and residuals from fitted item response curves, demonstrates that the assumption of common item parameters for all countries holds in 92 per cent of the cases, which is more than sufficient to support valid and reliable comparison.

What remains to be answered and suggestions for future measurement

The direct assessment of adult literacy at the population level is at a nascent stage of development. The suggested improvements laid out below would greatly enhance the quality and utility of the next generation of such assessments. In fact much of what is suggested has been incorporated into the design of ALL.

Broader linguistic, geographic and cultural representation

The empirical evidence flowing out of the psychometric and statistical analysis of the IALS data suggest that the attributes that underlie the difficulty of adult reading tasks are stable and predictable over a broad range of languages and cultures. This remarkable fact is crucial to the application of the IALS in countries and languages not represented in the sample of test items used to establish proficiency. Were it not so, the IALS assessment should have been applied in only the nine countries that contributed to its item pool. Nevertheless, if unimportant to the scientific validity of the assessment, the geographical, linguistic and cultural origin of assessment items contributes to the assessment's face validity in these countries. Ironically, broadly representative item pools are also important in North America – where most of the contributed items originate – which has large and diverse immigrant populations. For these reasons future survey cycles should seek to be far more systematic in seeking to achieve item pools that are culturally, linguistically and geographically representative. (Lafontaine in Chapter 2 and Murat and Rocher in Chapter 10 also discuss this issue extensively.)

Extension of Kirsch–Mosenthal grammar to other languages

As noted previously, the IALS assessment was based upon the groundbreaking insights of Kirsch and Mosenthal (1990) regarding the determinants of difficulty of adult reading tasks; their insights provided a theory that is capable of explaining fully 85 per cent of the variance in performance (Kirsch 2001). Application of the Kirsch–Mosenthal grammar in the English language has provided a rich body of empirical evidence in support of the underlying theory, evidence that has been independently validated by the massive body of evidence provided by the IALS data itself and that will likely be extended with ALL. To date, however, the Kirsch–Mosenthal grammar has seen only limited use in other languages.[1] Means should be sought to actively encourage linguists to apply and refine this work in their own languages.

Analysis of trend data

The IALS data have demonstrated that literacy is not a static commodity that is acquired in standard quanta during initial schooling. Rather, observed literacy proficiency is conditioned by strong social and economic forces that operate throughout one's life span and that cause literacy to be gained or lost. For example, data for Canada indicate a secular decline in average literacy proficiency beginning at the age of 45, a decline that is not observed in the Swedish population until later in life. These results could be the product of much more variable initial educational quality in Canada in older age cohorts or rather may reflect the impact of lower social and economic demand for literacy in Canada. In the former case, the problem of low literacy will disappear as older cohorts age and die, whereas in the latter case Canada will continue to 'manufacture' citizens with low literacy and all the related social and economic problems. Understanding which of these hypotheses is correct is of crucial importance to public policy.

IALS, being a single cross-sectional observation, is unable to provide the answer to this question. To understand such dynamic social processes, it is best to observe the same individuals over time longitudinally. However, while highly desirable, large-scale longitudinal assessments of the skills of entire adult populations would be technically and operationally complex as well as frightfully expensive. Fortunately, repeated cross-sectional assessments can provide much of the same information value as longitudinal data might by analysing how changes in literacy are related to changes in under-lying covariates. To enable such analysis, however, requires the literacy metric to be identical between the two observations. The Euroliteracy Project has already demonstrated that literacy ability is remarkably stable over a few years, at least in the four countries where respondents were retested (Carey 1999). It is for this reason that the prose and document lit-eracy measures being carried out by ALL in 2003 and 2005 are identical to those carried out by IALS and are designed to support psychometric link-age of the scales at the item level. Two studies currently under way may also shed light on the evolution of literacy skill in individuals. The first is a US Department of Education longitudinal study of American workers, half of whom receive developmental literacy instruction. The second study involves the longitudinal follow-up of Canadian youth assessed in PISA 2003.

A broader cross-section of countries

Analysis of IALS data revealed that literacy is a key determinant of individ-ual economic success and, in the aggregate, of the success of national economies (OECD and Statistics Canada 1995; OECD and Human Resources Development Canada 1997). Closely associated with wages, lit-eracy is clearly related to the productivity growth that is the primary source of increases in standard of living and one of the main economic forces which drive changes in the relative wealth of countries. Because of this importance, denying less developed nations access to the measurement tech-nology and related findings would be morally irresponsible. Because many of these nations have very young populations they could, through education reform, achieve large gains in literacy in a relatively short period. However, it will first be necessary to find the technical and financial support for such countries to participate in such studies.

More skill domains

One of the putative determinants of observed literacy profiles is the demand for literacy skill generated in the economy. IALS data show that this demand varies considerably from nation to nation, partly in response to differences in industrial and occupational structures and the technology of production that is utilised. As noted above, IALS data also show that advanced literacy attracts high wages in many labour markets, although the relationship is complex and seems to be mediated by a number of factors. Public policy makers have paid much attention over the past two decades to identifying and remedying skill deficits in the labour force, not only with respect to literacy, but also over a range of skills thought important to economic performance.[2]

Most of this debate, however, has been fuelled by anecdotal evidence rather than solid empirical evidence on the supply of skill actually available to employers, the demand for skill implied in industrial organisation or disequilibria in the market for skill. This has led to a call to expand the number of skill domains included in future rounds of literacy assessment. For this reason, ALL includes direct measures of problem-solving skill and numeracy, and behavioural measures of working with information and communication technology (Binkley *et al.* 1999). Research should continue to develop compact, valid and reliable direct measures of all skill domains thought to be of importance. The work conducted in the OECD/INES context to develop a conceptual frame of reference for defining and selecting key competences (Rychen and Salganik 2003) can be an important input to the process of identifying important skill domains.

Better understanding of skill demand

As noted above, IALS data suggest that the economic demand for the utilisation of skills leads to the acquisition of additional skill or at least the maintenance of existing skill levels. Conversely, low-skill demands may lead to skill loss. Analysis points to the existence of both skill deficits and significant skill surpluses (Krahn and Lowe 1998). The economic opportunity cost associated with the under-utilisation of skill is likely large. Such findings spark a call to explore how the demand for skill conditions the supply of skill, particularly in the context of individual firms. From a measurement perspective, two possibilities are implied. First, future survey cycles should include additional questions to determine how employees are called upon to use their skills. In fact, it is for this reason that ALL is exploring the incidence, frequency, criticality and complexity of behaviours over a range of skill domains. Second, a survey that assesses the skills of workers who have been selected from a representative sample of firms is essential to understanding the links of literacy with productivity, inter-firm variability in the demand and utilisation of skill and the way these are influenced by choice of technology.

Better statistical quality assurance

As noted in the IALS technical report (Murray *et al.* 1998) considerable resources were devoted to assuring the validity, reliability and comparability of data across countries. In the first cycle of data collection, most of these resources were directed towards the psychometric aspects of the study at the expense of the more mundane matters of sampling and data collection. Quality assurance in subsequent rounds has attempted to redress this imbalance with some success (OECD and Statistics Canada 2000). Such incremental improvement is crucial if international comparisons are to carry any significance. This goal is at the heart of the European Union's Euroliteracy project (Carey 1999) and to the panel of experts convened to provide advice and guidance regarding quality assurance in ALL.

However, serious impediments exist to achieving marked improvements to quality. First, standard survey practice in many countries leaves much to be desired. Second, the practice in many countries of subcontracting sampling and data collection to the lowest bidder often places serious restrictions on outgoing quality. Until countries are willing to invest more than minimal resources in these studies there is little chance that quality will improve. Finally, it must be acknowledged that studies such as IALS are collegial undertakings that are relatively free of meaningful sanctions for non-compliance to specified standards. This is not a problem unique to IALS, but one that is faced by all international comparative studies.

The answer to this latter problem seems to lie in two areas. First, quality standards must be established a *priori* which, if broken, precipitate a number of consequences, including non-publication and data qualification. TIMSS and PISA both used such an approach to some success. Second, the development and publication of a professional literature related to data quality would serve to educate potential participants regarding risks and best practice.

Additional theoretical development

The theory of adult literacy and of the related approach to assessment underlying IALS and ALL represents an important scientific advance. That being said, it is important to continue to explore the extent to which key assumptions pertain. Among these, the assumption about the unidimensionality of the scales is open to question, particularly at the lowest bands of the scales. Current evidence suggests that hybrid models may explain more overall variance than the single models employed in IALS. Suggestions have been made that other approaches to scaling, such as multi-level modelling, should be applied but there is no evidence to suggest that these models would yield substantively different results from the current models.

The redevelopment of the numeracy framework for ALL illustrates another dilemma: the need to continue to extend and refine the understanding of the factors that determine difficulty while preserving comparability of measurement. In this case an attempt was made to achieve both goals, but at the cost of some loss of precision. Another dilemma involves a need to understand better the sources of respondent error, both to detect poor adaptation of items to new languages and to inform the development of remedial curricula.

Notes

1 The author is aware of only two such applications, one by Jessiak in Polish and a second by a Dutch research team. Firmino da Costa and his team at the University of Lisbon have used the IALS framework to build a national adult assessment for Portugal. Isabel Infante and her colleagues have done similar work in six Latin American countries.
2 See, for example, the report of the US Department of Labour's Secretary's Commission on Achieving Necessary Skills (SCANS 1992).

References

Binkley M., Sternberg R., Jones S. and Nohara D., 1999. An overarching framework for understanding and assessing life skills. In *Frameworks. Working Drafts.* Briefing materials for ALL National Study Manager's meeting, Luxembourg, 23–24 September.

Bock D.R., 1997. A brief history of item response theory. *Educational Measurement and Practice*, 16 (4).

Carey S. (ed.), 1999. *The International Adult Literacy Survey in the European Context* (London: UK National Office of Statistics).

Jones S., 1998. Measuring adult basic skills: a literature review. In Wagner, Kirsch and Tuijnman (eds) *Adult Basic Skills. Innovations in Measurement and Policy Analysis* (Philadelphia PA: National Center for Adult Literacy, Hampton Press).

Kirsch I.S., 2001. The International Adult Literacy Survey (IALS). Understanding what was Measured (Princeton NJ: Educational Testing Service). Available from http://www.ets.org/all/Prose_and_Doc_framework.pdf (27 May 2003).

Kirsch I.S. and Jungeblut A., 1986. *Literacy. Profiles of America's Young Adults* (Princeton NJ: Educational Testing Service).

Kirsch I.S. and Mosenthal P. B., 1990. Exploring document literacy: variables underlying the performance of young adults. *Reading Research Quarterly*, 25, 5–30.

Kirsch I.S., Jungeblut A., Jenkins L. and Kolstad A., 1993. *Adult Literacy in America. A First Look at the Results of the National Adult Literacy Survey* (Washington DC: National Center for Education Statistics, US Department of Education).

Krahn H. and Lowe G.S., 1998. *Literacy Utilization in Canadian Workplaces* (Ottawa: Statistics Canada and Human Resources Development Canada).

Little R.J.A. and Rubin D.B., 1987. *Statistical Analysis with Missing Data* (New York: Wiley).

Mislevy R.J., Johnson E.G. and Muraki E., 1992. Scaling procedure in NAEP. *Journal of Education Statistics*, 17, 131–54.

Murphy R.T., 1973. *Adult Functional Reading Study*. PR 73–48 (Princeton NJ: Educational Testing Service).

Murphy R.T., 1975. *Adult Functional Reading Study*. PR 75–2 (Princeton NJ: Educational Testing Service).

Murray T.S., Kirsch I.S. and Jenkins L. (eds), 1998. *Adult Literacy in OECD Countries. Technical Report on the First International Adult Literacy Survey* (Washington DC: National Center for Education Statistics, US Department of Education).

OECD and Statistics Canada, 1995. *Literacy, Economy and Society. Results of the First International Adult Literacy Survey* (Paris and Ottawa: OECD and Statistics Canada).

OECD and Human Resources Development Canada, 1997. *Literacy Skills for the Knowledge Society. Further Results of the International Adult Literacy Survey* (Paris: OECD; Ottawa: Human Resources Development Canada).

OECD and Statistics Canada, 2000. *Literacy in the Information Age. Final Report of the International Adult Literacy Survey* (Paris: OECD; Ottawa: Statistics Canada).

Rychen, D.S. and Salganik L.H., 2003. *Key Competencies for a Successful Life and a Well-functioning Society* (Berne: Hogrefe & Huber).

Secretary's Commission on Achieving Necessary Skills (SCANS), 1992. *Learning a Living. A Blueprint for High Performance* (Washington DC: SCANS, US Department of Labour).

Statistics Canada, 1991. *Adult Literacy in Canada. Results of a National Study* (Ottawa: Statistics Canada).

Statistics Canada, 1992. *An International Assessment of Adult Literacy. A Proposal* (Ottawa: Statistics Canada).

Statistics Canada, Human Resources Development Canada and the National Literacy Secretariat, 1996. *Reading the Future. A Portrait of Literacy in Canada* (Ottawa: Statistics Canada, Human Resources Development Canada and the National Literacy Secretariat).

Stedman L.C. and Kaestle C.F., 1987. Literacy and reading performance in the United States from 1880 to the present. *Reading Research Quarterly*, 22 (1), 8–46.

Yamamoto K. and Kirsch I.S., 1998. Proficiency estimation. In Murray, Kirsch and Jenkins (eds) *Adult Literacy in OECD Countries. Technical Report on the First International Adult Literacy Survey*. 98–053 (Washington DC: National Center for Education Statistics, US Department of Education).

Chapter 4

Cross-curricular competencies

Developments in a new area of education outcome indicators

Jules L. Peschar

In the ongoing programmes to develop indicators of education systems, the measurement and presentation of education outcomes is one of the primary goals. This holds for national as well as for international programmes. However, to date the choice in available outcome indicators typically has been rather small. Researchers and policy makers have relied mainly on achievement measures in reading, mathematics or science, which have an internationally recognised level of quality. Nevertheless students learn more subjects than these three, and much of what they learn in school is not taught explicitly in one subject or another. Indicator and assessment programmes have begun to focus on competencies of a more cross-curricular nature. This chapter describes how and why cross-curricular competencies came to the forefront of international assessment development work, the present state of this development work and pertinent issues for continued development.

Perspectives on educational measurement

During the 1990s interest in information on the functioning of educational systems strongly increased, and this interest continues today (see also Chapter 1). Policy makers are interested in how various aspects of education relate to costs, participation and outcomes of schooling. Researchers continue to address issues on the effectiveness of schooling and the way school and family factors affect students' performance and achievement. These efforts have led to increased awareness that the main functions of education should and can be captured in relevant indicators. Some of these indicators report data on the macro- or national level; others focus on the effects of schools on performance (Spee 1999).

Various scientific disciplines address questions that are relevant for education and educational indicators. In fact, perspectives from at least five disciplines can be distinguished, which are enumerated in Box 4.1. Although the emphasis may be more on the societal dimension or more on the school or the individual, depending on which perspective education is being viewed,

Box 4.1   Perspectives on educational measurement

Educational statistics

First, in most OECD countries there is a strong tradition at the national level of collecting information on students and schools for educational statistics. Most of these statistics serve planning and administrative purposes. For example, a detailed account of numbers of and costs per students must be available for planning and financing purposes. Some of this information can be used effectively for developing indicators of outcomes (e.g. the number of students graduating with a diploma from a certain education level). However, to make international comparisons, these diplomas also have to be made transferable, for which purpose the International Standard Classification of Education (ISCED) system was developed. Yet even with such a standardisation, a main question remains to be answered: which competencies are associated with these diplomas and can they be compared across systems?

The measurement of performance and achievement

Second, the measurement of performance and achievement has been high on the agenda in many countries; educational researchers have been studying both processes and outcomes and focusing on the scholastic conditions under which students perform. This interest and study have led to an accumulation of expertise in national institutes of educational assessment and testing, as well as to the availability of internationally comparable assessments (e.g. the various IEA studies on mathematics, science and reading comprehension from the 1980s and 1990s). Most of the studies until recently focused on subject matter made available to students through the curriculum, with the appropriateness of such assessments being dependent, to a large extent, on the degree of fairness with which the test represents the curriculum. Through this approach two aspects of what students may learn are not being addressed: those competencies not explicitly addressed in a particular subject and those that are not explicitly part of the curriculum.

Psychology

Third, within the discipline of psychology, several approaches are relevant to education and school. Developmental psychology has focused on aspects of growth in education. Personality psychology has addressed issues of personality characteristics and the learning process. Cognitive psychologists have been intrigued with mapping the mental processes in problem solving, and advances in psychometrics have led to the improvement of instruments for both psychological and educational measurement. Much of the education-related work within psychology is related to individual processes and basically addresses two related questions: what is the predictive power of selection tests (or practices) and how are students or employees appropriately selected? In this respect the core business of educational psychologists is the predictive validity of tests.

The sociology of education

Fourth, the sociology of education examines both the social determinants of education careers and the effects of attained education on labour market and occupation outcomes. These two sequential processes became integrated with the development of path analysis (Blau and Duncan 1997), which like the later development of structural equation models allowed for the inclusion of additional relevant variables in the study of education and occupation attainment, which in turn has led to highly relevant longitudinal studies. The education variables, however, are rather restricted in scope: usually the number of years of schooling or the diploma is used as the main indicator of education achievement. Because much variation in terms of competencies will occur between students with the same amount formal schooling, predictive power improves when relevant competencies are directly measured.

Economics

Fifth, in economics the human capital approach has been a major perspective for studying education. In research on educational outcomes and the effect of education on the labour market, formal criteria of schooling also are used: again, diplomas acquired or amount of education. In an international context in particular, institutional differences between education systems remain underexposed, as in the case of general versus vocational training. A similar critique also applies to the sociological approach toward attainment, namely that much variation within these categories remains to be seen. A more direct measurement of what students really know (Healy 1997) improves the predictive power of human capital research.

the important commonality to notice across these perspectives is the shift in orientation from the processes of schooling towards the outcomes.

Much progress was made during the last several decades in terms of conceptual work, specification of theories and development of measurement models, all of which have had an enormous positive effect on the quality of education research. But only through this progress does it also become visible that there are underdeveloped areas of education measurement. Substantial work has occurred in measuring academic outcomes; countries have worked individually and collectively to develop direct measures of students' skills rather than rely on indirect measures through diplomas or education pathways. What remains, however, is to couple this focus on direct measures with a broader range of competencies – both in curricular subjects and in competencies that are across the curriculum. What is needed is specific attention to the international equivalence of these competencies to address important new questions. The next section elaborates on international efforts to develop measures of cross-curricular competencies.

Development of measures of cross-curricular competencies

The challenge to develop measures of cross-curricular competencies was undertaken within the OECD/INES context in the early 1990s because it was being recognised that education goals and outcomes were broader than just academics. Two key questions emerged: what kinds of competencies are needed for young adults to live as responsible citizens and to what extent do students possess these competencies (Trier 1991)? From the earliest discussions of these questions (Peschar 1993; Trier and Peschar 1995), four important cross-curricular competencies were identified:

- *Civics*, interpreted broadly to include not only knowledge of how governments are organised but also an understanding of democratic values and knowledge about how to co-operate with others.
- *Problem solving*, not just mathematical or scientific but any problem requiring analytical thinking and decision making in unclear situations.
- *Self-concept* (or, eventually, self-related cognitions), including the ability to know and judge oneself and one's skills and motivations and to have the self-confidence or disposition to persist.
- *Communication*, both orally and in writing.

Participants in the early development work recognised that some of these competencies could belong to what is generally a part of school curricula whereas others could be 'automatically' acquired and still others could not be taught at school at all.

From 1993 to 1997 a feasibility study was carried out within the OECD/INES context to find out whether the above mentioned competencies could be measured, whether instruments were available and of sufficient quality to measure them and whether these instruments could be administered in an international context. The results of the study were published by OECD under the title *Prepared for Life* (1997). After a broad discussion in the relevant governing bodies, the conclusions of the study were adopted. The study concluded that adequate instruments were available in at least two areas (civics[1] and self-related cognitions) and that a third area (problem solving) would require development work in the medium term. The theoretical elements of and empirical experiences with the self-related cognitions are presented in the remainder of this section.

A theoretical elaboration of dimensions of cross-curricular competencies

To move from the identification of self-related cognitions as an area ripe for development to the development of valid measurement required the development of a theoretical frame of reference within which to place these cognitions. This theoretical frame of reference (Baumert *et al.* 1998), drawing heavily on a review of literature on students' self-evaluation, learning competencies and outcomes commissioned of Fend (1998), distinguished various dimensions of cross-curricular competencies.[2] Formulated on a very general level, education systems aim to develop and improve students' mental dispositions that are helpful in coping with life tasks. These dispositions may be called competencies. Although the term *competencies* itself is in need of a more precise theoretical anchorage, as stressed by Fend (1998), in psychological paradigms *competencies* means endogenous structures as preconditions for performance and behavioural regulation (Weinert 2001). For the purposes of the OECD/INES development work, competencies were classified into three dimensions: task, degree of generality and psychological process of the individual learning. This classification is elaborated in Box 4.2.

These dimensions of education effect (task, degree of generality and psychological processes involved) constitute a preliminary step toward the theoretical underpinning of cross-curricular competencies. They may be defined as generalised functional systems of individuals in coping with strategic life tasks on the personal and community level. In fact these dimensions were in the background when the four domains were chosen for the feasibility test.

Because the three dimensions can be used in many combinations that are potentially useful, a first selection of indicators was based on pragmatic criteria: on which dimensions are instruments already available and on which will information be most useful or relevant? These criteria thus would allow

---

Box 4.2   Classifications of competencies

Tasks

- Technical and everyday problems.
- Social tasks, e.g. interpersonal and social requirements.
- Self-related tasks, in the sense of handling one's internal life, e.g. coping with needs, recognising self-worth.

Degrees of generality

In principle, competences classified according to degrees of generality can be mapped in a continuous way, although for practical purposes three levels are distinguished:

- Content domains within a subject area.
- School subjects.
- Cross-curricular or transcurricular areas.

Psychological processes

Heuristically competences can be divided into two groups of psychological processes, which can be subdivided according to the level of generality:

- Knowledge and beliefs:

  - Subject-related competences.
  - General competences in subjects.
  - General cross-curricular competences.

- Values, beliefs, attitudes, motivations, habits:

  - Attitudes towards whole subjects.
  - Attitudes within domains.
  - Attitudes towards learning in general.

Solving problems and coping with tasks always involve the functional systems mentioned above.

---

investment in new instruments to be relatively modest. There was a high priority for indicators that would provide information on processes over which the school had a high degree of control, which was certainly the case with self-regulated learning competencies, which generalise to life skills in mastering tasks (Fend 1998).

The next phase of development work, occurring between 1998 and 2001, was the development and elaboration of scales for self-related competencies. This was achieved through a multidisciplinary effort, building from the initial expert group, in which sociologists, social psychologists, education researchers and psychometricians brought their expertise together (see Baumert *et al.* 1998; Peschar and Molenaar 1999). This project was eventually presented as an optional component of PISA 2000.

Towards a conceptual framework for self-regulated learning

As has been noted elsewhere in this volume, PISA is a large international and multivariate study to assess students' literacy in reading, mathematics and science. The basic idea behind PISA is a dynamic model of continuous learning over one's life span; the model acknowledges that the knowledge and skills that are necessary for successful adaptation to changing personal, societal and economic circumstances are continuously acquired over the adult life span. Students cannot learn everything they will need to know in adulthood; however, they can acquire the prerequisites for successful learning in future life. These prerequisites are cognitive and motivational and include awareness of one's own thinking and learning, self-evaluation, knowledge of learning strategies and heuristics and ability to use these competencies to optimise the learning process. Also, because further learning and the acquisition of additional knowledge will increasingly occur in situations in which people work together and are dependent on one another, socio-cognitive and social competencies are of equal relevance.

Based on this dynamic model of knowledge acquisition, the first cross-curricular competencies component in PISA 2000 focused on self-regulated learning, an outgrowth of the developmental work begun in self-concept. Self-regulated learning can be conceived of as an interaction of cognitive, motivational and – if it occurs in social settings – socio-cognitive or social components. Table 4.1 maps the components of self-regulated learning that are most often dealt with in the research literature and for which instruments on at least the national level are available.

The most important resource for self-regulated learning is previous knowledge, its extent and the quality of its internal organisation. In PISA the declarative and procedural knowledge base in reading, mathematics and science are measured on the domain-specific level (e.g. solving an algebra problem), the domain-general level (e.g. thinking mathematically) and, by 2003, on the cross-curricular level (e.g. problem solving).

Five bundles of theoretical constructs formed the core of the field test for self-regulated learning in PISA (the letters in parentheses refer to the text in Table 4.1):

Table 4.1 Components of self-regulated learning

Cognitive components	Motivational components	Socio-cognitive components
Prior knowledge (declarative and procedural) *Domain-specific, domain-general* Reading, mathematical, and scientific literacy in PISA ***Cross-curricular*** Problem solving in PISA	**Motivational preferences (B)** ***General and subject-related:*** • Motivation by compliance • Instrumental motivation • Competitive motivation • Interest-based motivation	**Learning style preferences (F)** • Independent learning • Competitive learning • Co-operative learning
Learning strategies (A) • Memorising • Elaboration • Control strategies	**Goal orientations (C)** • Task orientation • Ego orientation	**Co-operation and conflict resolution / teamwork skills** No scales available yet To be developed in future
Implicit theories of learning and ability (G) • Stability of learning potential	**Attitude to lifelong learning** Some TIMSS scales available (Ramseier *et al.* 1999) To be extended in the future	
	Self-related cognitions (D) • Control beliefs/self-efficacy • Agency beliefs: effort • Agency beliefs: ability • Verbal self-concept • Mathematical self-concept • Academic self-concept • General self-concept	
	Action control / volitional strategies (E) • General effort and persistence in learning • Subject-specific effort and persistence	

Note

Shaded areas indicate that scales on the topic either are not available or are already being measured.

Source: Baumert *et al.* (1998).

- Strategies of self-regulated learning, which regulate how deeply and how systematically information is processed (A).
- Motivational preferences and goal orientations, which regulate the investment of time and mental energy for learning purposes and influence the choice of learning strategies (B, C).
- Self-related cognition mechanisms, which regulate the standards, aims and processes of action (D).
- Action-control strategies, particularly effort and persistence, which shield the performance of the action from competing intentions and help to overcome learning difficulties (E).
- Preferences for different types of learning situations, learning styles and social skills required for co-operative learning (F).

These components of self-regulated learning were measured in the field study on the subject-specific and cross-curricular levels. Theoretical and pragmatic considerations guided the later selection of specific indicators.

The basic theoretical model of self-regulated learning is a non-recursive interaction model (Harter and Connell 1984; Eccles and Wigfield 1995). This means that the theoretical constructs are treated as both criteria and predictors (or as both dependent and independent variables). They therefore not only widen the descriptive scope of the PISA study but also deepen its analytical potential.

The measures of self-regulated learning differ from one another in their proximities to behaviour. Together they cover the complete spectrum from self-reports on behaviour to self-reported preferences in virtual situations of differing specificity and from self-assessment of specific abilities to self-assessment of one's own personality. However, within the present context of large international assessment programmes, it is impossible to draw samples on behaviour (i.e. direct measurement versus self-evaluation) that would allow conclusions about latent competencies or personality features.[3]

This facet is important because the closer the measures are to behaviour the more suitable they are for descriptive purposes in international comparison because an equivalent anchoring of such scales across cultures has some plausibility. This equivalence probably cannot be assumed for either self-reports on capabilities or for other measures of self-evaluation. Different cultural norms in acceptable self-representation constitute different frames of reference, which can practically rule out comparisons of mean values.[4] Nevertheless, this does not necessarily restrict the cross-cultural construct validity and the analysis of causal relations, as shown in international self-concept and self-efficacy research (e.g. Marsh and Craven 1999). However, in selecting constructs within the PISA framework, there was a preference for constructs, which were operationalised close to behaviour and for which there was empirical evidence of cross-cultural construct validity.[5]

Finalising the instrument on self-regulated learning for PISA 2000

According to the plan described in Baumert *et al.* (1998), the self-regulated learning instrument was field tested in twenty-two countries in the spring of 1999. A number of theoretically relevant scales were selected and used to collect the data. In total, the instrument for measuring self-regulating learning originally included 112 items (captured in twenty-three scales), which required about thirty minutes of students' time. Based on statistical analysis and expert judgment, these 112 items and twenty-three scales had to be reduced in such a way that, within ten minutes, the most relevant dimensions could be implemented in PISA's student background questionnaire in 2000.

The analysis of the field-test data was carried out according to the procedures described in Peschar and Molenaar (1999). In selecting items, preference was given to items that had good or excellent psychometric properties, good conceptual coverage and a clear relevance to education policy makers. Based on classic reliability tests, confirmatory factor analysis and IRT, reducing the number of scales and items in an optimal way appeared feasible. An international expert group[6] critically reviewed the statistical analysis of the field-trial data and made recommendations for selecting items and constructing the final instrument.

The analysis of the field-study data concluded that three main dimensions of self-regulating learning could be distinguished empirically: learning strategies, motivation and self-concept. The scales selected within these dimensions also were deemed content relevant and met or exceeded the psychometric standards established for the analysis. These included the following:

- *For the learning strategies dimension:* memorisation, elaboration and control strategies.
- *For the motivation dimension:* instrumental motivation, interest motivation (subject-related), action control, effort and persistence in learning and co-operative and competitive learning.
- *For the self-concept dimension:* control expectation, self-efficacy, verbal self-concept, mathematics self-concept and overall academic self-concept.

The final instrument for PISA 2000 had fifty-one items and thirteen scales. For the total sample of the twenty-two countries in which they had been field tested more than 88 per cent of the final thirteen scales had a reliability of 0.70 or higher. No systematic differences were found for boys or girls, though for low-SES students the scales seemed to be somewhat less reliable than for the other SES groups (Peschar *et al.* 1999, p. 36). The validity of the scales also was extensively analysed. Estimated correlations of the scales (for the non-representative samples) with the achievement measures were all in the expected directions.

Results from PISA 2000

Twenty-six countries participated in the optional component on self-regulated learning in PISA 2000 and, thus, included the thirteen scales in the background questionnaires administered to students. This represented the first major international study of cross-curricular competencies and in total 170,000 students answered the questions.

The quality of the information and the reliability of the scales again were established. For all countries, the reliabilities of the scales varied from 0.71 to 0.87. Confirmatory factor analyses showed that the separate scales within the dimensions could easily be distinguished. The only overlap appeared to exist between the scales for control expectation and self-efficacy, and the academic self-concept showed – not unsurprisingly – great overlap with the mathematics and verbal self-concept,[7] In general, the instrument showed very good properties.

An in-depth analysis of the PISA 2000 self-regulated learning data recently occurred and is reported in an OECD report (Artelt *et al.* 2003). To get an impression of the potential richness and utility of these data, this chapter presents a selection of the preliminary results that were published in the PISA 2000 international report (OECD 2001).

The first example relates to the learning strategies that students apply, particularly their control strategies. Students were asked to report on how frequently they try to figure out what to learn, check to see what they remember, figure out which concepts are really understood, make sure they remember the most important things and look for additional information to clarify points. The top panel of Figure 4.1 shows the distribution of the scale scores when they are cut into four quartiles. Thus, it becomes visible that, compared with the OECD average, students in some countries – Austria, the Czech Republic, Germany, Hungary, Italy and Portugal – report more frequent use of control strategies. On the other hand, students in other countries – Finland, Iceland, Korea and Norway – report less frequent use of control strategies as compared with the average average (OECD 2001, p. 110). What accounts for such variation between countries is not clear.

Within-country variation also is apparent. In the lower panel of Figure 4.1 performance in reading literacy is plotted by quarters of the index of control strategies. This panel shows that in general the best-performing students also most frequently apply control strategies. Two other types of conclusion can also be drawn from these data. First, the variation within countries differs markedly, with countries showing different associations between control strategies and performance. The association is strongest in Australia, the Czech Republic, Germany, New Zealand and Portugal, whereas in Denmark, Iceland and Norway frequent use of control strategies does not appear to be associated with higher performance. Second, the magnitude of the differences between quartiles also differs across countries and

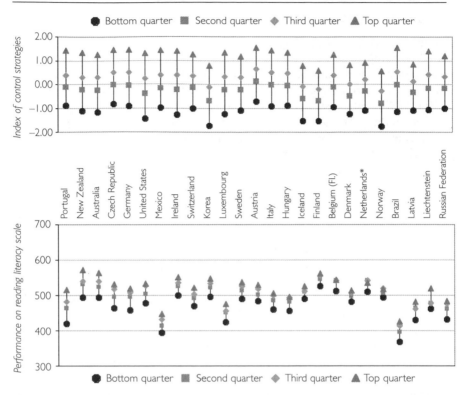

Figure 4.1 Index of control strategies and performance on the combined literacy scale of 15-year-olds, by quarters of the index (2000). *Response
rate too low to ensure comparability. *Note* OECD countries are sort-
ed in descending order of the magnitude of the difference in the
reading literacy scores of students in the top quarter of control
strategies and those in the bottom quarter.

Source: OECD, PISA 2000

reveals interesting information. In Finland, for example, students in the
three upper quartiles of use of control strategies perform equally well in
reading literacy and only those in the lowest quartile show a deviation.
Similar patterns can be seen in other countries, such as Belgium (Flemish
community), Germany, Italy, Luxembourg and the Netherlands. This suggests that students in the lower quartile in these countries, who do not apply
control strategies, may be at risk of poor performance. Identifying students
at risk and providing help for mastery of this competency may be an effective way of supporting poorly performing students.

The second example relates to students' self-concept. These scales were
based on the well known research of Marsh (e.g. Marsh and Craven 1999).
Because assumedly self-evaluations are relative measures, the comparisons

of absolute values must be done with caution, although the comparison of the magnitude of differences (e.g. between boys and girls) may be of interest. The first three columns in Table 4.2 show that the difference between boys' and girls' verbal self-concept within countries is quite large and significant.   In all countries except Korea, girls have a higher verbal self-concept. The last four columns of the table relate verbal self-concept and performance in reading literacy. While not large, there are differences in the mean performance of students who report a relatively high verbal self-concept and those who report a low verbal-self concept. In particular, students with the highest verbal self-concept also have the highest mean scores in reading literacy. Similar patterns emerge with respect to mathematics self-concept and performance in mathematical literacy.

Conclusions

These two examples from PISA 2000 demonstrate that it is possible to construct scales for self-regulated learning as a cross-curricular competency in a large-scale, international context. This allows relevant analyses within and between countries and illumination on important policy issues. These examples also show that causal order cannot be firmly established in the findings presented and possibly is less relevant then usually assumed. Do students have a 'high' self-concept because they are high performers? Or is it the other way round: having a 'high' self-concept helps students to achieve high scores in reading or mathematics? Regardless of the direction, because these aspects of self-regulated learning may also be seen as relevant outcomes of the education system in themselves and important for acquiring new knowledge in later life, the causality issue thus becomes less prominent. Further analyses in the previously mentioned thematic report elaborate on the results of this study (Artelt *et al.* 2003).

Issues for the near future

The foregoing sections showed that developing indicators on education outcomes in a new cross-curricular domain indeed has been successful. The analyses of the large body of self-regulated learning items from PISA 2000 showed that it was possible to develop a concise instrument that could provide indicators for this competency. Yet it is useful to turn back to the starting point of this chapter and discuss some issues that will emerge as the development of measures of other cross-curricular competencies is undertaken. The following section refers to cross-curricular competencies in general and, therefore, to self-regulated learning indicators specifically.

Table 4.2 Mean scores on the index of verbal self-concept, by gender and performance on the reading literacy scale, by national quarters of the index, of 15-year-olds (2000)

Country	Boys mean index	Girls mean index	Difference boys–girls[a]	Mean score of			
				bottom quarter	second quarter	third quarter	top quarter
Australia	-0.11	0.06	**-0.17**	499	519	538	572
Austria	-0.15	0.21	**-0.35**	484	492	513	547
Belgium	-0.24	-0.11	**-0.13**	514	529	553	548
Czech Republic	-0.45	-0.09	**-0.36**	478	490	511	536
Denmark	0.20	0.52	**-0.32**	456	491	510	548
Finland	-0.28	0.14	**-0.42**	509	531	560	593
Germany	-0.34	0.11	**-0.45**	477	476	503	534
Hungary	-0.30	0.02	**-0.32**	458	464	491	521
Iceland	-0.15	0.05	**-0.20**	474	495	522	551
Ireland	0.20	0.35	**-0.15**	513	527	533	542
Italy	0.08	0.52	**-0.44**	452	484	501	514
Korea	-0.34	-0.36	0.02	498	518	531	552
Luxembourg	0.06	0.26	**-0.21**	417	442	471	492
Mexico	-0.10	0.11	**-0.21**	410	415	425	441
New Zealand	-0.26	0.03	**-0.29**	514	510	544	573
Norway	-0.23	0.15	**-0.38**	470	490	523	561
Portugal	-0.23	0.08	**-0.31**	433	454	483	512
Sweden	-0.11	0.19	**-0.30**	481	503	528	559
Switzerland	-0.20	0.11	**-0.31**	473	482	511	524
United States	0.05	0.44	**-0.39**	469	496	526	558
OECD average	*-0.14*	*0.15*	*-0.29*	*473*	*490*	*513*	*539*
Brazil	0.11	-0.17	**-0.28**	391	392	407	424
Latvia	0.36	-0.15	**-0.51**	425	441	467	513
Lichtenstein	0.08	-0.29	**-0.37**	458	472	494	515
Russian Federation	0.37	-0.15	**-0.52**	435	447	471	505
Netherlands[b]	0.13	-0.11	**-0.25**	515	529	538	549

Notes

a Positive differences indicate that boys perform better than girls, negative differences indicate that girls perform better than boys. Differences that are statistically significant are indicated in bold.

b Response rate is too low to ensure comparability.

New questions

The most immediate impact of the availability of information on cross-curricular competencies are that new questions will be able to be answered. As with other macro-level data on outcomes, the distribution of competencies within countries and the breakdown for different sub-groups will be especially relevant at first. Do boys have similar level(s) of competencies to those of girls? Are these competencies equally distributed along social and ethnic lines? Is there a relationship between these competencies and personality factors or the availability of cultural and social capital? Do students in lower tracks or school types have a mastery of competencies equal to that of students in higher tracks? These are all new questions that can be addressed as indicators for cross-curricular competencies – including those on self-regulated learning – become available.

In a similar way, the relationship between cross-curricular competencies and performance in subject assessments is highly relevant. Are those students with high achievement in academic subjects also the ones who have strong cross-curricular competencies? Or is there a kind of compensatory mechanism that trades off competencies in subject areas against cross-curricular ones? This set of questions may be labelled as correlation versus compensation.

Researchers and policy makers also will be eager to learn whether or not curricula have some effect on the acquisition of cross-curricular competencies. Are schools that have organised activities explicitly referring to such competencies showing 'better' results than those that do not? Some researchers (Wesselingh 1997) have hypothesised that schools that explicitly prepare students for citizenship will have students who are more politically involved than will schools where students get no such preparation. Others have similarly argued that emphasising attachment, social competence and achievement at school will contribute to a student's participation in society later in life (Dijkstra *et al.* 1999). The issue of whether 'the school does matter' comes closer to having an answer with the availability of both cross-curricular and academic outcome measures. Principally, whether or not school practice could enhance these competencies should become clear. These are highly interesting issues and, fortunately, empirical evidence for exploring such assumptions is becoming available.

Until now, we have focused on relationships within countries, essentially looking into the microcosms of school and country. Another series of questions relates to macro-level differences, or those between countries. Can we extend the above-formulated questions to cross-country analysis as well? Are similar patterns visible between countries, and how can these patterns be explained?

Some issues become particularly pertinent on the macro-level, such as the issue of correlation versus compensation.[8] Do countries that perform well in terms of subject matter (reading, mathematics and science) also show high scores on the cross-curricular competency scales? Or should it be concluded that education is a zero-sum game: curricular time allocated to subject matter cannot be given at the same time to the development of other (cross-curricular) competencies? Using PISA 2000 data on self-regulated learning to test such hypotheses against the data of, for instance, Japan, Korea or Singapore versus the United States or the Netherlands will be highly relevant.

Studying in more detail whether education profiles of countries, for instance with regard to equality, match with scores on subject matter or with scores on cross-curricular competencies also becomes relevant. In such a way, maps of similarities and differences with regard to education may have to be drawn in new way, confronting education policy makers with a new reality and with the degree to which a variety of education goals are achieved.

Methodological issues

Several methodological issues are relevant for the further development of measures and indicators of cross-curricular competencies. First, there is a major issue in presenting a multitude of different – albeit relevant – outcomes of education. From the first issues of EAG, various ways of presenting data were developed, but these were mainly based on two-dimensional information (e.g. achievement per country, eventually broken down by gender). The availability and nature of data on cross-curricular competencies highlight the need for a more comprehensive picture that takes into account various dimensions of outcomes at the same time. These new, more sophisticated pictures need to be developed in such a way that the public audience and policy makers understand the findings.[9]

Second, the equivalence of instruments is a major concern in the domain of cross-curricular competencies. In principle, this is not different from similar concerns with regard to, for example, reading literacy. In reading, one tries to ensure that the instruments have the same meaning across countries and cultures (see Chapters 2, 8 and 10). However, for the cross-curricular competencies the scope of the argument is even wider. Not only may the meaning of the instrument vary across cultures, but also the content of the competencies themselves may also be different across cultures.[10] Citizenship may be measured in the same way but has different effects across countries. Problem solving may be measurable in the technical sense but may nevertheless miss the point of functional equivalence. One may even argue that the relevance of cross-curricular competencies varies over time, which adds another dimension to the problem of comparability and validity. Because the indicators of cross-curricular competencies intend to tap all these dimensions, extra focus on these issues of comparability and validity is needed. At the same time, some measures may be relevant only within a specified context. This may be the case with self-evaluations on the basis of relative classroom position.

Third, the PISA context, in which the experimentation with measures of such competencies has mainly occurred, restricts the scope of related indicators to 15-year-old students. Assessing additional target populations would be useful for two reasons. First, it can be argued that many cross-curricular competencies will be developed only at maturity. This implies that an older target population – for example, 18- or 21-year-olds – would be more attractive for study because it would allow the effects of education on the development of cross-curricular competencies to be investigated.[11] Second, the development of cross-curricular competencies in a person's life span should become a major issue: how do students develop these competencies and what is the (added value) role of schools? Such an issue can be studied only by launching longitudinal research that enables researchers to track personal growth and the formation of human capital.[12]

Fourth, regular monitoring for indicator purposes requires a stable infrastructure and long-term commitment to these issues. Though these requirements apply to any of the activities in the OECD/INES context, they are particularly important for the newly developing area of cross-curricular competencies. Investing in the monitoring of these competencies for a few years, only to discontinue it later, would not be useful.

Finally, the development of instruments and indicators is not accomplished overnight. A constant effort has to be made, which is not something extraordinary because the present generation of mathematics indicators have a thirty-five-year tradition in the IEA.

Political and policy issues

Political and policy issues also arise when cross-curricular competencies are to be measured as a regular part of assessment systems. There is broad agreement on which entities are responsible for the academic outcomes in subjects such as reading, mathematics or science. Because the relationship between the curriculum and an assessment and the resulting indicators is often close (or at least identifiable), responsibility can easily be taken by Ministries, school boards or inspectorates both for implementing the studies and for celebrating or trying to improve the results.

The question of which entities are responsible may be less obvious with regard to cross-curricular competencies, which almost by definition do not belong to curricula. As long as cross-curricular competencies are considered relevant outcomes of schooling, authorities can easily see them belonging to the educational domain. But as soon as the same authorities consider these competencies as belonging outside their locus of control, then it is not completely clear who would adopt final responsibility for collecting the information. This is not completely fantasy. The feasibility study referenced earlier indicated that certain survey questions relating to knowledge of politics and self-concept could not be asked in some countries because the schools did not want to be evaluated on these aspects because they were seen as outside their control.[13] This must be seen as a serious issue that needs to be settled in time.

Parallel to this argument, the question may be raised of what to do with the results. Must results be made public in the same way as achievement results are published in some countries in the form of 'league tables' of schools? Are some schools indeed better in maths and science and cross-curricular competencies? Is high performance on a range of outcomes a virtue of the school, or is it mainly generated by the student intake of the school? Though the technical issues can be handled appropriately by multi-level analyses, whether such political aspects must be solved at a national level or at a school level is less clear.

Parallel developments and future directions

Interestingly, most of the above-mentioned issues match quite well with ongoing or programmed activities. In the framework of the European Union, discussions are occurring on instruments that cover competencies wider than school achievement. No decisions have been made yet with regard to developmental activities, but it is clear that the focus is on competencies similar to those cross-curricular competencies discussed within the OECD/INES context (EC Basic Skills Working Group 2003).

Parallel to the development of the self-regulated learning instruments for PISA 2000 and the problem-solving instrument for PISA 2003 (see Chapter 5), the DeSeCo Project was under way. This study aimed at improving the theoretical basis for the definition and selection of key competencies. In this project, experts from psychology, sociology, education, economics and philosophy were asked to give a description of the state of the art in their respective disciplines with regard to theories of basic competencies (Salganik et al. 1998). In addition, two large international symposia were organised and additional expert perspectives were sought. It became clear that a great variety of experiences exist. Competencies, for example, may be defined as abstract or concrete; may refer to general or specific skills; or may relate to the workplace or to the 'good life' (Rychen and Salganik 2001). However, by the end of the five-year project the group was able to provide a theory-grounded concept of competence and to elaborate three categories of key competence (Rychen and Salganik 2003).

Several national studies of similar scope to the OECD/INES work have also been conducted, and they have adopted the terminology and label of cross-curricular competencies as well. In Finland large-scale data were collected in 1998 on a nationwide sample of sixth- and ninth-grade students by the Centre for Educational Assessment at the University of Helsinki.

Achievement measures were accompanied with extensive testing on motivations, self-concept, learning strategies and knowledge (Hautamäki 1999). In the context of the evaluation of lower secondary education in the Netherlands, measures were developed to evaluate students' capacity to solve everyday life problems, so-called 'general skills' (Meijer and Elshout-Mohr 1999a). It appears that there is indeed a high correlation of the general skills scale with scholastic achievement (0.82), raising the question of the conceptual and instrumental overlap between scholastic achievement and these general skills (Meijer and Elshout-Mohr 1999b).

This list of examples can undoubtedly be expanded. The point is that, indeed, researchers and policy makers have become interested in widening the criteria for successful schooling and measuring that the criteria are being met.

However, new measures of additional cross-curricular competencies have to be developed in the future, and the process of identification of new competencies of interest has just started. For example, the knowledge of and attitudes toward ecological issues were seen as important at the very early stages of the OECD/INES cross-curricular competencies work, but then no indicators were or are available. At the same time, the existing areas must be developed further, such as problem solving (see Chapter 5).

That most indicators refer to individual competencies may not be entirely logical: much of the 'performance' of a school or of a school system refers to an aggregation of individual performances. Thus there is no special need to evaluate only individual activities. On the contrary, one would be interested, for example, in how students as a group co-operate and find solutions for problems. Also, in later professional life, such co-operation is likely to occur and to be valued. Group work could thus be developed as an area for future indicators. The outcomes of the DeSeCo Project, which identified functioning in socially heterogeneous group as one of three categories of key competence, will be useful in moving forward in this area.

Summary

This chapter has discussed a new area of educational indicators, cross-curricular competencies and specifically self-regulated learning. The main argument of the movement to develop these indicators is that schools do a lot more than subject teaching and students learn a lot more than subjects in school. In education research and in the development of education indicators, the attention to measures of cross-curricular competencies has greatly increased. Yet the number of empirical studies that have measured cross-curricular competencies at the national or international level is still small.

Of course, various technical issues have not been discussed in this chapter. How must instruments be validated to allow international comparisons? How do national or cultural stereotypes with regard to (social) competencies affect measurement? Do we have to control for social desirability effects because national patterns may differ in this respect? Such questions will be addressed in further analysis of available data and future development work. Investment in new instruments may also be necessary, as the experiences with instruments on problem solving have shown.

In the OECD/INES context, developmental activities have been ongoing since 1993 and have led to empirical evaluations of potential instruments. In PISA 2000, for the first time on an international scale, subject achievement (reading, mathematics and science) was accompanied by appropriate measurement of one set of cross-curricular competencies, self-regulated learning competencies. The availability of large-scale data on self-regulated learning competencies is allowing researchers to develop new indicators that are relevant for lifelong learning, the flexibility of the work force and personality building. It also is providing the international community with empirical evidence on the issue of to what degree schools and education systems equip students with learning competencies that are relevant for later life. That is what schools are for but it has not yet been demonstrated empirically in detail.

Notes

1 It was decided not to undertake additional development work in the realm of civics because a study of civic education (CivEd) was already being planned in the IEA context. The results of the two phases of the CivEd study are described in Torney-Purta *et al.* (1999) and Torney-Purta *et al.* (2001).

2 This section is extended in Artelt *et al.* (2003).

3 This is in contrast with, for instance, the problem-solving component of PISA (see Chapter 5), which focuses on actual problem-solving capacity and not on self-reports.

4 This is an explicit subject in the thematic report on self-regulated learning from PISA 2000 (Artelt *et al.* 2003). For about half the scales it seems to be possible to compare country means directly.

5 This was one of the main issues in the stage of instrument validation in the field study for PISA 2000 (see Peschar and Molenaar 1999).

6 Jürgen Baumert (Germany), Helmut Fend (Switzerland), Herbert Marsh (Australia), Harold O'Neil (United States), Luc Van de Poele (Belgium) and Jules L. Peschar (Netherlands) served on this expert group.

7 See *A Review of the CCC Analysis Plan* (OECD working document 2001) for details.

8 Fend (1995, pp.133-7) points to a related issue of 'risk indicators'. These indicators may reflect aspects of mental health, anxiety, delinquent or offensive behaviour or suicide rates among students. Such indicators may very well correlate with country differences in indicators of cross-curricular competencies.

9 In *Prepared for Life* (OECD 1997, pp. 72-6) various suggestions have been made.

10 This is the classic issue already extensively documented in Verba *et al.* (1978).

11 It is only for practical and budgetary reasons that PISA focuses on 15-year-olds who can be approached via school surveys. Household surveys, such as the adult literacy studies applied (see Chapter 3), would not be a realistic option for a cross-sectional study in over thirty countries.

12 In the Netherlands such a study is being undertaken for a national cohort of 15-year-olds who will be approached several years later (Van der Wal and Peschar 1999).

13 This led a prominent member of Network A to the conclusion that there was censorship in that country.

References

Artelt C., Baumert J., Julius-McElvany N. and Peschar J.L., 2003. *Learners for Life. Student Approaches to Learning* (Paris: OECD).

Baumert J., Fend H., O'Neil H. and Peschar J.L., 1998. *Prepared for Lifelong Learning. Frame of Reference for the Measurement of Self-regulated Learning as a Cross-curricular Competency (CCC) in the PISA Project* (Paris: OECD).

Blau P.M. and Duncan O.D., 1997. *The American Occupational Structure* (New York: Wiley).

Dijkstra A.B., Van Oudenhoven J.P. and Peschar J.L., 1999. Attachment, Competencies and Achievement in the Life Course. Ongoing research programme at the University of Groningen, funded by Dutch National Science Foundation (NWO).

EC Basic Skills Working Group, 2003. Key documents, available from http://www.eaea.org/wg03b3.html (23 August 2003).

Eccles J.S. and Wigfield A., 1995. In the mind of the achiever: the structure of adolescents' academic achievement-related beliefs and self-perceptions. *Personality and Social Psychology Bulletin*, 21, 215–25.

Fend H., 1995. Personality theories and developmental processes: their implications for indicators of the quality of schooling. In *Measuring What Students Learn* (Paris: OECD).

Fend H., 1998. *A Theoretical Framework for the Development of Cross-curricular Competencies* (Zürich: University of Zürich).

Harter S. and Connell J.P., 1984. A model of children's achievement and related self-perceptors of competence, control, and motivational orientation. In Nicholls (ed.) *Advances in Motivation and Achievement* XXIII (Greenwich CT: JAI Press), pp. 219–50.

Hautamäki J., 1998. *Learning to Learn as Part of Cross-curricular Competencies. Studies of Sixth and Ninth Graders in Finland* (Helsinki: Centre for Educational Assessment, University of Helsinki).

Healy T., 1997. *Measuring What Students Know* (Paris, OECD).

Marsh H.W. and Craven R., 1999. Academic self-concept: beyond the dustbowl. In Phye (ed.) *Handbook of Classroom Assessment* (San Diego CA: Academic Press).

Meijer J. and Elhout-Mohr M., 1999a. *Validering van AlvaBavo, een toets voor algemene vaardigheden in de Basisvorming* (Validation of AlvaBavo, a test to assess cross-curricular skills of students 14–16 years of age) (Amsterdam: SCO-Kohnstamm Instituut).

Meijer J. and Elshout-Mohr M., 1999b. An Instrument for the Assessment of Cross-curricular Skills. Unpublished paper (Amsterdam: SCO-Kohnstamm Instituut).

Niemivirta M., 1999. *Habits of Mind and Academic Endeavours. The Role of Goal Orientations and Motivational Beliefs in School Performance* (Helsinki: Centre for Educational Assessment, University of Helsinki).

OECD, 1997. *Prepared for Life?* (Paris: OECD).

OECD, 2001. *Knowledge and Skills for Life. First Results from PISA 2000* (Paris: OECD).

Peschar J.L., 1993. Prepared for Real Life: Establishing Indicators for Non-curriculum-bound Indicators (NOBs) in a Comparative Setting. Presented at the OECD/INES/Network A meeting, Vilamoura, Portugal, 10–12 February.

Peschar J.L. and Molenaar I.W., 1999. Plan of Analysis of Self-regulated Learning as a Cross-curricular Competency in PISA's Field Study (Groningen: University of Groningen; Washington DC: American Institutes for Research).

Peschar J.L., Veenstra D.R. and Molenaar I.W., 1999. Self-regulated Learning as a Cross-curricular Competency. The Construction of Instruments in Twenty-two Countries for the PISA Main Study, 2000 (Groningen: University of Groningen; Washington DC: American Institutes for Research).

Ramseier E., Keller C. and Moser U., 1999. *Bilanz bildung* (TIMSS) (Chur and Zürich: Rüeger).

Rychen D.S. and Salganik L.H. (eds), 2001. *Defining and Selecting Key Competencies* (Berne: Hogrefe & Huber).

Rychen D.S. and Salganik L.H. (eds), 2003. *Key Competencies for a Successful Life and a Well-functioning Society* (Berne: Hogrefe & Huber).

Salganik L.H., Rychen D.S., Moser U. and Konstant J., 1998. Project on Competencies in the OECD Context. Analysis of Theoretical and Conceptual Foundations (DeSeCo) (Neuchâtel: Swiss Federal Statistical Office).

Spee A.A.J., 1999. *Vaardigheden internationaal vergeleken* (Competences in International Comparison). Submitted paper (The Hague: Ministry of Education, Culture and Sciences).

Torney-Purta J., Lehmann R., Oswald H. and Shultz W., 2001. *Citizenship and Education in Twenty-eight Countries. Civic Knowledge and Engagement at Age Fourteen* (Amsterdam: IEA).

Torney-Purta J., Schwille J. and Amadeo J-A., 1999. *Civic Education across Countries. Twenty-four Case Studies from the IEA Civic Education Project* (Amsterdam: IEA).

Trier U.P., 1991. Non-curriculum-bound Outcomes. Presented at the OECD/INES/Network A meeting, Paris.

Trier U.P. and Peschar J.L., 1995. Cross-curricular competencies: rationale and strategy for developing a new indicator. In *Measuring What Students Learn* (Paris: OECD), pp. 99–107.

Van der Wal M. and Peschar J.L., 1999. Development of Cross-curricular Competencies in Adolescence. Ongoing research project at the University of Groningen, funded by the Dutch National Science Foundation.

Verba S., Nie N.H. and Kim J.O., 1978. *Participation and Political Equality. A Seven-nation Comparison* (Cambridge: Cambridge University Press).

Weinert F., 2001. Concept of competence: a conceptal clarification. In Rychen and Salganik (eds) *Defining and Selecting Key Competencies* (Berne: Hogrefe & Huber).

Wesselingh A.A., 1997. *De school als oefenplaats voor burgers* (School as a Testing Ground for Citizens). Presented at Dutch National Science Foundation conference, The Hague.

Chapter 5

Assessment of cross-curricular problem-solving competencies

Eckhard Klieme

Problem solving is a highly popular topic in the human resources literature as well as in educational policy, pedagogy and curriculum development. It is ranked as an important key qualification by labour market experts (see Binkley *et al.* 1999) as well as in the literature on vocational training and education (e.g. Didi *et al.* 1993). Problem solving was classified as an important outcome of schooling by OECD experts (OECD 1997) and is often stated as a high-level goal of school curricula (e.g. Svecnik 1999). Likewise, problem solving is relevant to many – if not all – school subjects, including for example, mathematics, because 'solving problems is an activity at the heart of doing mathematics' (De Corte *et al.* 1996).

But what kind of relationship exists between solving problems of a certain kind (e.g. mathematical problems) and problem solving as a general capability? Although problem solving seems to be crucial for academic, professional and everyday performance, defining what problem solving as a general competence or life skill means, and how it might be measured in large-scale assessments, especially in contrast to domain-specific competencies like mathematical or scientific literacy, is unclear. This chapter reviews the state of the art with regard to the concept and development of measures of problem solving.

Because there is a considerable body of research on problem solving in general cognitive psychology as well as in differential psychology, the first section of the chapter defines problem solving in psychological terms and discusses related issues, such as the domain-specificity of problem solving and its relation to intelligence. The second part discusses the notion of problem solving as a cross-curricular or non-curriculum-bound competence and outlines a framework for problem-solving assessment within educational evaluation and systems monitoring. The third section provides an overview of other experiences in measuring problem solving in large-scale settings, including a description of the German national enhancement of PISA 2000, which field-tested and validated a broad set of problem-solving instruments.

The concept of problem solving

The definition in Box 5.1 is based on an understanding of problem solving as it is established in psychology (Hunt 1994; Mayer 1992; Mayer and Wittrock 1996; Smith 1991). Although relatively broad, the definition makes clear that problem solving is to be understood as a cognitive process. This is in contrast to the everyday understanding of the term or to the clinical psychological concept in which 'problem solving' is associated with the resolution of social and emotional conflicts. The concern here is with cognitive-analytical problem solving only. Social context plays a role here too, for example when problems have to be approached interactively and resolved co-operatively – and motivational factors, such as interest in the topic and task orientation, influence the problem-solving process. However, the quality of problem solving is primarily determined by the comprehension of the problem situation, the thinking processes used to approach the problem and the appropriateness of the solution.

Box 5.1   A psychological definition of problem solving

Problem solving is goal-directed thinking and action in situations for which no routine solution procedure is available. The problem solver has a more or less well defined goal, but does not immediately know how to reach it. The incongruence of goals and admissible operators constitutes a problem. The understanding of the problem situation and its step-by-step transformation, based on planning and reasoning, constitute the process of problem solving.

This definition encompasses a wide range of problem-solving processes, including the following:

- *Scope* of a problem, which can range from working on limited parts of a task to planning and executing actions to completing extensive projects.
- *Context*, which can reflect different domains (e.g. school subjects, topic areas, areas of experience), may be theoretical or practical in nature, may be related to academic situations or to the real world (e.g. school life, students' out-of-school activities, games, adult life or professional situations) and may be more or less authentic.
- *Complexity*, which is determined by the characteristics of the problem itself, which can have a closed or open format, a well defined or an ill defined goal or a transparent (explicitly named) or intransparent constraint and which can involve a few isolated elements or numerous interconnected ones.

Following Pólya (1945, 1980), the process of problem solving has frequently been described in terms of the following stages: (1) defining the goal; (2) analysing the given situation and constructing a mental representation; (3) devising a strategy and planning the steps to be taken; (4) executing the plan, including controlling and, if necessary, modifying the strategy; (5) evaluating the result. Such a sequential model may be useful for training purposes or for the implementation of problem-solving heuristics in everyday life.

However, the cognitive processes that are activated in the course of problem solving are certainly more diverse and more complex than these categories, and they are most probably organised in a non-linear manner. Among these processes the following components may be identified: searching for information; structuring and integrating it into a mental representation of the problem (i.e. creating a 'situation model'); reasoning, based on the situation model; planning actions and other solution steps; executing and evaluating those solution steps; and continuously processing external information and feedback. Baxter and Glaser (1997) present a similar list of cognitive activities, labelled *general components of competence in problem solving*, which are problem representation, solution strategies, self-monitoring and explanations.

Psychological models of these processes and the mental structures (representations) on which they operate have changed over the history of psychology, each being tailored to the problems that were the focus of the respective research paradigm. In the early years of cognitive psychology, for example, 'insight' was seen as a major mechanism for problem solving. This notion was appropriate in limited but ill defined problem situations, where a sudden restructuring or reinterpretation could solve the problem. In their seminal book *Human Problem Solving*, which served as a framework for numerous studies in information processing psychology and artificial intelligence, Newell and Simon (1972) described problem solving as a process of search in a 'problem space' consisting of states (including given state and target state) and operators. This model was appropriate to the study of well defined, puzzle-type problems. While Newell and Simon believed they had discovered rather universal mechanisms, research on scientific reasoning and expertise later proved that problem solving depends heavily on the use of domain-specific knowledge, which was described in terms of rule systems, schemata, mental models or 'mental tools' (e.g. Chi *et al.* 1988; Weinert and Kluwe 1987). At the same time it became clear that metacognition, defined as the process of planning, monitoring, evaluating and regulating ongoing cognition as well as the knowledge and beliefs about cognitive functioning, is of crucial importance to the process and product of problem-solving activities (Brown 1987; Flavell 1976).

To study how well students can solve particular types of problems, identifying mental structures or components of the process in detail is not necessary. Assessment frameworks need not meet the sophistication of cognitive psychological models. However, even a purely functional approach to assessing problem solving should take into account some important results of psychological research associated with the key terms 'general intelligence', 'complex problem solving' and 'domain specificity'. The following sections briefly review these findings and discuss their consequences for the design of assessments of problem solving.

Problem solving, reasoning and related constructs

Problem solving as defined above is quite similar to some other constructs in modern psychology. Among them are critical thinking (Ennis 1996; Norris 1989), which means judging the credibility of arguments, and naturalistic decision making (Zsambok and Klein 1997), which is defined as the use of knowledge and expertise to act under complex and uncertain conditions. Each of these constructs describes some kind of intellectual activity, based on reasoning and the application of knowledge. Therefore they are closely linked with the construct of intelligence, which is understood by many modern psychologists as a general ability to acquire, integrate and apply new knowledge. Intelligence, in turn, is linked with more basic features of the human information processing system, such as working memory capacity or mental speed (Neisser *et al.* 1996).

In the tradition of psychometric research, the core of general intelligence is reasoning (Carroll 1993) or information processing capacity (Süss 1999). It is operationalised by tests using mathematical word problems, number series (e.g. 1, 2, 4, 7, 11, _?) and analogical reasoning, in particular by figural analogies (e.g. / is to \ as # is to _?). All these may be subsumed under the broad concept of problem solving as defined above, with the exception of rare cases in which highly trained persons solve such tasks using special algorithms. Thus whichever indicators of problem-solving competence are used will be correlated to psychometric measures of reasoning ability. The strength of this correlation and, hence, the extent to which problem-solving competence can actually be distinguished from reasoning is an open question in cognitive psychology research. Even with respect to complex, dynamic, computer-based problem-solving tasks (e.g. Frensch and Funke 1995) several studies suggest that inter-individual differences in performance can be fully explained by reasoning ability and basic features of the human information processing system (Süss 1999).

Another recent perspective on this controversy is taken from differential psychology, namely Robert Sternberg and his associates (e.g. Sternberg and Kaufman 1998). Sternberg supports a broad concept of intelligence, basically equating it with problem-solving abilities. He identifies three subcomponents of intelligence: (1) analytical abilities, such as 'identifying the existence of a problem, defining the nature of a problem, setting up a strategy for solving the problem and monitoring one's solution process'; (2)

creative abilities 'required to generate problem-solving options'; (3) practical abilities needed to apply problem-solving strategies to real-life tasks. Sternberg assumes that practical intelligence is clearly discernible from intelligence assessed by means of the classic psychometric measures (IQ). However, a method of measuring the practical aspects of intelligence and problem-solving abilities independently has yet to be devised. In computer-based complex problem solving the practical and the analytical aspects presumably mix. The procedure Sternberg proposes to measure practical intelligence cannot be regarded as a performance test. Rather he presents respondents with descriptions of real-life or job-related problem situations and asks them to evaluate different response alternatives. If a respondent's evaluations correspond to those of a reference group ('experts' in an occupational field or representatively selected control groups for real-life problems), the respondent is said to have 'tacit knowledge', which Sternberg sees as the core of practical intelligence (Sternberg and Wagner 1986).

The assessment of the third aspect in Sternberg's triarchic concept of intelligence – creativity – appears to be just as difficult a task, judging by the present state of research. Because problem solving emphasises novel situations that cannot be dealt routine, it always requires a certain degree of creativity. Attempts to measure creativity independently, as originality, flexibility and fluency of ideas (e.g. Krampen 1993), or to assess it as a distinctive feature of problem-solving performance (Mumford et al. 1997), however, have not yet yielded convincing results.

Addressing the complexity and dynamics of problem solving

In recent years psychological research on problem solving has turned to increasingly complex, authentic problems with broad scopes (Sternberg and Frensch 1991). Research on problem solving is no longer concerned with well defined puzzles (e.g., in the extreme case, reasoning tasks as used in psychometric tests of human intelligence), which can be solved by the application of suitable operations. Instead, research on problem solving incorporates the thinking of experts in scientific and professional domains (Reimann and Schult 1996; Zsambok and Klein 1997) in planning and problem solving in real-life contexts (Funke and Fritz 1995; Jeck 1997; Lave 1988) and in complex ecological, economic and technical systems (Dörner et al. 1983; Frensch and Funke 1995).

Computer simulation has proved to be an important tool for investigating complex problem-solving performance. When interacting with the computer, the problem solver explores the simulated system, generates and tests (more or less systematically) hypotheses about relationships and regularities, acquires knowledge and is finally able to govern the system by purposeful intervention. Systems used include realistic simulations of highly interconnected ecological or economic systems (Dörner *et al.* 1983) or, for school contexts (e.g. Leutner 1992), systematically constructed, discrete, smaller-scale systems (i.e. 'finite state automata': Buchner and Funke 1993) and virtual experimental environments. From the perspective of educational psychology, such systems can be understood as environments for discovery learning (Boshuizen *et al.* 1997; Leutner 1992). From the perspective of problem-solving research, these instruments provide a new quality of problems, distinguished by high levels of complexity and, in particular, by a dynamic character.

These dynamic tasks have three advantages over static paper-and-pencil tasks. First, the demands of the tasks are enhanced by requiring active searching and continuous processing of external information and feedback. Although solving written problem-solving tasks may also involve applying, evaluating and modifying processing strategies, respondents' interaction with the computer, however, makes such a course of action inevitable. Second, in this medium the problem situation can be made much more authentic than in a written test. Third, not only the results but also the course of the problem-solving process can be recorded and assessed (i.e. the type, frequency, length and sequence of interventions made by the subjects). This provides process-based indicators of problem-solving strategies.

These three advantages are mutually independent and demonstrate the benefits of using computers in the assessment of problem-solving performance. There are, however, serious theoretical and methodological problems when measuring 'strategies'. The definition of such measures, their reliability, the extent to which they are comparable across different simulated systems and the impact of motivational factors are research questions that are not yet fully answered. Both the advantages and disadvantages mentioned above also apply to so-called performance assessment where students engage in hands-on activities or experiments (Linn 1994). In fact computer-based discovery tasks may be understood as a variant of performance assessment.

Mumford and his colleagues (1998) suggest that the degree to which problem solving is focused on salient and eventually contradictive features of the problem situation may be an important indicator of strategic behaviour. However, their attempt to operationalise this kind of strategy in paper-and-pencil tasks resulted in rather low correlations between strategy indicators and external criteria. Veenman and his associates (1997) proposed a set of indicators for metacognitive skilfulness, namely orientation, systematic orderliness, evaluation and elaboration, based on extensive qualitative analyses of think-aloud protocols. Veenman reports rather strong predictive power of these indicators for academic success. Most other research on metacognition has focused on reading or it has been based upon self-reported learning strategies. (For an adaptation to large-scale assessment see Chapter 4 and Baumert *et al.* 1998.) The assessment of problem solving, especially the evaluation of processes and strategies, overlaps these paradigms, but it is based on behavioural data (i.e. on problem-solving performance rather than on questionnaires, as in the previous examples). The German framework for assessing problem solving in PISA 2000 (Klieme *et al.* 2001) aimed to identify strategy indicators by automatic analysis of the respondents' operations in computer-simulated scenarios.

Domain specificity of problem-solving performance

One of the most important insights of recent research in cognitive psychology is that demanding problems cannot be solved without knowledge in the domain in question. The concept of a problem space through which a general problem solver moves by domain-independent search strategies (Newell and Simon 1972) turned out to be too simple to describe the understanding of problem situations and the process of finding solutions. Efforts to identify a general, domain-independent competence for steering dynamic systems ('operative intelligence') within the framework of complex problem-solving research were also unsuccessful; performance with such systems can only partially be transferred to other systems (Funke 1991).

Problem solving is dependent on knowledge of concepts and facts (declarative knowledge) and knowledge of rules and strategies (procedural knowledge) in the relevant subject domain. Empirical support for the importance of knowledge is provided by comparison of the problem-solving strategies used by experts and those used by novices (Gruber and Mandl 1996; Reimann and Schult 1996; Schunn and Anderson 1999), by analysis of the factors affecting the development of school performance (Helmke and Weinert 1997), by laboratory experiments on learning in the natural sciences (Glaser *et al.* 1992) and by studies of real-world problem-solving performance – for example, studies of Brazilian street vendors who use complex rules, detached from those learned in school maths lessons, to do demanding price calculations (Lave 1988).

The amount of relevant previous knowledge available could also account for the relationship between intelligence and problem-solving performance, as shown in the work of Raaheim (1988) and Leutner (1999). People with no relevant previous knowledge cannot explore the problem situation and plan a solution in a systematic manner but must rely on trial and error. Those who are already familiar with the task are able to deal with it routinely. General intellectual ability, as measured by reasoning tasks, plays no role in either of these cases. When problem solvers are moderately familiar with the task, however, reasoning strategies can be successfully implemented, thus resulting in clear correlations between intelligence and problem-solving performance.

These findings are crucial for the assessment of problem-solving competencies. They show that the idea of universal problem-solving competence is not tenable. (Box 5.2 summarises the author's recommendations for an assessment framework based on the research described in the three previous sections.) If the idea of a universal problem-solving ability must be abandoned, however, how can problem solving be viewed and assessed as a cross-curricular competence? This issue is addressed in the next section.

Box 5.2 Research-based recommendations for problem-solving assessment frameworks

Problem solving, reasoning and related constructs

In accordance with the research on problem solving, reasoning and related constructs, the author recommended that a framework for assessing problem solving should cover practical as well as analytical components. Some components will be close to psychometric reasoning, while others – especially strategy indicators, such as from computer-based complex problem solving – may prove to make unique contributions to the cognitive profile of students. Work done in related areas, such as critical thinking, could also be helpful for developing or adapting instruments for use in large-scale assessment.

Complex and dynamic problem solving

After reviewing the research on complex and dynamic problem solving, the author concluded that frameworks for the assessment of problem solving should – in addition to more traditional multiple-choice or extended-answer formats – incorporate complex, dynamic tasks that require continuous processing of information in more authentic settings, which could allow for the assessment of the strategies as well as the outcomes of problem-solving behaviour. Portable computers with simulation software, which under present conditions would be accessible at least for some sub-populations within large-scale assessments, serve this purpose. Strategy indicators may be in part derived from research on metacognition. Another way to enhance problem-solving tasks in terms of complexity and dynamics is to implement them in small group settings where participants must reach a common solution by negotiating goals and strategies and by considering the information (contributed by different participants) that is available. This approach has been widely used in job placement and selection (e.g. at assessment centres) and may benefit from recent research in distributed co-operative problem solving. Scoring would be based on solutions generated by the groups of students (not on individual performance) and would be interpreted as a measure of complex problem-solving outcomes which implicitly also measures strategic qualities and some aspects of social competence.

Domain-specificity of problem solving

Following research on the domain-specificity of problem solving, the author recommends that frameworks for problem-solving assessment should aim at defining a profile of competencies in particular domains (whether subject or real-world). The selection of these domains and the balance between high specificity and proximity to general intelligence, in the sense of psychometric reasoning, is of great importance. Problem-solving tasks should be carefully directed at the target population to ensure that they neither can be solved as a matter of routine nor place excessive demands on students, thus triggering trial-and-error behaviour. Students' relevant previous knowledge should, if possible, be controlled for empirically.

Problem solving in PISA

As noted in previous chapters, when OECD countries' policy makers set out to define an international programme to assess the outcomes of schooling, they address the following guiding question: 'What do young adults at the end of education need in terms of skills to be able to play a constructive role as citizens in society?' (Trier and Peschar 1995). Thus they crossed the boundaries of school curricula as well as the limitations of classical models of human ability. They neither restricted the scope of assessment to knowledge and skills within a few school subjects nor referred to psychological theories of general intellectual abilities. Instead they took a functional view, seeking to learn whether young adults are prepared to cope with the challenges of their future lives. Such a disposition for mastering unforeseen demands and tasks has been called life skills (Binkley *et al.* 1999), non-curriculum-bound outcomes or cross-curricular competencies (OECD 1997; Trier and Peschar 1995).

In using the term 'competencies' rather than 'abilities' the PISA effort fitted into a scholarly discussion in psychology launched by McClelland (1973), Bandura (1990) and others (Barrett and Depinet 1991), which has been reviewed by Weinert (2001). These authors claim that the measurement of general, domain-independent skills or traits is of little use when performance in real-life situations is to be understood or optimised. As Bandura (1990) stated, 'there is a marked difference between possessing knowledge and skill and being able to use them well under diverse circumstances, many of which contain ambiguous, unpredictable and stressful elements'. Being able to cope with a certain range of situations is called a competence. Weinert (2001) suggested that a similar, purely functional approach should be used in large-scale assessments of education outcomes. Competences should be defined by the range of situations and tasks that have to be mastered, and assessment might be accomplished by confronting the student with a sample of such (eventually simulated) situations. Such an assessment would be of greater practical use because it would go beyond compartmentalised and inert knowledge.

In fact the functional understanding of competencies became central to PISA as it has been implemented. For example, the PISA framework for the 2003 cycle defines mathematical literacy as 'an individual's capacity to identify and understand the role mathematics plays in the world, to make well-founded judgments and to use and engage with mathematics in ways that meet the needs of that individual's life as a constructive, concerned and reflective citizen' (OECD 2003). Likewise, reading literacy and science literacy are related to everyday applications and authentic tasks. Obviously such competencies rely heavily on non-routine, goal-oriented, high-level cognitive processes, and thus they incorporate problem solving in the broad sense of our definition. This becomes more clear when one examines the sub-components of the literacy dimensions described within the frameworks. For mathematical literacy, for example, the framework distinguishes between three competency clusters: reproduction, connections and reflections. Roughly, the distinction between the first cluster and the latter two may be understood as a distinction between non-problem (i.e. routine or reproductive) and problem-type tasks. Within the framework for scientific literacy, among the science processes 'understanding scientific investigation' and 'interpreting scientific evidence and conclusions' most probably address some sort of domain-specific problem-solving competence.

The assessment of problem-solving competencies in PISA and similar programmes has to include an explicit approach to problem solving within the literacy domains (i.e. domain-specific problem-solving competencies). In general the assessment items within each domain will be anchored on a latent scale that fits to the Rasch model so that each student's performance can as well be anchored on that scale. What is the position of problem-type tasks within these latent scales? Theoretically, for each of the domains three different structures are possible.

One possibility is that there is one latent dimension, and the different types of tasks (i.e. the components of the respective frameworks) form a hierarchy within the dimension. This would imply that problem-type tasks consistently have higher difficulty parameters than routine or reproductive items. A second possibility is that problem-type tasks vary in difficulty as routine-type tasks do, and they form independent sub-dimensions of the literacy domain. This would imply that, for example, the connections cluster of mathematical literacy items would constitute a unique Rasch scale, distinct from reproductive items, which may be interpreted as a 'mathematical problem solving' scale. A third possibility is that both routine and problem-type tasks vary in difficulty across a wide range but do not represent independent competency dimensions. Those students who can do routine and reproductive tasks are, in most cases, also good problem solvers, and vice versa. This would mean that problem-solving competence cannot be distinguished from routine or reproductive competencies within the domains – neither as a higher level of proficiency (as in the first scenario) nor as a distinctive sub-dimension (as in the second scenario).

The PISA frameworks for reading, mathematical and scientific literacy mainly argue against the first scenario but leave the ultimate answer to be answered by empirical investigation. Findings from psychology about the dependence of problem solving on domain-specific knowledge would support the first scenario, and in fact German research on proficiency scales in TIMSS (Klieme and Köller 2000) as well as analyses of national data from PISA 2000 are in accordance with this hypothesis. Results from PISA 2003, in which mathematical literacy is the focus of the assessment and problem solving is being assessed as a cross-curricular competency, are forthcoming in 2004.

Assuming that an approach to identify domain-specific problem-solving dimensions or levels within the three literacy domains has been developed, discriminating it from problem solving as a cross-curricular competence can be attempted. Here again, there seem to exist several alternatives.

One alternative is that cross-curricular problem solving is made up of all problem-solving indicators from the three domains, combined into one latent dimension. Thus the term 'cross-curricular competence' is understood in the rather narrow sense of being measured across curricular domains. Another alternative is that problem solving as a cross-curricular competency is understood as problem solving in contexts that clearly go beyond (or cross) the boundaries of the three literacy domains into what could be regarded as transfer domains. These domains may include school subjects other then mathematics or science, integrative domains/subjects (e.g. the combination of science, mathematics and geography when students have to work in a simulated environment), extra-curricular activities (e.g. editing a school journal, which is part of school life but not part of a particular domain) or games. A third alternative is that problem solving as a cross-curricular competency is assessed within certain settings that are not used for the literacy domains. These settings may be distinguished by their complexity. On one hand, measures of cross-curricular competencies may include more complex, computer-based or small-group settings, while on the other hand they may include more constrained, reasoning-type tasks. Thus cross-curricular problem solving would be characterised by particular performance expectations, such as the continuous processing of external information and feedback and analogical or combinatorial reasoning.

Based on psychological research as discussed in this chapter, the expectation that problem-solving indicators from different domains will constitute a general problem-solving competence is highly unreasonable. If, indeed, a broad range of problem-solving tasks could be scaled on a single latent dimension, that dimension most probably would be identical to general intelligence or reasoning. Thus the first alternative is ruled out, and context (the second alternative) and setting (the third alternative) are used to specify cross-curricular problem solving.

The following summarise the discussion on domain-specific and cross-curricular problem-solving competencies:

- Frameworks for assessing problem-solving competencies should define a profile of competencies rather than a unique competence.
- Domain-specific problem-solving competencies related to the traditional literacy domains should be part of the profile, although whether or not they can be characterised as proficiency levels or sub-dimensions of the respective literacy scales is open to investigation.
- Cross-curricular problem-solving competencies should be assessed by tasks that differ from literacy measures in terms of context (focusing various transfer domains) and setting (focusing complex, dynamic environments as well as reasoning tasks).
- These cross-curricular assessments again will result in a profile of competencies rather than in a single dimension. Most probably, discriminating between reasoning-like problem solving and strategic behaviour (including metacognitive regulation) in dynamic problem situations will be possible.
- To discriminate cognitive problem-solving competencies from motivational factors and from effects of domain-specific knowledge, both types of prerequisites should be assessed independently (e.g. through questionnaires) and controlled for in statistical analyses.

One example of such assessment that incorporates all the recommendations is given later in this chapter when the German national option for PISA 2000 is described. An example in which several of the recommendations are evident is the problem-solving assessment developed as an international option for PISA 2003.[1] (For reasons of feasibility and financing, dynamic settings are not addressed.) PISA 2003 defines problem solving as 'an individual's capacity to use cognitive processes to confront and resolve real, cross-disciplinary situations where the solution path is not immediately obvious and where the literacy domains or curricular areas that might be applicable are not within a single domain of mathematics, science or reading' (OECD 2003, p. 156). The domain is organised by problem type, context, disciplines involved, processes used and reasoning skills applied.

The benefits of implementing such a framework within large-scale assessments (as in both PISA and the German example given later) are threefold. First, student performance can be described and evaluated in domains and settings that go beyond classic areas of cognitive functioning into transfer domains and into new kinds of settings, such as the exploration and regulation of complex, dynamic environments. The use of new contexts and settings is appropriate for the life skills orientation of PISA. Second, the structure of cognitive capabilities, including reasoning, literacy domains and cross-curricular competencies can be better understood. The kind of relationships that can be empirically identified might even differ across countries. For example, low correlations between competency domains and general reasoning can be expected when the system is successful in fostering domain-specific competencies for all students, independent of their general intellectual level. Low correlations between curriculum-bound and cross-curricular competencies would be expected if the system is *not* successful in supporting links and transfer between domains. Third, the impact of personal prerequisites (e.g. domain-specific knowledge and motivation), social background and school-related variables on competencies of different scope, context and complexity can by studied, thus enhancing the analytical power of the assessment and providing insight into how problem-solving competencies may be fostered.

Problem solving in large-scale assessments

According to the broad definition in Box 5.1, problem solving can occur in any domain, so there is abundant experience with problem-solving tests in education research and practice. Most stimulating may be tests that use innovative formats such as the 'clinical reasoning test' (Boshuizen *et al.* 1997), based on case studies in patient management; the 'overall test' of complex, authentic decision making in business education (Segers 1997); or the 'what if ?' test, which addresses intuitive knowledge – apart from declarative knowledge – attained in exploring simulations of science phenomena (Swaak and de Jong 1996). In science, Baxter and Glaser (1997) provide a systematic approach to performance assessment tasks, allowing the analysis of cognitive complexity and problem-solving demands. The domain of mathematics has a long tradition of problem-oriented thinking and learning (Hiebert *et al.* 1996; Schoenfeld 1992) and related assessment strategies (Charles *et al.* 1987; see Klieme 1989 for an integrated discussion from an education, cognitive-psychological and measurement perspective). For example, Collis and colleagues (1986) developed a 'mathematical problem solving test' which used so-called 'super-items', each composed of a sequence of questions that address subsequent levels of cognitive complexity. Since the seminal work by Bloom and his colleagues (1971) there have been various attempts at differentiating task complexity levels, a recent example being the structure of observed learning outcomes (SOLO) taxonomy (Collis *et al.* 1986). The literature on the SOLO taxonomy and related tasks does not contain any category like 'problem solving', since Bloom and his colleagues conceptualised problem solving as an integration of all the levels they proposed (reproduction, understanding, application and so on). Later work such as the test rubrics developed for TIMSS 1995 (Robitaille and Garden 1996) and PISA 2000 and 2003 (OECD 1999, 2003), in specifying performance expectations included some kind of problem-solving category within domains, and left the question of whether this may constitute a separate dimension or level open (see earlier discussion).

There have been several recent attempts to implement measures of cross-curricular problem solving in large-scale assessments. For example, Meijer and Elshout-Mohr (1999) developed a general test of cross-curricular competence based on 'critical thinking' inventories, but it seems to be rather heterogeneous. Trier and Peschar, working in the OECD/INES context (1995, OECD 1997), identified problem solving as one of four important cross-curricular competencies. The 'item' in the related feasibility test, which at the same time served as an operationalisation of skills in written communication, was an essay-like planning task, based on various documents presented to the students. For this task the respondent had to plan a trip for a youth club. This task turned out to be too difficult for the target population, and rather weak levels of objectivity were reached in scoring the answers.

The idea of planning tasks as typical instances of cross-curricular problem solving was independently invented by other research groups as well. In Germany, Funke and Fritz (1995) devised several experimental variants of planning tests, while Klieme and his colleagues (in press) developed a multiple-choice test of problem-solving competence for a large-scale assessment programme in one of the German federal states. For the latter, a 'project' such as arranging a party or planning a trip was decomposed into five action steps: (1) clarifying goals, (2) gathering information, (3) planning, (4) making decisions and (5) executing the plan and evaluating the result. These steps were addressed by a sequence of items. A typical item within this project approach required respondents to judge the consistency of goals, analyse maps, schedules and other documents, reason about the order of activities, diagnose possible errors in the execution of actions, and so on. While the tasks made heavy use of seemingly authentic material, answering the questions (most often in closed formats) required analytical and combinatorial reasoning. Structural models proved that performance on this test was not confounded with mathematical and language competencies – that is, it added a specific branch to the overall profile of students' competencies.

The project approach is also part of the ALL study. Ebach *et al.* (1999) developed several projects for this large-scale assessment and succeeded in establishing Rasch scores. Analysis of critical item elements showed that the number and connectivity of information elements, as well as the cognitive complexity of the reasoning, accounted for item difficulty. Thus the project approach is an example of a reasoning-like, analytical, though contextualised, test of cross-curricular problem solving.

Also within the ALL context, pilot versions of Sternberg's 'practical cognition' measure and a problem-solving test developed by Baker (1998), O'Neil *et al.* (1999) and colleagues at the Centre for Research on Evaluation, Standards and Student Testing (CRESST) in the United States were pilot-tested. The latter is based on a framework that defines (1) domain-dependent strategies, (2) metacognition, (3) content understanding and (4) motivation as components of problem solving. (Only the first two of these are understood as aspects of problem-solving competence in this chapter, while the third and fourth are understood as prerequisites that have to be assessed independently.) To assess strategies, these authors confronted respondents with information on a technical device (tyre pump) or a similar biological system which was described as malfunctioning, and asked them to think about trouble-shooting actions. To assess content understanding, respondents were asked to explain how the device works by drawing a knowledge map. Several field trials showed that the instrument was feasible in principle, although its difficulty (with less then 25 per cent of the adults being able to solve the trouble-shooting questions) and reliability were not fully convincing.

From the preceding overview, it becomes clear that the existing approaches to large-scale assessment of cross-curricular problem solving by no means address the full range of tasks, contexts and (more or less dynamic) settings that are covered by the general framework outlined in the second section of this chapter. In fact, the only cross-curricular approaches that so far have been shown to be feasible for large-scale implementation and to be theoretically sound are the project approach and the CRESST problem-solving test (i.e. the 'tyre pump task'). Therefore the national expert group for problem-solving assessment in PISA/Germany[2] started a major research and development enterprise, adapting instruments from various paradigms of experimental psychology and integrating them in a large validation study that was conducted with the 1999 field test of PISA and that was modified and conducted in final form with the main PISA data collection in 2000. The intention was to use as much input from basic cognitive research on problem solving as possible for the development and validation of new instruments.

Instruments used for the German validation study of problem solving

The expert group followed the recommendations outlined earlier in this chapter that cross-curricular problem-solving competencies should be assessed by tasks that differ from literacy measures in terms of context (focusing on transfer domains that are more or less distant from school subjects) and setting (focusing on complex, dynamic environments as well as reasoning tasks). The group also wanted to vary the paradigm of psychological problem-solving research from which the tasks would be drawn.

As illustrated in Table 5.1, several variants of context were implemented in the validation study: (1) fictitious, game-playing contexts (e.g. a space scenario), which are none the less meaningful and authentic for today's students, and real-world contexts (e.g. repairing a simple technical instrument; planning); (2) school- but not curriculum-related contexts (planning and reasoning about extracurricular activities); (3) cross-curricular or integrated contexts, which relate to topics dealt with in school but that cross the borders of individual subjects (e.g. a simulated eco-system requiring geographical, economic, arithmetic and real-world knowledge and a virtual laboratory in which the fundamental principles of hypothesis generation and hypothesis testing are employed).

Also, several different settings implemented variants of complexity and dynamics: (1) transparent and well defined tasks with a closed format, which mainly called for combinatorial reasoning; (2) less well defined tasks with an open format, in which conceptual relations had to be understood, analogies, drawn or approaches to a practical problem outlined; (3) dynamic computer-assisted learning environments that could be explored freely and provided the student with continual feedback on the effects of his or her interventions. Co-operative problem solving was another setting implemented, which can be thought of as a variant of

Table 5.1 Variation of task characteristics in the German validation study of problem solving

Setting (ordered by complexity, high to low)	Context (ordered by proximity to curricular domains, high to low)		
	Integration of curriculum-related domains	School-related extra-curricular domains	Out-of-school domain and games and puzzles
Exploration and decision making in dynamic environments	Virtual laboratory Ecological simulation	Co-operative project tasks	Space game
Understanding and solving open-ended problems		Troubleshooting	Analogical transfer problems
Reasoning on closed, transparent problems		Project tasks	Transformation problems

dynamic environments. In the co-operative scenario, students first had to work on individual subsections of a problem, on which they each had specific information, and then agree on a common solution in which all relevant aspects were integrated. Here, the problem-solving process gains complexity and dynamics from the group discussions in which the differing perspectives are introduced.

A total of eight different problem-solving tasks were used in the German problem-solving validation study. Table 5.2 identifies the paradigms within experimental psychological research on which the tasks were based and the instruments that were administered. As the table indicates, the first four tasks were presented in the form of written tests, and the remainder were computer-assisted or involved a simulated or dynamic environment.

Table 5.2 Overview of the German validation study of problem solving

Problem-solving paradigms within experimental psychological research	Problem-solving instruments designed or adapted for the validation study
Problem solving in static, well defined situations	**Paper-and-pencil tasks**
As a search in a problem space with well defined states and operators	➡ Transformation problems, by Dörner and Leutner (test 8)
As planning and combinatorial research	➡ Project tasks, by Klieme *et al.* (test 4)
As analogical reasoning	➡ Analogical transfer problems, by Wirth and Klieme (test 7)
As reasoning in mental modes	➡ Trouble shooting, adapted by Wirth from O'Neil *et al.* (test 6)
Problem solving as reasoning and action in dynamic environments	**Computer-based, simulated and small-group tasks**
As dual-space search (forming hypotheses and performing experiments)	➡ Virtual laboratory, by Reimann and Schmitt (test 1)
Complex problem solving in simulated naturalistic scenarios	➡ Ecological simulation, by Leutner and Schrettenbrunner (test 2)
Complex problem solving with well defined tasks (finite state automata)	➡ Space game, by Funke (test 3)
Collaborative	➡ Co-operative project tasks, by Klieme (test 5)

Note
The table identifies the authors of the various tasks; no citations appear in the reference list.

Box 5.3 Tasks in the German validation study of problem solving

1 Virtual laboratory

In this test the student identifies certain regularities in a series of simulated experiments. He or she specifies the experimental conditions and is played a video of the experiment. The sequence of the experiments and their results are recorded in a table. On the basis of this information, the problem solver formulates hypotheses, which can then be either confirmed or rejected. The experimental environment thus consists of three components: a virtual laboratory (shown in the videos), a table of results and a hypothesis window. Evaluation is based on whether the problem solver generates hypotheses central to the subject domain and on how systematically he or she proceeds

2 Ecological simulation

In this test, topics from various subject domains are addressed in a planning game that consists of a computer simulation of a small farm. The system is relatively complex (i.e. extensive, interconnected, non-transparent, changing during the problem-solving process) and is thus able to reflect the research tradition of complex problem solving. Experts in the field have judged that the system represents reality well. Here evaluation is based on how efficiently the system is explored, how much knowledge is acquired and how well the student managed his or her concern in a concluding test.

3 Space game

Within complex problem solving, dynamic systems with quantitative variables (such as the ecological simulation described above) and discrete systems have both been studied. Discrete systems consist of a series of states that can be altered by certain interventions (represented as the pushing of 'buttons') and are referred to as finite state automata – real-world examples of which are ticket machines and electronic appliances. A variant of this is embedded in a computer-based space game in which students must learn to navigate a spaceship by learning the system. Here, too, evaluation is based on the efficiency with which the system is explored, the knowledge acquired and performance in control tasks.

4 Project tasks

The validation study includes two project tasks in which students must use analytical and combinatorial reasoning to complete a project that has been decomposed into action steps around which test items are focused. For example, one task asks respondents to organise a class party.

5 Co-operative planning

A new variant of the project task also was developed, in which three students work on the project together. The three students are given different introductory information and are each responsible for different goals. Each student first works out a partial solution for his or her part of the problem, then a common solution has to be arrived at in group discussion. The result is interpreted as a combination of problem-solving competence and co-operative abilities.

6 Troubleshooting, or technical problem solving

This task is adapted from the examples from CRESST (e.g. tyre pump) described earlier in the chapter. The adaptation modified the 'knowledge mapping' instruction as well as the scoring rubric, and resulted in the addition of two new items for respondents to answer.

7 Analogical problem solving

The validation study also uses several short planning and ordering tasks, each of which is embedded in a real-world context. For each target task, a more or less analogous base task with a worked-out solution is provided. The problem solver has to recognise the relationship between the target task and the base task and transfer the solution strategy. The success of this analogical transfer (Vosniadou and Ortony 1989) is evaluated.

8 Transformation problems

This rather short, puzzle-like test presents a fictitious biological object that can be altered by means of certain operations ('genetic transformations'). In a series of tasks, the given state and the goal state are identified, and the problem solver is asked to find the shortest possible sequence of operations leading from the given state to the goal state.

Selected results of the German validation study of problem solving

The validation study, given as a national enhancement to the field test of PISA 2000, allowed extra testing time within a sub-sample of about 650 15-year-old students from different *Länder*, representing the full range of school types and intellectual and socio-economic backgrounds. A balanced matrix design was used where each student worked on some of the problem-solving instruments. To administer the computer-based instrument, a team from Max Planck Institute visited approximately twenty schools in three German *Länder* with a set of thirty laptops.

In addition to the problem-solving tests, students completed the PISA booklets for reading, mathematical and scientific literacy, worked on a psychometric reasoning test (of figure and verbal analogies) and answered – in addition to the PISA questionnaires – questions regarding task-specific knowledge, motivation and metacognitive regulation. This allowed performance on the various problem-solving tests to be correlated with other indicators of cross-curricular competence, to the literacy scores and to general reasoning scores, and allowed sophisticated analyses of the structure of competencies. Effects of motivation and knowledge also could be considered, as could the whole set of socio-cultural, individual and educational background variables.

The two aspects that were of greatest concern for the evaluation of the instruments were feasibility and convergent and discriminant validity. To assess the feasibility of the instruments for the target population, the project team calculated the difficulty level (which on an average should be close to 50 per cent of the maximum score) and index of reliability (Cronbach's alpha should be above 0.70) and examined whether there were biases for certain sub-groups of students, such as by gender. The project team also examined whether the indicators of cross-curricular problem-solving competence showed generally high intercorrelations with one another but somewhat lower correlations with reading, mathematical and scientific literacy scores (which were expected). Appropriate structures also were expected when the team differentiated between types of literacy items (problem solving versus routine tasks) as well as types of cross-curricular indicators (reasoning-like versus dynamic).

As Table 5.3 indicates, most of the tasks – especially the knowledge tests for computer-based learning and the co-operative planning task – behaved well with respect to difficulty level and reliability. The project tasks were rather easy for the target population, and the knowledge test for the ecological simulation was not reliable enough. (*A posteriori* inspection showed that the ecological simulation task contained several questions that could be answered by domain-specific knowledge alone, without having explored the system – a flaw amenable to modification.) Troubleshooting (i.e. technical problem solving) had some shortcomings, replicating the findings reported

Table 5.3 Difficulty and reliability of tasks in the German validation study of problem solving

Task	Difficulty (mean % correct)	Reliability (Cronbach's alpha)
Transformation problems	32	0.88
Analogical transfer problems	33	0.79
Troubleshooting / technical problem solving	36	0.63
Project tasks	68	0.74
Co-operative project tasks	60	0.71
Space game (knowledge acquired)	53	0.82
Virtual laboratory (knowledge acquired)	50	0.78
Ecological simulation (knowledge acquired)	62	0.63

by Baker (1998), despite the attempts in the German study to make the knowledge-mapping task easier and the scoring more reliable. The two new paper-and-pencil tasks (transformation and analogical transfer problems) had high reliability but were rather difficult for the majority of students.

Task-specific motivation had no effect at all, with one significant exception: performance in the virtual laboratory depended upon pre-task motivation. Observation of student behaviour indicated that this task, as it had been implemented, was too demanding for students in lower-school tracks. However, both the space game and ecological simulation (computer-based) were highly self-motivating. Most students – independent of their background – enjoyed working on the tasks, so motivational differences had no impact.

There were some gender effects, favouring boys, for technical problem solving ($r = 0.16$, $p < 0.05$) and for three of the eight computer-based problem-solving tasks (r was between 0.28 and 0.35, $p < 0.001$). When computer experience (which is higher for boys) was controlled for, all the gender effects were reduced to values below 0.30 and thus – by applying standard rules from psychological research – were qualified as 'weak'. The more computer experience students reported the more efficiently they controlled the space game and the ecological simulation ($r = 0.36$ and $r = 0.28$, $p < 0.001$). However, performance in the space-game control tasks was the only indicator (out of the eight tasks) that showed 'medium size' effects of computer experience. Thus, in accordance with expectations, both gender and computer experience were relevant to computer-based problem solving-processes, but in no sense did they determine the test results.

Some first insights into the validity of problem-solving indicators based on the German study are illustrated in Figure 5.1. This diagram is based on an analysis of the correlational pattern between seven competencies, each of

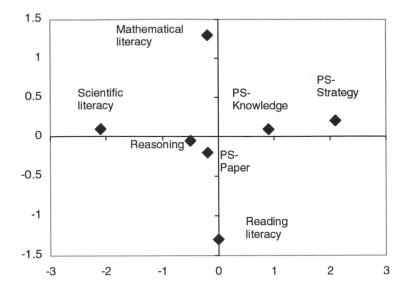

Figure 5.1 Visualisation ('non-metric' scaling) of the correlations between sev-
en competences in the German validation study of problem solving.
Note The closer two factors are in this diagram the higher they are
correlated.

Source: PISA/Germany validation study of problem solving (1999)

them measured by two or three measures in the study design. These competence factors were reading, mathematical and scientific literacy, reasoning
(measured by figure and verbal analogies), and three components of cross-
curricular problem solving: (1) PS-Paper, which is based on
paper-and-pencil tests (technical problem solving, analogical transfer, transformation and project tasks) (2) PS-Knowledge, which integrate the tests
that assessed knowledge acquired in exploring simulated environments, and
(3) PS-Strategy, which is based on indicators of efficient and systematic processing from the two computer-based tasks. This model, which
differentiates between reasoning, literacy domains and cross-curricular
problem solving (which is decomposed into three components), fits the data
better than models without such differentiation. Thus separating several
domain-specific and cross-curricular competencies seems to be reasonable,
as proposed earlier in the chapter.[3]

The diagram also shows that reasoning is indeed the very core of the
structure of competencies, and the paper-and-pencil problem-solving tests
are close to that centre. In searching for a more unique type of problem-
solving competence, knowledge and strategy indicators based on
computer-based instruments should be used.

Problem solving in PISA 2000/Germany

The German problem-solving validation study demonstrated the feasibility of both paper-and-pencil and computer-based instruments for problem-solving assessment in transfer domains. These instruments addressed competencies that were clearly distinct from literacy domains. As expected, several propositions were supported. First, there was no way to define a general, unique 'problem-solving competence'. Rather, problem-solving assessment produced a profile of competencies, varying in terms of context and setting. Second, problem-solving indicators, especially those based upon paper-and-pencil tasks, were strongly correlated with reasoning, which, in fact, is the core of problem solving. Finally, strategy indicators derived from students' behaviour in simulated environments did provide specific additional information.

Based on the results of the validation study, the problem-solving study finally administered as a national option in PISA 2000 included a written test (comprising project tasks), a co-operative problem situation and – for a sub-sample of about 800 students – the two computer-based tests (i.e. the space game and ecological simulation).

Conclusion

The experience of the German study as well as similar experience in other assessment projects indicates that developing an international framework that integrates both domain-specific and cross-curricular problem solving seems a reasonable proposition. In doing so, new challenges will arise, such as the question of whether or not such assessments can be conducted fairly and reliably across cultural settings. However, theoretical concepts as well as assessment techniques are ready for new developments.

References

Baker E.L., 1998. *Final Report for Validation of Teamwork Skills Questionnaire using Computer-based Teamwork Simulations*. 85300-97-0056 (Los Angeles CA: National Centre for Research on Evaluation, Standards, and Student Testing, CRESST).

Bandura A., 1990. Conclusion: reflections on nonability determinants of competence. In Sternberg and Kolligian Jr (eds) *Competence Considered* (New Haven CT: Yale University Press), pp. 315–62.

Barrett G.V. and Depinet R.L., 1991. A reconsideration for testing for competence rather than for intelligence. *American Psychologist*, 46, 1012–24.

Baumert J., Fend H., O'Neil H. and Peschar J.L., 1998. *Prepared for Lifelong Learning. Frame of Reference for the Measurement of Self-regulated Learning as a Cross-curricular Competency (CCC) in the PISA Project* (Paris: OECD).

Baxter G.P. and Glaser R., 1997. *An Approach to Analyzing the Cognitive Complexitiy of Science Performance Assessments*. CSE Technical Report 452 (Los Angeles: CRESST).

Binkley M.R., Sternberg R., Jones S. and Nohara D., 1999. An overarching framework for understanding and assessing life skills. In *Frameworks: Working Drafts*. Briefing materials for ALL National Study Manager's meeting, Luxembourg, 23–24 September.

Bloom B.S., Hastings J.T. and Madaus G.F., 1971. *Handbook on Formative and Summative Evaluation of Student Learning* (New York: McGraw Hill).

Boshuizen H.P.A., van der Vleuten C.P.M., Schmidt H.G. and Machiels-Bongaerts M., 1997. Measuring knowledge and clinical reasoning skills in a problem-based curriculum. *Medical Education*, 31, 115–21.

Brown A.L., 1987. Metacognition executive control, self-regulation and other more mysterious mechanisms. In Weinert and Kluwe (eds) *Metacognition, Motivation and Understanding* (Hillsdale NJ: Earlbaum).

Buchner A. and Funke J., 1993. Finite state automata: dynamic task environments in problem solving research. *Quarterly Journal of Experimental Psychology*, 46A, 83–118.

Carroll J.B., 1993. *Human Cognitive Abilities. A Survey of Factor-analytic Studies* (New York: Cambridge University Press).

Charles R., Lester F. and O'Daffer P., 1987. *How to Evaluate Progress in Problem Solving* VI (Reston VA: National Council of Teachers of Mathematics).

Chi M.T.H., Glaser R. and Farr M.J. (eds), 1988. *The Nature of Expertise* (Hillsdale NJ: Erlbaum).

Collis K.F., Romberg T.A. and Jurdak M.E., 1986. A technique for assessing mathematical problem-solving ability. *Journal for Research in Mathematics Education*, 17 (3), 206–21.

De Corte E., Greer B. and Verschaffel L., 1996, Mathematics teaching and learning. In Berliner and Calfee (eds) *Handbook of Educational Psychology* (New York: Simon & Schuster Macmillan).

Didi H-J., Fay E., Kloft C. and Vogt H., 1993. *Einschätzung von Schlüsselqualifikationen aus psychologischer Perspektive*. Gutachten im Auftrag des Bundesinstituts für Berufsbildung (Bonn: Institut für Bildungsforschung).

Dörner D., Kreuzig H., Reither F. and Stäudel, T., 1983. *Lohhausen. Vom Umgang mit Unbestimmtheit und Komplexität* (Berne: Hogrefe).

Ebach J., Hensgen A., Klieme E. and Sidiropoulou E., 1999. Analytical reasoning in real world contexts. In *Frameworks: Working Drafts*. Briefing materials for ALL National Study Manager's meeting, Luxembourg, 23–24 September.

Ennis R.H., 1996. Critical Thinking (Upper Saddle River NJ: Prentice Hall).

Flavell J.H., 1976. Metacognitive aspects of problem solving. In Resnick (ed.) *Nature of Intelligence* (Hillsdale NJ: Erlbaum), pp. 231–5.

Frensch P.A. and Funke J. (eds), 1995. *Complex Problem Solving. The European Perspective* (Hillsdale NJ: Erlbaum).

Funke J., 1991. Solving complex problems: exploration and control of complex systems. In Sternberg and Frensch (eds) *Complex Problem Solving: Principles and Mechanisms* (Hillsdale NJ: Erlbaum), pp. 185–222.

Funke J. and Fritz A. (eds), 1995. *Neue Konzepte und Instrumente zur Planungsdiagnostik* (Bonn: Deutscher Psychologen Verlag).

Glaser R., Schauble L., Raghavan K. and Zeitz C., 1992. Scientific reasoning across different domains. In de Corte, Linn, Mandl and Verschaffel (eds) *Computer-based Learning Environments and Problem Solving* LXXXIV (Belin: Springer), pp. 345–71.

Gruber H. and Mandl, H., 1996. Das Entstehen von Expertise. In Hoffmann and Kintsch (eds) *Lernen* VII (Göttingen: Hogrefe), pp. 583–615.

Helmke A. and Weinert F. E., 1997. Bedingungsfaktoren schulischer Leistungen. In Weinert (ed.) *Psychologie des Unterrichts und der Schule* III (Göttingen: Hogrefe), pp. 71–176.

Hiebert J., Carpenter T.P., Fennema E., Fuson K., Human P., Murray H., Olivier A. and Wearne D., 1996. Problem solving as a basis for reform in curriculum and instruction: the case of mathematics. *Educational Researcher*, 25 (4), 12–21.

Hunt E., 1994. Problem solving. In Sternberg (ed.) *Thinking and Problem Solving* (San Diego CA: Academic Press), pp. 215–32.

Jeck S., 1997. *Planen und Lösen von Alltagsproblemen* (Lengerich: Pabst).

Klieme E., 1989. *Mathematisches Problemlösen als Testleistung* (Frankfurt: Lang).

Klieme E. and Köller, O., 2000. Mathematisch-naturwissenschaftliche Grundbildung. Erfassung und Skalierung von Kompetenzen. In Baumert, Bos and Lehmann (eds) *TIMS. Mathematisch-naturwissenschaftliche Bildung am Ende der Sekundarstufe* II (Opladen: Leske & Budrich).

Klieme E., Ebach J., Didi H-J., Hensgen A., Heilmann K. and Meisters, K-H., in press. Problemlösetest für die 7. Jahrgangsstufe. In Lehmann and Steinbach (eds) *Hamburger Schulleistungstest für sechste und siebente Klassen* (Göttingen: Hogrefe).

Klieme E., Funke J., Leutner D., Reimann P. and Wirth J., 2001. Problemlösen als fächerübergreifende Kompetenz. Konzeption und erste Ergebnisse aus einer Schulleistungsstudie (Problem solving as a transdisciplinary competence: conception and first results of a study on school achievement). *Zeitschrift für Pädagogi*, 47 (2), 179–200.

Krampen G., 1993. Diagnostik der Kreativität. In Trost, Ingenkamp and Jäger (eds) *Tests und Trends. Jahrbuch der pädagogischen Diagnostik* X (Weinheim: Beltz), pp. 11–39.

Lave J., 1988. *Cognition in Practice* (Cambridge: Cambridge University Press).

Leutner D., 1992. *Adaptive Lehrsysteme* (Weinheim: Beltz and PVU).

Leutner D., 1999. 'Discovery Learning, Intelligence, and Problem-solving Ability. Presented at the EARLI conference, Göteborg, September (Erfurt: Erfurt Educational University).

Linn R.L., 1994. Performance assessment: policy promises and technical measurement standards. *Educational Researcher*, 24 (9), 4–13.

Mayer R.E., 1992. *Thinking, Problem Solving, Cognition* (2nd edn, New York: Freeman).

Mayer R.E. and Wittrock M.C., 1996. Problem-solving transfer. In Berliner and Calfee (eds) *Handbook of Educational Psychology* (New York: Simon & Schuster Macmillan), pp. 47–62.

McClelland D.C., 1973. Testing for competence rather than for 'intelligence'. *American Psychologist*, 28, 1–14.

Meijer J. and Elshout-Mohr M., 1999. 'An Instrument for the Assessment of Cross-curricular Skills. Presented at the EARLI conference, Göteborg.

Mumford M.D., Baughman W.A., Supinski E.P. and Anderson L.E., 1998. A construct approach to skill assessment: procedures for assessing complex cognitive skills. *Beyond Multiple Choice. Evaluating Alternatives to Traditional Testing for Selection* (pp. 75–112).

Mumford M.D., Supinski E.P., Baughman W.A., Costanza D.P. and Threlfall K.V., 1997. Process-based measures of creative problem-solving skills. *Creativity Research Journal*, 10 (1), 73–85.

Neisser U., Boodoo G., Bouchard T. J. Jr, Boykin A.W., Brody N., Ceci S.J., Halpern D.F., Loehlin J.C., Perloff R., Sternberg R.J. and Urbina S., 1996. Intelligence: knowns and unknowns. *American Psychologist*, 51, 77–101.

Newell A., and Simon H.A., 1972. *Human Problem Solving* (Englewood Cliffs NJ: Prentice Hall).

Norris S.P., 1989. Evaluating critical thinking ability. *History and Social Science Teacher*, 21 (3), 135–46.

OECD, 1997. *Prepared for life?* (Paris: OECD).

OECD, 1999. *Measuring Student Knowledge and Skills*. A New Framework for Assessment (Paris: OECD).

OECD, 2003. *The PISA 2003 Assessment Framework. Mathematics, Reading, Science and Problem Solving Knowledge and Skills* (Paris: OECD).

O'Neil H.F., 1999. 'A Theoretical Basis for Assessment of Problem Solving'. Presented at the annual meeting of the American Educational Research Association, Montreal, 19 April.

O'Neil H.F., Chung, K.W.K.G. and Herl H. E., 1999. *Computer-based Collaborative Knowledge Mapping to measure Team Processes and Team Outcomes* (Los Angeles: University of Southern California).

Pólya G., 1945, 1980. *How to Solve it. Deutsche Übersetzung. Schule des Denkens. Vom Lösen mathematischer Probleme* III (Berne: Francke).

Raaheim K., 1988. Intelligence and task novelty. In Sternberg (ed.) *Advances in the Psychology of Human Intelligence* IV, pp. 73–97.

Reimann P. and Schult, T.J., 1996. Turning examples into cases: acquiring knowledge structures for analogical problem solving. *Educational Psychologist*, 3 (2), 123–32.

Robitaille D.F. and Garden R.A. (eds), 1996. *Research Questions and Study Design* (Vancouver: Pacific Educational Press).

Schoenfeld A.H., 1992. Learning to think mathematically: problem solving, metacognition, and sense making in mathematics. In Grouws (ed.) *Handbook of Research on Mathematics Teaching and Learning*, pp. 334–70.

Schunn C.D. and Anderson J.R., 1999. The generality/specificity of expertise in scientific reasoning. *Cognitive Science*, 23 (3), 337–70.

Segers M.S.R., 1997. An alternative for assessing problem-solving skills: the overall test. *Studies in Educational Evaluation*, 23 (4), 373–98.

Smith M., 1991. *Toward a Unified Theory of Problem Solving* (Hillsdale NJ: Erlbaum).

Sternberg R.J. and Frensch P.A. (eds), 1991. *Complex Problem Solving. Principles and Mechanism* (Hillsdale NJ: Erlbaum).

Sternberg R.J. and Kaufman J.C., 1998. Human abilities. *Annual Review of Psychology*, 49, 479–502.

Sternberg R.J. and Wagner R.K. (eds), 1986. *Practical Intelligence. Nature and Origins of Competence in the Everyday World* (New York: Cambridge University Press).

Süss H-M., 1999. Intelligenz und komplexes Problemlösen. Perspektiven für eine Kooperation zwischen differentiell-psychometrischer und kognitionspsychologischer Forschung. *Psychologische Rundschau*, 50 (4), 220–8.

Svecnik E., 1999, 'Stellenwert der Problemlösefähigkeit im österreichischen Schulwesen'. Unpublished Bericht des EU-Netzwerk, New Assessment Tools for Cross-curricular Competencies in the Domain of Problem Solving (Graz).

Swaak J. and De Jong T., 1996. Measuring intuitive knowledge in science: the develoment of the what-if test. *Studies in Educational Evaluation*, 22 (4), 341–62.

Trier U.P. and Peschar J.L., 1995. Cross-curricular competencies: rationale and strategy for developing a new indicator. In *Measuring What Students Learn* (Paris: OECD), pp. 99–109.

Veenman M.V.J., Elshout J.J. and Meijer J., 1997. The generality v. domain specificity of metacognitive skills in novice learning across domains. *Learning and Instruction*, 7, 187–209.

Vosniadou S. and Ortony A., 1989. Similarity and analogical reasoning: a synthesis. In Vosniadou and Ortony (eds) *Similarity and Analogical Reasoning* (Cambridge: Cambridge University Press), pp. 1–18.

Weinert F.E., 2001. Concept of competence: a conceptual clarification. In Rychen and Salganik (eds) *Defining and Selecting Key Competencies* (Berne: Hogrefe & Huber).

Weinert F.E. and Kluwe R.H. (eds), 1987. *Metacognition, Motivation and Understanding* (Hillsdale NJ: Erlbaum).

Zsambok C.E. and Klein G. (eds), 1997. *Naturalistic Decision Making* (Mahwah NJ: Erlbaum).

Notes

1 The framework for assessing problem solving as a cross-curricular competency in PISA 2003 was developed by an expert group led by John Dossey (retired from Illinois State University) and including Beno Csapo (University of Szeged), Ton de Jong (University of Twente), the author and Stella Vosniadou (University of Athens), with consultation from the chair of the mathematics expert group, Jan de Lange (Freudenthal Institute).

2 The author is indebted to Professors Joachim Funke, Detlev Leutner, Peter Reimann and Peter Frensch for serving on the expert group, providing instruments and contributing to the theoretical framework. The design, implementation and analysis of the study were indeed a joint activity of this group, supported by Joachim Wirth, Thomas Schmitt, Stefan Wagener and other staff at the Max Planck Institute.

3 This analysis is a preliminary one because not all the test components have been integrated so far. In particular, the collaborative planning task cannot be included here because it does not provide individual performance indicators.

Chapter 6

Reflections on the use of indicators in policy and practice

Friedrich Plank and Douglas Hodgkinson

OECD first published EAG in 1992. Since then EAG has been published regularly, providing OECD countries, and now countries participating in the World Education Indicators programme, with education indicators that allow them to compare themselves with others on measures of education inputs, processes and outcomes. Many countries also produce national or, in some cases, regional indicator publications.

This chapter presents two case studies which consider how indicators are used in the national context.[1] The first, from Austria, focuses on the use of assessment measures, both nationally at the classroom level and internationally through participation in large-scale assessments, such as COMPED and TIMSS. The Austrian case study also considers media responses to the reporting of assessment results and the value of further co-operation within the framework of international assessment. The second case study presents the Canadian experience with indicator publications and data by examining how policy makers have used provincial and territorial indicators publications, *Education Indicators in Canada*, the pan-Canadian indicators publication, and EAG. The questions at issue are how indicators are used in general, whether distinctions can be drawn with respect to using different types of indicator and what suggestions arise from the case study for developing and improving education indicators at all levels.

Reflections from Austria

Austria's school system, one of the first to impose universal compulsory school attendance, has retained a high differentiation of tracks and programmes. Beginning at ISCED level two, students are taught by two different categories of teachers. Students in the *Gymnasium* (university stream) are taught by *Professoren* (university-trained specialists), while students in the *Hauptschule* (mainstream) and *Berufsschule* (apprentice) programmes are taught by subject teachers trained in shorter but highly charged pedagogical programmes at the *pädagogische Akademien*. Generally, in this system of separate 'higher' (i.e. academically oriented) and 'intermediate' tracks for students of the same age group, the differentiation of university- and non-university-trained teachers essentially continues at ISCED levels three through five.

On a spectrum of traditional outcome measures of education, Austria holds its place in a country grouping that has put its trust primarily in the teacher's professional competence. The teaching staff of the higher schools that prepare students for university study being academically trained themselves has traditionally served as the major guarantee of quality (a phenomenon that is seen throughout all academically trained professions); these teachers' competence in marking (or grading) and power to promote or retain students from an early age are still generally undisputed. This model of determining students' careers on the basis of individual experts' teaching and assessing students' performance in class has been structurally reinforced through an elaborate national legal framework, which is designed to ensure that standards of teaching and marking are the same throughout the country at all levels and ages of the non-university education and training sectors.

At key points in students' careers the national system goes beyond its specialists' assessment practice: class teachers jointly determine their students' yearly pass or fail standing (a fail standing results in retention), and boards of examiners preside over the leaving and matriculation examinations[2] at the end of students' secondary schooling. These boards' actions are bound nationally by a detailed and rigid legal framework that defines examination content and procedures; the observation and enforcement of these rules are the key responsibilities of the school inspectorate.

An assessment system that is based solely on the teachers' individual or joint judgement can yield statistics that are based only on their monitoring and marking, and Austria has recorded statistical indicators based on students' end-of-grade results and matriculation examination results for many years. As well as being presented in the statistical education publications, this judgement-oriented outcome statistic has been nationally utilised in the labour market context, where information on, for example, the distribution of general and professional graduations in *Gymnasium* and higher technical and vocational schools at the end of secondary education, has contributed to the political debate by confirming the merits of strategic policy points. In the latter field, these statistics have typically served as a reminder of the prevalence of conventional technical studies and of the underrepresentation of ICT studies. This kind of quantitative statistic, and the types of indicators based upon its findings, still largely dominate the national discussion and indeed continue to be the international state of the art when tertiary education is dealt with.

The first impact of participating in EAG on Austria

In Austria OECD's EAG was welcomed by those with expertise in the area as a means to indicate policy-relevant issues across the whole spectrum of education; for the first time, Austria's education was highlighted in an international system of indicators that reflected on all levels of education, irrespective of which Austrian Ministry happened to be responsible. (Until recently a separate Ministry dealt with the universities.)

The Austrian media seized on political 'sensations', such as the unit cost of education, which were shown as higher than average in primary and secondary education and lower in tertiary education. The media more or less completely overlooked indicators which – when read and interpreted in their political context – could have given rise to a sustained domestic political discussion. Thus indicators that went beyond information on the education system itself passed largely unnoticed (e.g. indicators on gender differences in salary for people equally qualified or on the relatively short periods many Austrians spend in their active professional lives between very late graduation from university and very early retirement). The 'strong points' as indicated in EAG (e.g. the relationship between low youth unemployment and a strong vocational element in the upper secondary sector) also went largely unreported because EAG, for lack of data, could not illustrate the public budget savings in connection with the dual apprentice system.

As a consequence, the nationally most quoted and used outcomes indicators were 'non-assessment effectiveness' indicators such as:

- Census-based indicators on highest formally attained level of education.
- Graduation indicators (intermediate and higher schools and colleges, non-university and university).
- Employment by highest/lowest attained level of formal education.
- Proportion of general and vocational formal training.

Gender differences were also considered in the reporting of the above indicators.

Extending assessment beyond classrooms in Austria

A system where the measurement of the individual knowledge and skills of students is done by highly qualified, competent and reliable teachers leaves little room for external assessment (not unlike the situation in higher education); only when there is reason to believe that the system is not working the way it should that questions of quality of assessment practice will be asked and listened to.

From within the system, there have persistently been signals that all was not as well as it appeared. Not surprisingly in teachers' circles, cases were reported on how specialist teachers had assessed the same essay of a student differently, how what was assessed was often based on personal interpretations of curricula by teachers and how students could pass in one school with less effort than students in another school.

Involved parents have always been instrumental in securing teachers' attention for a 'fair' assessment for their own children; informed parents and students look at a teacher's assessment even more critically and note any shortcomings that could work to a student's disadvantage.

One early attempt to get a more systematic grip on the objectivity of testing and assessment was the *Lehrzielbank*, an item-banking project of teaching objectives, which started as early as the mid-1970s in Austria. The item-banking project covered the upper secondary technical and vocational curricula, established what the core objectives were in the key subject domains and illustrated them with model test instruments which teachers could use for building their own teaching and testing paradigms on.

Because this project stopped short of being developed into a national assessment project, the gap between the model instruments and teachers' real world of assessment remained by and large unbridged, and if any effect was felt, it was through the enhanced quality of the schoolbooks published by authors who had been part of the project. Yet its impact on the quality of the instruments used in schools throughout Austria cannot be overestimated because these books have also been used throughout secondary education, including general (and indeed, to a limited extent, in tertiary) education.

Education policy and international assessment in Austria

That Austria should have persistently distanced itself from international projects to monitor education is not surprising. The first international assessment Austria took part in was IEA's COMPED, both the equipment and the student surveys. However, because of the small number of countries in the student survey, COMPED country results never qualified for inclusion in the EAG indicators.

When the results were published, the media were quick to spot a section of teachers' complaints about insufficient and outdated equipment, overlooking the fact that a new generation of computers had been introduced on the basis of a complete curriculum overhaul after the survey had been carried out. That Austria's students had outperformed those in the few countries that had participated in the students' questionnaires went largely unnoticed by the media, and any interest in these results was difficult to sustain because of weak international evidence. (It did not help that any international evidence there might have been was not brought forward at the time.)

COMPED as a study was not sufficiently convincing to turn the tide in favour of international assessment in Austria, and mainstream educational scientists, with the sole exception of the newly formed University of Salzburg IEA Austria Unit, continued to advise against embracing the competence measuring school. Even so, the ice had been broken, and participation in TIMSS 1995, which was presented as a research project, was secured for all three population groups, including apprentice education.

Budget restraints and a general reluctance to reply to yet more surveys were major reasons for Austria's choosing not to participate in the IEA RLS. Another major reason for Austria's not choosing to participate was that the Bamberger school of reading still held the centre stage of educational policy in Austria. Although it is true that Bamberger does measure reading skills, he uses the results mainly as a predictor of students' careers. Bamberger actively promotes the skill at an early age, emphasising that this policy holds the key to success in school and in later life. Austria also missed out on the IEA CivEd study because it was perceived as competing for focus and funds with the traditional emphasis of providing schools and teachers with the materials that were considered to be needed to promote the case of model citizenship.

While still struggling with what TIMSS 1995 could or would not say about mathematics and science teaching in Austria, agreement to take part in PISA, an assessment that the OECD had put considerable weight behind, was a foregone conclusion. (Austria did not participate in TIMSS 1999 or PIRLS 2001.)

Austria's neighbours as models and facilitators

Neighbouring countries participated much earlier and more extensively in IEA surveys. Looking at just a few selected countries gives some background.

In Switzerland, unlike in Austria, education is not the responsibility of a strong central government; Switzerland is a European example of what a small but influential and engaged group of persons can accomplish in and for a country that clearly belongs among the 'diverse education systems'. At an early stage of international assessment practice, these people understood the importance of being involved in international comparative studies on the quality of education systems. Their interest was methodical (what could possibly be done?) as well as aimed at gaining a more valid assessment of Swiss education by using the international studies for intranational comparisons between regions and cantons. The Swiss educationalists were also aware that this kind of comparison requires extensive internal secondary analysis of the implications of the results in the national context. As a result, corresponding research programmes to address such analysis have been carried out.

During the mid-1990s there was a remarkable shift in the official policy of the Swiss Conference of Cantonal Directors of Education, from a very reserved, conservative position (not viewing a need for comparisons with others) to a more rational one. After that gaining the financial support of all twenty-six cantons was not too difficult (evidently, some lobbying was required).

What was perhaps unique in the case of Switzerland was the link that could be established between administrative management and innovative and research-oriented perspectives, which was the basis of the Swiss initiatives in the OECD/INES context. The Swiss initiatives were systematically probing the INES framework for missing elements, and proposals for concrete activities to fill in the gaps were favourably received. Important activities led or actively supported by the Swiss have included early work on non-curriculum-bounded skills and knowledge, later work on cross-curricular competences (namely self-concept and self-efficacy), an *ad hoc* group on equity and finally the DeSeCo project, which was to support research on and elaboration of theoretical foundations for the examination of competencies. Without these contributions from Switzerland, PISA might not have gained European and international backing to the extent it did. This certainly holds true for Austria, where a merely conventional subject-bound assessment would not have won the support it has.

Germany is both similar to and different from Switzerland. With each of the *Länder* responsible for its education policies, secondary education is not organised uniformly. There are some remarkable differences in structure, with the exception of the one common track of vocational education and training,[3] though students across Germany sit the final examination at the general upper secondary level (*Abitur*) under comparable conditions and general standards. Germany (unlike Switzerland, which was mainly represented in assessment activities by its scientific community in IEA) has been one of the strongest participants in international assessment. This strong scientific involvement is also apparent in PISA, where Germany has been pioneering problem solving (see also Chapter 5). Akin to what occurred in Austria, not too favourable TIMSS results caught the attention of politicians, the media and the public at large, and the question of the quality of schooling and instruction has been at the top of the agenda in the *Länders'* Standing Conference of Ministers of Education and Cultural Affairs.

Hungary has enjoyed a much longer tradition of partaking in international surveys than its neighbours Austria and the Czech Republic. It is interesting to see how already in once communist-ruled Hungary key educationalists were eager to test their country's 'adapted' education system against the 'outside world' of Western countries as well as how they undertook these endeavours. To an Austrian it is still astonishing that – for long almost unnoticed by its immediate neighbours – Hungary was able to participate actively in IEA studies and build up a competence in large-scale assessment, which was reinvested in direct contact with IEA.

Other post-communist countries that are immediate neighbours of Austria, including the two republics of the former Czechoslovakia, joined IEA right after 1989, more or less about the same time as Austria, with TIMSS 1995 being the first international survey for each. It is remarkable to see that these small countries, with little prospect of help in translating instruments into their languages, quickly became top players in international assessment. Given the common roots and old, re-emerging close ties with its neighbours to the east and south-east, Austria was, of course, interested how its educational system would now compare with those of adjacent countries.

Austria's practical utilisation of COMPED and TIMSS 1995 results

The assessment aspect of the COMPED study was difficult to interpret because of the small number of countries that participated and because the 'horse race' test results, meagre as they were, were too good to prompt national analysis. Results that indicated shortcomings, such as inadequate access to and use of computers in the classroom and outdated equipment, were almost irrelevant and had little impact because conditions had changed between the time of instrument application and the time of data release: during that period considerable efforts had been made to train teachers and install a new generation of equipment. In addition, because COMPED was the first international assessment project in which Austria had participated, and because a cautious approach was chosen to introduce assessment, the stakeholders reacted in sporadic bouts of attention, the data were not put to use analytically and the matter was not pursued.

Related to the TIMSS 1995 findings, the ongoing project Innovations in Mathematics and Teaching (IMST) was initiated and extended to the end of secondary education (see also Chapter 7). The project is based on a thorough analysis of the end-of-secondary results because they were, at first, particularly disappointing and, at the same time, largely puzzling, if not inexplicable, because results in primary and lower secondary schools were better than average. On the basis of this analysis, an assessment of the status quo of Austrian mathematics and science teaching was carried out, and the reforms of other countries (e.g. the Netherlands) where the results prompted such an assessment were discussed. The respective conclusions and expert opinions were formulated by way of policy recommendations in IMST² (the extra T in 'T²' accounting for the important role of technology). IMST² was designed to foster innovations that aim at improving the quality of learning and teaching, to focus on mathematics and science and to address all stakeholders in the Austrian educational system.

Given that a vast wealth of TIMSS 1995 data lay dormant for some time (i.e. all the lower-grade populations), it was disappointing to see that by the time they could have been put to use, most data were already out of date. (Politics is very critical of 'old' data.) Because tighter public budgets do not help the situation, future assessments should consider the countries' need to use their data in a timely manner. This need, in part, impacted the decision to conduct PISA on a three-year cycle.

What added value Austria expects from participation in PISA

The main reason why Austria embraced international assessment was hope of help in the areas where greatest benefit of international co-operation is anticipated, including system monitoring, assessment anchoring, international placement of system effectiveness, international agreement on competence standards and on benchmarking, assessment measurement expansion into more complex domains and encouragement of its scientific community for measurement-driven research in education, a truly international documentation of best practices in knowledge and skills acquisition (instruction types and practices; attitudes; interactions of teachers, students, parents, and schools).

Additionally, several bi- and multinational co-operations within the framework of international assessment are imagined, including the following:

- Evaluation of common system characteristics, which could better explain results and which are not dealt with internationally (e.g. domain organisation, student flows, classroom assessment and national marking systems effects).
- Identification of the key elements that determine the quality of the interaction process between teachers and students.
- Identification of the degree of satisfaction of stakeholders concerning national system characteristics.
- Co-operation in developing assessment areas that are of national interest but have not yet been internationally accepted (e.g. foreign language, democratic skills, communication).
- Co-operation in assessing supplementary populations.
- Co-operation in innovating assessment methods and in developing a comprehensive system of quality control in education.

Reflections from Canada

This section examines how education indicators are used in Canada, a country that, in contrast to Austria, has a decentralised system of education. Canada has no national-level department of education, and policy decision making is concentrated at the provincial and territorial level, although school districts and schools also have some responsibility for certain areas. At the time the interviews on which this analysis is based were conducted Canada consisted of a federation of ten provinces and two territories (the jurisdictions).[4] The Canadian constitution divides government responsibility between the jurisdictions and the federal government. Responsibility for education is allocated to the jurisdictions. The term 'pan-Canadian' is used to refer to the Canada-wide context involving participation by provinces and territories. In recognition of the value of having a mechanism for inter-action among the twelve education systems at the pan-Canadian level, the Council of Ministers of Education, Canada (CMEC) was created in 1967, to share information and undertake projects in areas of mutual interest and concern. CMEC is an intergovernmental body comprising the Ministers responsible for elementary/secondary and tertiary education from the provinces and the territories.

Although the Canadian jurisdictions share many areas of similarity and common interest, the structure of the education system and of its adminis-tration vary considerably from jurisdiction to jurisdiction. For example, some provinces have separate systems of education for students learning in the official language (either English or French), which is not the majority language of the province, while others provide such education opportuni-ties within one system. Administratively, three provinces choose to establish separate Ministries of elementary/secondary education and tertiary educa-tion, while the other jurisdictions combine the two areas in one Ministry. Interviews were conducted with individuals within each jurisdiction across Canada who are involved in policy development.[4]

Canada has participated in the OECD/INES project since its inception and Canadian jurisdictions use EAG as a source of international indicator information. The Pan-Canadian Education Indicators Program (PCEIP) performs a similar function within Canada. The primary objective of the PCEIP is to 'develop statistical measures that will provide the public and policy makers with information about the performance of education sys-tems in Canada and support decisions about priorities and directions' (Canadian Education Statistics Council 1994). The structure of the PCEIP is also closely aligned with the OECD/INES framework.

The other pan-Canadian indicator vehicle is the School Achievement Indicators Program (SAIP), which is an assessment of the performance of 13- and 16-year-old students in mathematics, reading and writing, and sci-ence. The aim of the programme is to provide the jurisdictions with information that can be used 'to set educational priorities and plan program improvements' (CMEC 1999). SAIP is focused on assessing student achieve-ment, and SAIP data are used as a source of output indicators for the PCEIP.

Seven of the twelve jurisdictions either have or are developing their own indicators programme. Three jurisdictions, Newfoundland and Labrador, Quebec and Alberta have been publishing education indicators reports since before the publication of the first edition of EAG in 1992.

Use of indicators in Canadian jurisdictions

Canadian policy makers consult indicator information from all three lev-els – international, pan-Canadian and jurisdictional – as part of their decision-making process. However, the primary indicators that policy makers look to tend to be those of their own jurisdiction, where available. Pan-Canadian and international indicators are consulted for additional external reference as needed.

As with all indicator systems, jurisdictional indicators in Canada fulfil an important monitoring function, providing information on changes in the education system over time. In every case, accountability was one of the main reasons given for developing a jurisdictional indicator programme. Politicians, students, parents and teachers want to know how well the system is performing, as does the general public. Indicator programmes provide a vehicle for jurisdictions to disseminate their expectations of the system to the public. Consultations with stakeholders are important, respondents noted, both in enlisting co-operation in obtaining data and in ensuring that the indicators chosen will provide appropriate and useful information.

Jurisdictional indicators also assist in developing policy. The data contained in the indicators may suggest areas for improvement or justify existing policy trends. Respondents stated that internal results, such as high-school graduation examinations and rates of completion, play an important role in policy direction, primarily because they allow a jurisdiction to track progress over time and monitor the results of policies and programs.

Jurisdictional indicators alone are not sufficient, however. To fully analyse and evaluate the data provided at a jurisdictional level, external factors must be considered. The performance and programmes of other jurisdictions, and other countries, provide an essential context for evaluating jurisdictional results. For some issues, such as the Atlantic Education Indicators Project, which was a programme involving the four Atlantic provinces, regional comparisons have been seen as important and useful. For other issues, comparison may most usefully be made between provinces geographically distant but systemically similar, such as between the francophone minority students of Manitoba and New Brunswick.

Comparisons between jurisdictions are not always easy. Jurisdictions with well established indicator programmes have developed certain methods of data collection and indicator calculation, which may not mesh with those used by other jurisdictions. The PCEIP is, in part, an attempt to remedy this situation, presenting data that are, to the extent possible, consistent in collection and calculation methodology across the jurisdictions. The concern most often mentioned about using indicators from outside the individual jurisdiction was variability in the definition of terms and in the methodology used for collecting the data. For example, in Quebec, *enseignant* (educator) refers strictly to a classroom teacher. Some other jurisdictions use a broader definition of an 'educator' and include staff other than classroom teachers in their data, creating potential comparability problems. The need for consistency in order to obtain reliable, comparable data was stressed by all respondents, in both the pan-Canadian and the international context.

How are the broader sets of indicators, the OECD indicators and the PCEIP used by the jurisdictions? EAG and EPA were characterised as important documents which provide background material on the international context of education and are an excellent reference source. Respondents voiced strong support for the level of detail and comprehensiveness currently provided, which are needed for the richer international analysis around specific topics for which the material is often used. Several jurisdictions pointed out that even though their direct use of EAG might be infrequent, the publication was nevertheless highly valuable because the international arena is becoming increasingly important. Ontario's accountability goals, for example, are explicitly 'benchmarked against the best in the world' (Government of Ontario, Ministry of Education and Training, 1998). Policy makers use international data both in assessing policy internally and in answering the question 'How are we doing?' for the media and the public.

Quebec, which refers to the OECD indicators several times a week, makes the greatest use of EAG in Canada. This intense use by Quebec reflects the cultural and linguistic uniqueness of its position within Canada and its interest in international francophone comparison. Larger jurisdictions, such as Ontario and Alberta (Advanced Education), use EAG regularly for comparisons and provision of perspectives on provincial policy and programmes. In other jurisdictions it tends to be read with interest when first issued, and functions thereafter primarily as a reference tool consulted when questions with an international dimension arise. Here the effects of working in a decentralised system can be seen. Information is provided to the OECD and reported in EAG at a national level, but the information is primarily used at a jurisdictional level within the country.

International indicators are used in several ways for the development of policy. They provide a perspective for discussion of issues by showing where the jurisdiction stands in relation to similar countries with respect to a particular indicator, although the first consideration in making such comparisons is generally the activities of other jurisdictions within Canada. Programme-specific indicators, such as those on special education, are useful for generating ideas, indicating areas for further inquiry and demonstrating the international policy spectrum on a particular issue. International information is used both by politicians and policy makers to provide a broad perspective and benchmark against which to measure policy in an individual jurisdiction. While EAG cannot give the total picture, it does provide necessary comparative information that allows judgements and assessments to be made.

Respondents who work in tertiary education noted that international comparisons are especially important at that level. Even though jurisdiction-level information is generally the starting point when using indicators in policy development, global analysis is included where possible. Universities and colleges must compete in the international arena, not only for students from other countries who might choose to pursue their studies in Canada, but also with institutions from other countries which may attract Canadian students.

The finding that emerged most clearly was that indicators are of the greatest value when they provide information at the primary locus of decision making. In a decentralised education system such as Canada's, most policy is made at the provincial and territorial level. Canada-level data, such as that in EAG and some indicators in *Education Indicators in Canada*, the PCEIP publication, are of benefit, but their direct usefulness for policy development is limited. In the same way, for example, information about education in the European Union as one entity might be of interest and be both pertinent and useful in certain contexts, but would not provide Education Ministries in individual countries with a picture of how their particular education system was functioning. As with EAG, pan-Canadian indicators that provide information at a Canadian level are considered less useful than jurisdiction-level data because Canadian data fail to provide the level of detail required for education policy work in jurisdictional Ministries and departments of education.

The policy use of the pan-Canadian indicators in *Education Indicators in Canada* is similar to that of EAG, although the pan-Canadian indicators tend to be consulted more often because they provide jurisdiction-level data. The pan-Canadian indicators have been regularly used, for example, in preparing briefing notes for Ministers, for comparing and ranking a particular jurisdiction against other Canadian jurisdictions and in responding to issues raised by the media and political opposition. In some cases, jurisdictions have passed *Education Indicators in Canada* on to schools in order to provide information about the education system to stakeholders and the public. The pan-Canadian indicators have also stimulated debate within jurisdictions about education policy by generating ideas and concerns based on observations of what other jurisdictions may or may not be doing. The comments about the sector-specific OECD indicators, mentioned above, demonstrate a similar use of indicators at the international level.

One type of indicator which tends to have a high profile because it is easily understood by the media and the public is the results of large-scale assessments, such as PISA, TIMSS and the SAIP. Reflecting the comments above about the importance of inter-jurisdictional comparison, the jurisdictions which make the most use of results from assessments, such as TIMSS, are those which oversampled to allow stable estimates at the jurisdictional level.[6] Quebec has also participated in large-scale international assessment of francophone populations and finds those results particularly pertinent to its unique situation because of the problems which arise in the pan-Canadian context of making comparisons across different languages.

SAIP results have been used by jurisdictions for the assessment of curriculum and policy, particularly the evaluation of any changes in policy made after the release of the first set of SAIP results. For example, in the

1994 reading and writing assessment, the results of New Brunswick franco-phone students were considered to be below expectations. An external committee was immediately created to make recommendations to the Minister and within the following year a new curriculum and new instructional material had been introduced. Results for the 1998 reading and writing assessment showed higher percentages of students at or above the anticipated levels than did the 1994 results. The results from SAIP provide a strong tool for policymakers to use when advocating changes in programmes. Results are used to spur Cabinet interest in, for example, programmes for early intervention to prevent the development of inequities in achievement between boys and girls. The results also assist in the analysis of results of provincial/territorial exams in those subjects.

Assessments such as SAIP, TIMSS and PISA play a valuable role as a support for public information and accountability. Quebec, for example, reports the results of both SAIP and TIMSS in its annual indicators report. The results can be used to support and justify existing policies and to provide stakeholders, including the public, with information about how the system is performing relative to other jurisdictions and to itself over time. The results also provide politicians and the media an opportunity to raise questions about education.

The federal context

Although Canada has no federal department of education, some areas of federal responsibility involve education issues. Federal concerns over equality of access, citizenship and labour, for example, are informed by education data.[7] Federal concerns tend to centre on pan-Canadian issues that generally require either interjurisdictional or international comparison order to look for national variation or to evaluate Canada's performance in the international context. The federal respondents indicated that they focus primarily on international and pan-Canadian indicators, turning to jurisdictional indicators only for specific questions. Consideration of indicator data may generate policy initiatives in areas where Canada's performance seems to differ from that of other countries. For example, rates of secondary school completion, which are of direct interest to the jurisdictions, also affect federal concerns for youth at risk and school to work transitions.

Conclusions

One of the most interesting comments from those interviewed regarding the role of indicators related to their indirect and 'unofficial' impact. One respondent stated that preparing and circulating multiple drafts for a provincial indicator report was perhaps the most valuable part of an indicators programme. As people offered commentary and suggestions to the various drafts they thought more about the education system in general, raised questions and came up with new ideas. The indicators became a part of the conceptualisation of the issues, enriching the process and helping to crystallise thinking around issues. Similar comments were made with respect to EAG about the importance of simply circulating it and making people aware of the indicators and concepts it contains. The information indicators provide about other education systems and their performance is generally looked to not as a model or blueprint but as a guide and inspiration. The value of indicators lies not only in the data and in their direct use in the policy context, but in their role as a source of information about possible approaches to education, as a stimulus to begin questioning and as an opportunity to look at one's own education system with fresh eyes.

The trend in Canada appears to be towards a larger role for indicators in developing education policy. Most jurisdictions now have their own indicator programmes, and all jurisdictions have been involved in the process of developing and reviewing the indicators for *Education Indicators in Canada: Report of the Pan-Canadian Education Indicators Program, 1999*. Discussions have been held at various levels about the possibility of creating broader-based indicators and of combining education indicators with those on health, community services, citizenship and justice. Indicators provide a structure for reporting on elements of the education system and on the well-being of children to show where progress has been made and where attention needs to be focused.

One of the primary functions of these indicators is accountability. In part, this is public accountability. Indicator data allow governments to give concrete results to a sometimes sceptical public. It is far more convincing to show that more students are completing high school than ten years ago than simply to state that the education system is doing well. Accountability within governments is also a factor. The past few years have seen a climate of fiscal restraint, and programmes need to be demonstrably effective in order to continue to receive funding.

Notes

1 These case studies were originally prepared in 2000 and only minor updating has occurred since then.
2 'Leaving' refers to obtaining a vocational qualification; matriculation (from 'higher' schools and colleges) qualifies a student for direct and unlimited university access.
3 The federal government has responsibility for the practical part of the dual system; the vocational college system is under the responsibility of the *Länder*.
4 As of 1 April 1999 the eastern section of the North West Territories became the territory of Nunavut.
5 Where a jurisdiction divides responsibility for elementary/secondary education and tertiary education between two Ministries, individuals from each Ministry were contacted. The answers referred to reflect the knowledge of the individual interviewed and, as such, may not present a complete picture.

6 For TIMSS 1995, students were assessed in three population groups: Population 1 (grades 3 and 4), Population 2 (grades 7 and 8) and Population 3 (final year of secondary school). British Columbia, Alberta, Quebec and Ontario oversampled to produce data for all three populations. New Brunswick and Newfoundland and Labrador did not participate fully in the Population 3 study.

7 The two federal departments which probably make the greatest use of education indicators are Statistics Canada, which also assists in the production of the data for the pan-Canadian indicators, and Human Resources Development, Canada, whose mandate covers a broad range of issues, including literacy.

References

Canadian Education Statistics Council, 1996. *Education Indicators in Canada* (Toronto: Canadian Education Statistics Council), p. 4.

CMEC, 1999. *SAIP Report on Reading and Writing, 1998* (Toronto: Council of Ministers of Education, Canada).

Government of Ontario, Ministry of Education and Training, 1998. *Ontario Government Business Plans 1998–1999* (Ottawa: Government of Ontario, Ministry of Education and Training), p. 2.

Chapter 7

Gender differences in achievement

Overview and examples of data use in five countries

Contributions by Konrad Krainer, Helga Jungwirth and Helga Stadler, Steve May and Lynne Whitney, Arnold A.J. Spee, Anita Wester, Douglas Hodgkinson; compilation by Maria Stephens

Policy makers from countries participating in international studies of student performance often cite two reasons for involvement in such endeavours – they are interested in (1) obtaining data to inform policy decisions about national programmes and practices and (2) comparing their students with those in other countries. The results of international assessments serve not only to flag potential educational problems, as other diverse data sources can do, but also to illustrate the magnitude of these problems relative to a country's trading partners or regional or cultural counterparts.

One persistent concern among policy makers in OECD countries is to ensure that boys and girls are receiving equal opportunities to learn and are achieving at equal rates so that all students can contribute to society and reap the rewards of an education (e.g. OECD 1998, 2000, 2003). The first section of this chapter describes basic findings about gender differences in mathematics and science in OECD countries, drawing mainly from TIMSS 1995.[1] The second section presents examples of national analyses, conducted in five countries, that explored the issue of gender and achievement in more depth. These examples draw mainly on the experiences of various countries with TIMSS 1995 because there has been sufficient time to observe and document national uses of these data. Together the five profiles demonstrate a range of valuable uses to which data from international assessments have been put over the years to address questions of national importance.

Gender differences in OECD countries

Gender differences in mathematics at the fourth-grade level were small to moderate, as reported from TIMSS 1995. The mean difference across all countries participating in the assessment was two points.[2] Among the seventeen OECD countries[3] where fourth-grade students were assessed, differences were statistically significant in only three countries – Japan, Korea and the Netherlands – where boys outscored girls by an average of eight, fifteen and fifteen points respectively. In Greece, Ireland and New Zealand the gender gap appeared to favour girls, although the differences were not statistically significant.

With regard to achievement in science among fourth-grade students, a somewhat larger gender gap was evident in 1995, with a mean difference of nine points across all countries. The differences were statistically significant in nine of the seventeen participating OECD countries, in each of which boys outperformed girls. The results of TIMSS 2003 (which will be available in December 2004) will show whether or not differences at the fourth-grade level have changed over time for the ten OECD countries that repeated the assessment.

Gender differences at the eighth-grade level in TIMSS 1995 were less pronounced and less frequently statistically significant in mathematics than they were in science. Among eighth-grade students the average gender gap in mathematics across countries was eight points. In six of the twenty-five OECD countries[4] participating the differences were statistically significant and favoured boys. Only in Canada, Australia and Belgium (Flemish community) did girls score higher than boys, although these differences were small and were not to be statistically significant. For the twelve OECD countries that administered both TIMSS 1995 and TIMSS 1999, three countries (Japan, Korea and the Netherlands) with significant differences favouring boys in mathematics in the 1995 data, when it is reanalysed on the 1999 scale, showed no statistically significant gender differences in 1999.[5] However, only Korea showed a reduction in the magnitude of gender differences between the two studies.

In contrast to the modest differences in mathematics at the eighth-grade level, a considerable gap was evident in TIMSS 1995 with regard to achievement in science. Boys outperformed girls by an average of seventeen points across countries. In eight OECD countries the differences exceeded twenty score points, and in seventeen OECD countries the differences were statistically significant.

TIMSS 1995 also showed that, by the end of secondary school, gender differences favouring boys were considerable in both mathematics and science, with average differences of thirty-three points in mathematics and thirty-nine points in science across countries. In mathematics, the differences were statistically significant in all but two of the sixteen participating OECD countries (Hungary and the United States), and in science the differences were statistically significant in every OECD country. In three cases (Denmark, Norway and the Netherlands) the differences between boys and girls in mathematics exceeded fifty points, which is half the standard deviation. The same can be said of Austria and Norway with regard to science achievement.

More recent data from PISA 2000, which cannot be compared directly with TIMSS because of differences in the respective assessment frameworks, items, target populations and groups of participating countries, showed a slightly less extreme pattern for 15-year-old boys and girls on its assessments of mathematical and scientific literacy. In mathematical literacy in PISA 2000 boys outperformed girls by an average of eleven points, with statistically significant differences favouring boys in thirteen of the

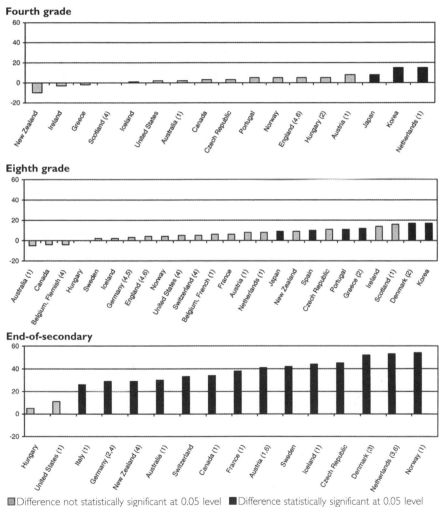

Fourth grade

Eighth grade

End-of-secondary

■Difference not statistically significant at 0.05 level   ■Difference statistically significant at 0.05 level

Figure 7.1 (a) Differences in mean mathematics achievement between boys and girls (1995). *Note* Countries are ranked in ascending order of difference in means between boys and girls. 1 Did not satisfy sampling guidelines. 2 Unapproved sampling plan or procedures or age group. 3 Unapproved sampling plan and low participation rates. 4 Sampling guidelines met only after replacement included. 5 National population does not cover all of desired population. 6 National population covers less than 90 per cent of desired population.

twenty-eight OECD countries participating. In scientific literacy, there was no difference in the average performance of boys and girls overall or in any OECD countries except four – three of which (Austria, Denmark and Korea) favoured boys.

What can be concluded overall about gender differences in OECD countries (see Figure 7.1a–b)?[6] Moreover, what can be said about gender differences in the five countries that contributed profiles to this chapter?

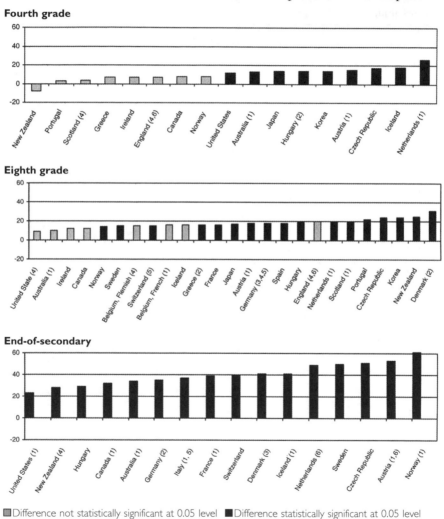

■Difference not statistically significant at 0.05 level ■Difference statistically significant at 0.05 level

Figure 7.1 (b) Difference in mean science achievement between boys and girls (1995). *Note* Countries are ranked in ascending order of difference in means between boys and girls. 1 Did not satisfy sampling guidelines. 2 Unapproved sampling plan or procedures or age group. 3 Unapproved sampling plan and low participation rates. 4 Sampling guidelines only met after replacement included. 5 National population does not cover all of desired population. 6 National population covers less than 90 per cent of desired population.

First, the average differences between boys and girls tended to be larger in science than in mathematics at the three grade levels assessed in TIMSS 1995. Furthermore, the average differences in both mathematics and science tended to be larger at the higher grade levels, with successively larger numbers of countries in which gender differences were statistically significant in each of the grades. Beyond these generalisations, TIMSS 1995 offers examples of individual countries that deviate from the overall patterns.

In some countries the relative advantage for boys 'increases' between grade levels. For instance, in both mathematics and science the gender gap favouring boys in Scotland was much larger in the eighth grade than in the fourth grade. And in New Zealand and Greece a possible advantage in mathematics for girls at the fourth grade was a statistically significant advantage for boys in the eighth grade. Similarly, in science, New Zealand's gender gap seemed to favour girls in the fourth grade but was the second largest among OECD countries favouring boys in the eighth grade.

For other countries, the relative advantage for boys was smaller at the higher grade. In mathematics, both the Netherlands and Hungary had smaller gender differences favouring boys in the eighth grade than they had in the fourth grade. The Netherlands exhibited a similar pattern for science. Although in the Netherlands, despite 'improvement' between the two grades, gender differences were above the OECD mean and statistically significant at both.

In a few countries, gender differences were small and 'changed' little between the fourth and eighth grades. For example, the United States exhibited relatively stable gender differences in mathematics between the two grades and was at or below the mean for both grade levels. The same could be said of Ireland or Canada in science.

Finally, at both grade levels and in both subject areas, girls in some countries – even those with large within-country gender differences – outperformed boys in other countries. The most notable example of this in TIMSS 1995 was in Korea, where, despite having the largest gender gap in OECD countries in mathematics at the eighth grade (seventeen points), the average achievement of Korean girls exceeded that of boys in all other OECD countries except one (Japan). Similar general patterns also were observed in the later TIMSS and PISA studies.

National uses of international data on gender differences

The remainder of this chapter presents information from analyses performed in five countries – Austria, New Zealand, the Netherlands, Sweden and Canada – to answer questions of particular national importance. Austria and New Zealand, although responding to different stimuli, explored the factors that contribute to gender differences. The Netherlands and Sweden answered more research-oriented questions. The Netherlands conducted a study of primary schools in response to a disturbing finding from TIMSS, and Sweden studied results from a national option to learn about the possible impacts of item format on student performance. Finally, Canada provides an example of how national assessment data were analysed to confirm and contextualise results from international assessments.

Austria

Innovations in mathematics and science teaching study

Following the administration of TIMSS 1995 in Austria, the Ministry of Education and Cultural Affairs was interested in further data analysis to provide valuable information for teachers. In contrast to Austria's results for the primary and lower secondary populations of TIMSS 1995, which placed its students above the average of OECD countries, results for end-of-secondary students were disappointing, both with regard to the percentages of correct responses and to overall mean scores.[7]

The Ministry initiated two projects. The first was to deliver the end-of-secondary data on compact disc, to disseminate all released items and results via the Internet and to develop software to support teachers' self-evaluation. The second was to further analyse the end-of-secondary school results, to encourage self-evaluation by professional staff in schools, to analyse reforms in selected countries, to analyse the strengths and weaknesses of mathematics and science teaching (e.g. through workshops with teachers and teacher educators) and to develop proposals to improve the quality of mathematics and science teaching (IFF 1999). This profile focuses mainly on national analyses of end-of-secondary data. Although only a small part of Austria's work related to TIMSS, these analyses were of major interest to policy makers.

Results from the Austrian Innovations in Mathematics and Science Teaching project[8]

One focus of the IMST project was to explore the effects of school type and content area on gender differences. For mathematics and science achievement at the end of secondary school, differentiating between the types of schools revealed that the difference between the performance of boys and girls is largest in the intermediate technical and vocational schools. There the average score for girls, in both mathematics and science, was only 80 per cent of the average score for boys, whereas in the other schools (academic secondary, higher technical and vocational and dual vocational training) the girls' average score was closer to 90 per cent of the boys' average score. Differentiating by science content area, boys and girls performed equally with regard to items with a strong emphasis on biology. However, boys outperformed girls with regard to items with a strong emphasis on physics, with girls achieving only 72–83 per cent of the boys' scores (depending on school type and on the amount of physics instruction). In mathematics the differences across content areas were not so marked.

In the advanced mathematics and physics assessments (an additional TIMSS 1995 component), the gender gap was more notable than in the general mathematics and science assessments and varied greatly between the two major school types in Austria. Whereas in the academic secondary schools girls achieved 83 per cent and 85 per cent of boys' scores in mathematics and physics respectively, in the higher technical and vocational schools they achieved only 60 per cent of boys' scores in both subjects. Content area analysis shows that in advanced mathematics boys outperformed girls most substantially in calculus. In the physics assessment gender differences were the smallest in the content areas that were taught during the final year of secondary school (e.g. radioactivity or quantum mechanics).

Neither the findings in general mathematics and science nor those in advanced mathematics and physics provide definitive explanations for the gender differences observed in Austria. However, the amount of instruction over the years in secondary schooling may explain for the differences in achievement because, in the schools preferred by girls, there is less mathematics and science instruction than in other schools (BMUK 1998). Some achievement differences remain none the less, independent of this factor.

In many cases, interpretations of the TIMSS 1995 data concurred with the more anecdotal feedback of Austrian teachers and teacher educators. For example, a comparison of students' achievement levels in the TIMSS 1995 general mathematics assessment (Baumert *et al.* 1998, p. 308) showed that fewer students from Austria and Germany, in cross-national comparison with those from Switzerland and the Netherlands, achieved levels of performance where mathematical reasoning, model building and networking of operations were necessary. These data conformed with the experts' views, which indicated that in Austria and Germany such competences were not emphasised as much as they were in Switzerland and the Netherlands, where earlier reform movements (e.g. the 'realistic mathematics education' movement in the Netherlands) greatly influenced teacher education and curriculum and brought about change in mathematics teaching.

New Zealand

Factors affecting gender differences in mathematics and science

In New Zealand the media consistently paint a simple picture of the relative performance of boys and girls in the country's schools: girls outperform boys across most achievement areas (Education Review Office 1999). Using information from a range of sources, including TIMSS 1995, the Ministry of Education demonstrated that the picture is, rather, a complex one, with the relative performance of boys and girls being influenced by a range of factors related to both school and student characteristics (Praat 1999).

The Ministry of Education (1993a) published National Education Guidelines that form part of the charter of every New Zealand school. These guidelines place an obligation on schools and teachers to implement programmes that enable all students to realise their full potential and to provide equality of educational opportunity for all New Zealanders by identifying and removing barriers to achievement. Information provided to schools on the relative achievement of boys and girls assisted schools in selecting and implementing such programmes. For example, in revising the national curriculum for the 1990s the Ministry of Education made specific mention in the official documents of gender issues and their management in relation to mathematics (1992, p. 12) and science (1993b, pp. 11–12).

To shed light on the issue of the performance of boys and girls in mathematics and science, researchers at the Ministry of Education also looked at the international results from TIMSS 1995. Contrary to impressions painted by media reports, the relative performance of boys and girls changed over time and differed by grade level. At the year 4 and 5 levels,[9] for example, the TIMSS 1995 results showed that there were no significant gender differences for either mathematics or science. However, at years 8 and 9 boys outperformed girls in both mathematics and science. The difference for mathematics at these levels was not statistically significant, but for science New Zealand had the second largest gender difference among participating OECD countries. At the school-leaver level (i.e. years 12 and 13) the gender differences in mathematics and science were significantly in favour of boys in both subjects, although the differences were significantly below the respective international averages.

Having established that the picture of the relative achievement of boys and girls in mathematics and science was more complex than the simple achievement bias in favour of girls reported in the media, policy makers wanted to investigate which factors could be operating to produce these results.

Explaining gender differences

Research published in the international and New Zealand national reports for TIMSS 1995 (Garden 1996a, 1996b, 1997) found that overall performance could be affected by the content area being assessed, the ethnic identity of the student and the attitudinal shifts that occur at different points in the school system.

In mathematics at years 4 and 5 New Zealand girls scored significantly higher than boys in geometry and patterns, relations and functions, and significantly lower in the curricular area of measurement. In year 5 girls also outperformed boys in data representation, analysis and probability, but again not in measurement or in fractions and number sense. Boys' superior performance on the measurement tasks probably accounted for their overall significantly better performance as school-leavers because of the emphasis on measurement items in the end-of-secondary general mathematics assessment.

In science at year 5 girls scored significantly higher on life science and on environmental issues and the nature of science. At year 9 this difference was still apparent, but no longer statistically significant. At year 9 boys outperformed girls in the areas of earth science, physics and chemistry.

In the mid-1990s about one-quarter of students in years 4 and 5 were Maori. At these levels and in year 9 Maori girls scored significantly higher than Maori boys in mathematics. By contrast, results for European-descended students at years 4 and 5 and years 8 and 9 showed no significant differences between boys and girls.

In science there was a significant gender difference in favour of Maori girls at years 4 and 5 and correspondingly there were no significant gender differences between European boys and girls. At year 9 the situation for both groups of students had changed. Although boys significantly outscored girls among European students, there was no significant difference between Maori girls and Maori boys.

With regard to students' attitudes, changes in boys' and girls' attitudes toward science were evident between years 8 and 9. At year 9 girls reported being slightly less positive about science and boys reported being slightly more positive about science than did their counterparts in year 8. These changes enhanced the already present difference in attitudes between the two groups and, as described above, was reflected in girls' lower performance relative to boys in science at this level.

Interpreting the results

These results confirmed that the relationship between performance and gender in mathematics and science assessment is not a simple one. Relative strengths and weaknesses among boys and girls can be influenced by a number of factors. By identifying some of the factors, as described above, awareness can be raised among policy makers in government, practitioners and parents in the broader education sector, and results can be used to inform and address issues relating to the teaching and learning of students.

The TIMSS 1995 data were compared with other student outcome data generated within New Zealand and were found to be consistent with the results for gender from the National Education Monitoring Project (NEMP)[10] at years 4 and 8 for science (1995) and mathematics (1997). On the other hand, the report on school leavers from TIMSS 1995 was inconsistent with the picture from national external examinations at year 11. A number of factors may have accounted for this difference, including the content of the tasks, the type of tasks, the nature of the sample for each subject (self-selected in the external examination as opposed to randomly selected in TIMSS) and the relatively high-stakes nature of the national programme as compared with the relatively low-stakes nature of the international programme.

As a result of the findings from TIMSS 1995 and other studies, the Ministry of Education reviewed the literature to further explain gender differences and to document strategies to address these differences. Continuing analysis of more recent international assessments contributes to this ongoing work.

The Netherlands

Bridging the gender gap

Pupils in the Netherlands have demonstrated relatively high performance on international mathematics and science assessments. In fact Dutch pupils performed in TIMSS 1995 as 'the best of the West', competing with top-performing East Asian countries such as Japan and Korea. Unfortunately, in this case high achievement was not coupled with much gender equity: there were large differences within the country between boys and girls. This called for pedagogical and curricular reforms to bridge the achievement gap between boys and girls in primary and secondary school.

Gender differences at the fourth grade

The Netherlands participated in the fourth-grade assessment in TIMSS 1995 and, more recently, TIMSS 2003. TIMSS 1995 showed that at the fourth-grade level differences in mathematics and science achievement between boys and girls were larger (in favour of boys) than in any other country (except Korea in mathematics), with differences reaching fifteen and twenty-six points for the two subjects respectively. By contrast, the international averages were two and nine points respectively, and in most other countries the gender differences at this level were small and not statistically significant. In view of the wide differences in achievement between boys and girls, the Ministry of Education, Culture and Science commissioned a research study (conducted by researchers at the Universities of Leiden and Utrecht) to examine the characteristics of schools with a range of gender differences.

From the 5,000 Dutch schools that participated in the international assessment, the study identified 2,134 for having relatively stable gender differences over the previous three years, using national data. Among these schools, twenty were selected where boys significantly outperformed girls, and twenty were selected where there was no difference in the performance of boys and girls. Ultimately the sample was narrowed to four schools, two of which favoured boys and two of which had no gender differences, and all four of which shared similar structural characteristics (e.g. size, percentage of non-Dutch students, availability of counselling in mathematics), similar student characteristics (e.g. SES, attitudes towards mathematics, self-perception) and similar teacher attitudes and expectations.

The hypothesis of study was that the introduction of 'realistic mathematics' – the well known Dutch reform strategy in which pedagogy is based on real situations and students learn mainly by doing – in primary education contributed to the differences in achievement between boys and girls. The research, however, concluded that it was not the 'realistic mathematics' approach as such but poor implementation and the didactic failures of teachers that accounted for girls lagging behind the boys (van den Heuvel-Panhuizen and Vermeer 1999). Behaviours such as time spent in the classroom on instruction, posing questions, thinking and replying, practising and exercising – hallmarks of 'realistic mathematics' – were measured. One of the most marked differences between the sets of schools was in the time spent on 'thinking', where the schools without gender differences spent 9 per cent of time on this activity, compared with only 1 per cent of time in the schools in which there were gender differences. The research concluded that schools in which girls and boys performed equally well were characterised by a favourable and safe class atmosphere, clear and instrumental instruction by teachers and sufficient opportunities to learn.

To respond to the study's findings and to create better learning opportunities for girls, the Freudenthal Institute (the Institute of Mathematics Education, University of Utrecht) developed a teacher training course to improve the implementation of the curriculum for 'realistic mathematics'. The course was given in three regions in the Netherlands (de Goei and van den Heuvel-Panhuizen 2002). Hopefully, TIMSS 2003 will shed light on whether these regional teacher training courses may have helped bridge the gender gap in primary schools at the national level.

Gender differences at the eighth grade

To obtain data on students at the eighth-grade level, the Netherlands participated in SIMS and SISS in 1982 and 1984 and, more recently, in TIMSS 1995, 1999 and 2003. SIMS and SISS showed that in the Netherlands gender differences in mathematics were higher than any other country except France and in science higher than in any other OECD country.

This large gender gap in mathematics and science performance in the first years of secondary school in the 1980s was one of the reasons the government introduced a new curriculum for basic secondary education in 1993. Its core consisted of fifteen subjects that were compulsory for a maximum of three years. New subjects in this curriculum were technology, ICT studies and self-care. It was expected that by having a better balance of 'girls' subjects' and 'boys' subjects' the class climate would be more gender-balanced and the differences in achievement between boys and girls on all subjects would be smaller.

When TIMSS 1995 and 1999 data were placed on the same scale for comparative purposes, gender differences in mathematics performance at the eighth grade were twelve points for 1995 and five points for 1999. Similar results were observed for science as well, where the difference between boys and girls was twenty-six points in 1995 and eighteen points in 1999. This difference between 1995 and 1999 was caused by an increase among girls and no change among boys. In the 1999 assessment, gender differences in mathematics were not statistically significant, not different from the average differences across OECD countries and quite comparable with those in countries such as Belgium (the Flemish community), Korea and Hungary. Gender differences in science performance remained statistically significant, above the OECD average and statistically similar to those in Belgium (Flemish), Australia and Italy. Thus the international data indicated that in 1999 in the eighth grade girls and boys were performing equally well in mathematics, and girls were perhaps catching up in science.

Many education researchers doubted whether the relatively better performance in 1995 (compared with SIMS fourteen years earlier) was caused by the introduction of the basic secondary education curriculum, because the curriculum was not fully implemented then (Inspectorate of Education 1999). However, the absence of statistically significant gender differences in mathematics in TIMSS 1999 provided a strong argument for those who believed that the curriculum reforms were making a difference.

Gender differences at the end of secondary school

With regard to students near the end of secondary school, the Netherlands participated in TIMSS 1995 and PISA 2000 and 2003 (the results of which are not available until 2004). According to TIMSS 1995, gender differences were relatively large at the end of secondary school as well. In PISA 2000 (which cannot be compared with TIMSS for reasons enumerated earlier in the chapter), differences between boys and girls were not statistically different from the average OECD difference for mathematics as well as for science. Although there is no way to determine whether the smaller gender differences reported in PISA signify a real reduction in gender differences or whether they were a product of the differences in the make-up of the two assessments (or both), politically speaking there is a sense in the country that girls are catching up with boys.

In 1995 gender differences in achievement may have been related, in part, to the relatively small number of girls taking mathematics and science courses at the end of secondary school. The percentage of girls that were taking mathematics in their final year in 1995 was lower than in any other country. Since then the promotion campaign 'Exactly your choice' (in Dutch 'exact' means 'correct' and is short for 'exact sciences') stimulated the number of girls taking mathematics and science. The structure of mathematics programmes has also changed since then, being split into three levels (ordinary, intermediate and advanced), with all students in upper secondary education now taking at least the ordinary level mathematics.

The gender differences in 1995 may have been attributable to the lack of feedback given by teachers. Dutch research indicates that, in upper secondary science classes, girls prefer more extensive feedback on exercises than do the boys. But in the Netherlands girls did not receive the feedback they needed. The reasons for this, in the case of science, were an overburdened curriculum and the speed at which science was taught (de Bruijn 1997). Since 1997 the curriculum load in upper secondary education has been reduced and the pace of teaching has been slowed, giving girls the opportunity to match their performance with the boys' (de Bruijn 2001).

Again, although it is not technically sound to directly compare the results of TIMSS 1995 and PISA 2000, another hypothesis for the different pattern of results is that the students taking PISA are from a cohort close to those students who participated in the TIMSS 1999 lower secondary assessments, in which gender differences appeared to be smaller than in TIMSS 1995 and SIMS.

The poor performance of girls compared with that of boys in the past was one of the reasons for reforms such as those that have been mentioned in this profile. The pedagogical and curricular reforms aimed at creating better learning opportunities for girls in primary education, a better balance of subjects in basic secondary education and coherent packages of subjects in upper secondary education. From the perspective of policy makers, these measures have not been without success – gender differences were reduced between TIMSS 1995 and 1999 and were not observed in PISA 2000. Girls perform similarly to boys in mathematics and science in secondary education and outperform boys in several aspects of education, such as overall participation, entry into higher education, retention and transition (Ministry of Education, Culture and Science 2002). The effect of the low performance of girls in the past has not disappeared entirely, however. The participation of women compared with that of men in mathematics and natural science faculties in universities is still among the lowest in the world (OECD 2002). Hopefully, this statistic will also change in the near future, building on the equivalence of mathematics and science performance achieved by girls and boys in secondary education today.

Sweden

Item format and gender differences in mathematics and science

The issue of significance of item format for explaining gender differences in academic achievement has been the focus of many studies. (Chapter 2 discusses this issue in brief as well.) In many of these studies the results have shown that the multiple-choice format, relatively speaking, favours boys, while the open-ended format contributes to a relatively higher performance among girls (Bolger and Kellaghan 1990; Bell and Hay 1987; Murphy 1982). These findings have given rise to the suggestion that gender differences on assessments might be eliminated by using performance assessment and not multiple-choice items (e.g. Jovanovic *et al.* 1994).

The National Agency for Education (Skolverket) in Sweden designed a national option (i.e. a special study administered with the international study) as part of its participation in TIMSS 1995, which included grades 6, 7 and 8. The purpose of the study was to examine the effect of different item formats on gender differences in performance in mathematics and science. The following research question was addressed: does a change in item format from the multiple-choice format to the open-ended format, using identical item stems, favour the performance of girls compared with boys?

The study's design specified twenty TIMSS multiple-choice items (ten mathematics and ten science) as experimental items distributed across the eight test booklets and twelve TIMSS items as core (or anchor) items[11] (six mathematics and six science) in each booklet. Additionally a ninth booklet was developed – collaboratively with Denmark and Norway – which consisted of the twenty experimental items converted from their initial multiple-choice format to an open-ended format and the twelve anchor items. Thus the items used in the study were identical except for their format. In the open-ended format, students had to produce their own solution, which could be a single number or a word or a sentence to explain a certain phenomenon.

The results of the study showed no changes in gender differences when the item format was changed from multiple-choice to open-ended. In mathematics, girls performed slightly better than boys (see Figure 7.2), a difference that remained the same when using open-ended items. The two lines representing girls' and boys' achievement are parallel, indicating no interaction between gender and item format.

In science, boys performed somewhat better than girls on multiple-choice items, a difference that, again, remained when the format was open-ended. Furthermore, as was shown for mathematics, the lines representing girls' and boys' performance are parallel for science as well. No evidence in this national study from TIMSS 1995 indicates that changing the item format from multiple-choice to open-ended, relatively speaking, would have favoured the performance of girls.

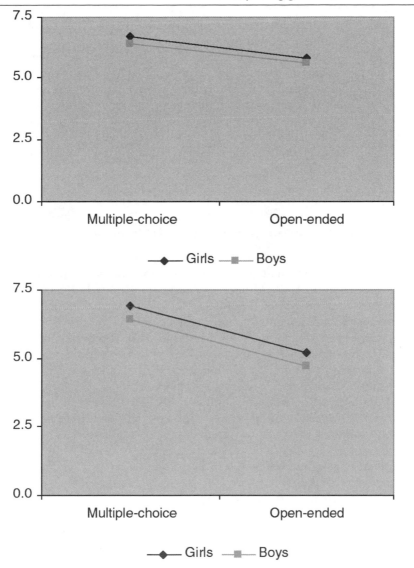

Figure 7.2 Mean score for females and males on ten items in the multiple-choice and the open-ended format.

The results imply that, when dealing with Swedish students in mathematics and science, the question of item format and gender differences in performance are not as simple as has been suggested by some previous research. The data contradict, for example, the suggestion of a strong interaction between the multiple-choice item format and certain personality traits (Hellekant 1994). Also, the idea that boys are more prone to guessing, whereas girls are more inclined to leave items unanswered, as an explanation for gender differences in performance on tests (Ben-Shakar and Sinai 1991) was not supported in this study.

In conclusion, defining what is meant by an 'open-ended item' seems crucial to further studies. It is somewhat surprising that, in most of the research on gender and item format, no distinction has been made between different types of open-ended items, although there is no disagreement about the significant difference between performing a mathematical computation and writing an essay. It may also be necessary to differentiate between subjects, for example, between natural science subjects and verbal/language subjects in such studies in the future.

Canada

Gender and achievement in the School Achievement Indicators Program

In the late 1980s the Canadian provinces and territories (i.e. jurisdictions) began to develop the SAIP. Ministers of education wanted to maximise the effectiveness and quality of Canadian education systems and agreed that achievement in fundamental school subjects would be one appropriate performance indicator for the school systems. SAIP was designed to measure the achievement of a sample of 13- and 16-year-olds from each jurisdiction in mathematics, reading and writing and science.[12] These three subject areas were chosen because they are ones in which students across the country learn many similar skills. All students write components of the same test (there are several booklets of differing levels of difficulty) and all the tests are graded on the same scale. The results, reported at the Canadian and jurisdiction levels, not only show the findings for each age group for each jurisdiction, but also provide both gender and linguistic breakdowns.

The first assessment, in mathematics content and mathematics problem solving, was administered in 1993. A second and third mathematics assessment in 1997 and 2001 allowed trends over time to be examined. Likewise, two reading and three writing assessments have taken place, in 1994, 1998 and 2002. The first science assessment, which contained both written and practical components, was administered in 1996 and was followed with a second assessment in 1999.

Results according to gender are reported only at the country level. Knowing that both age groups take essentially the same test, the test developers thought that the largest proportion of 13-year-olds would achieve at performance level 2 and the largest proportion of 16-year-olds would achieve at level 3. (The tests are graded on a five-level scale, with 5 being the highest level.) The results can be examined for each level, or for an aggregate of all levels at or above the predicted level of performance. For the second round of assessments, beginning with mathematics in 1997, an expectation-setting process was carried out in which a broadly based national panel reviewed the assessment and actual student results. They were attempting to determine the percentage of students from each age group who would be expected to achieve at each of the five levels for each component of the assessment.

The two age groups that take the SAIP assessments are somewhat similar to the eighth-grade and end-of-secondary populations of TIMSS 1995, although the 16-year-olds are slightly younger than the comparable TIMSS population. Although these two assessment-based studies were not intended to be comparable, they measured similar skills, and both used a combined problem-solving and general-knowledge approach. One significant difference between SAIP and TIMSS 1995 was that each of the three TIMSS populations took a different test, unlike SAIP, where both ages took components of the same test.

Results for TIMSS 1995 in Canada showed no significant differences in mathematics or science achievement at the eighth-grade level. There also were no statistically significant differences in mathematics or science between boys and girls at the end of secondary school, except in physics, where boys' results were higher.

Similarly, in the SAIP mathematics and science assessments, no statistically significant gender difference among 13-year-old students appeared in the results, with the exception of the problem-solving portion of the 1997 mathematics assessment, where more boys than girls achieved level 4. Among the 16-year-olds, in all assessments except the practical portion of the science assessment, where no differences appeared, more boys than girls achieved the higher levels (levels 4 and 5). This result suggests that between the ages of 13 and 16 the learning gain of girls does not match that of boys. This may be due to a number of factors, including choice of courses, in those situations where students have choice, and the effect of peer pressure and perceived societal expectations.

Results of both TIMSS 1995 and SAIP in the 1990s showed little gender discrepancy among the younger age group, but a gap in performance at the upper secondary level. The SAIP 2001 mathematics assessment largely confirmed this pattern, though some small gender differences in favour of boys were detected in the 13-year-old population.

The SAIP programme explicitly aimed to assist jurisdictions with information that could be used 'to set educational priorities and plan program improvements' (CMEC 1999). In the jurisdictions, SAIP results have led to an explicit examination of curriculum and policy. For example, in the 1994 reading and writing assessment the results of New Brunswick francophone students were felt to be below expectations. An external committee was immediately convened to make recommendations to the Minister and within the following year a new curriculum and new instructional material had been introduced (Wagner, verbal discussion, 1999). In response to the results of the 1993 SAIP mathematics assessment, along with results from the 1991 second IAEP and provincial assessment results, Alberta noted that although its students had performed well, they had not performed as well in mathematics as in science. The province made improvement in mathematics a priority and developed a more rigorous mathematics curriculum (McEwen 1998).

It is hoped that (1) national (as well as international) assessment will continue to impact education policy and learning as in the examples above and that (2) as Canada implements the new streamlined Pan-Canadian Assessment Program, which will replace SAIP (while preserving its trend lines and focus on key subjects) and better link with PISA, providing internationally benchmarked information for 'improving learning' is the explicit goal.

International comparative assessments can provide information that is valuable for benchmarking and for identifying strengths and weaknesses in education systems, as shown in the first section, which reviews the general findings with respect to gender differences. Although many secondary analyses performed on the TIMSS 1995 data set seek to explain the findings and patterns across countries, the second section provides a reminder that some explanations must be examined within the context of a single country. The five profiles show but a sample of the types of research that can be and is being conducted to explore questions of national importance with international data.

Appendix

Methodological notes

Austria. For the end-of-secondary assessments, Austria had the lowest school participation rate before replacement (Mullis *et al.* 1998), which warrants caution in comparing Austria's results with those of other countries and in making generalisations about Austrian students. Other contextual factors may affect the interpretation of comparisons, as well. For example, Austria had the second highest (curriculum) coverage index and the highest rate of students reporting that they had no mathematics or physics in the final year of secondary school (Mullis *et al.* 1998). Austria also has very few upper secondary schools that specialise in mathematics and science; the lack of such schools perhaps contributes to their having one of the lowest relative differences between mean achievement of the top 5 per cent and top 10 per cent of all students in the advanced subject areas (Mullis *et al.* 1998). Finally, Austria has a great variety of school types at the upper secondary level, which greatly affects the amount of mathematics and science instruction students receive.

Sweden. The Swedish sample consisted of 8,851 students, 4,334 of whom were girls and 4,517, boys; from grade 6 (n = 2,825), grade 7 (n = 4,081) and grade 8 (n = 1, 945) – the three grades which, in Sweden, correspond to the TIMSS target population. Each of these students completed one of the eight TIMSS booklets. An additional 928 students, 446 females and 482 males, completed the ninth booklet (i.e. the booklet with open-ended items).

Canada. The assessments are administered to a large random sample of students from all jurisdictions. In some jurisdictions where the population is small, all 13- and 16-year-old students are assessed. Students take the assessment in their first official language. French and English versions of the assessments are harmonised to the extent possible.

Achievement is measured on a five-level scale. Level 1 attainment means that the student has reached early stages of competence in the subject; level 5 means that the student has achieved the full competence acquired by a student who has completed a specialised course at or near the end of secondary school. The developers of SAIP thought that the largest proportion of 13-year-olds would achieve at level 2 and the largest proportion of 16-year-olds would achieve at level 3 on all assessment instruments. For the second round of assessments, beginning with mathematics in 1997, an expectation-setting process based on a modified Angoff approach was carried out in which a broadly based eighty-nine-member national panel reviewed the assessment and actual student results to determine the percentage of students of each age group who should achieve at each of the five levels for each component of the assessment.

Where possible, the second assessment in a subject used the same criteria, instruments, administrative procedures, scoring procedures and exemplars as were used in the first assessment. If changes occurred, they were tested to establish whether they were likely to affect test results, and any such effects were noted in the report. Two reports are produced for each assessment, a public and a technical report. The results of the SAIP assessments are published by CMEC.

Notes

1 For more comprehensive information on gender differences see the 1998 and 2003 editions of EAG, as well as Mullis, Martin, Fierros *et al.* (2000).

2 All assessments described in this section have means set at 500 points, with standard deviations of 100 points.

3 For ease of reference, England and Scotland are counted separately in the number of OECD countries because their results are reported separately.

4 This total includes four communities counted separately: England and Scotland from the United Kingdom and the Flemish and French communities of Belgium.

5 To compare the scores of those countries that participated in both TIMSS 1995 and TIMSS 1999, the scores from TIMSS 1995 were re-scaled to be comparable with the TIMSS 1999 scale.

6 TIMSS assessed students at the end of secondary school in mathematics literacy, science literacy, advanced mathematics and physics. For the purpose of providing a broad overview, this section focuses almost exclusively on the mathematics and science literacy results, referred to here only as mathematics and science to avoid confusion with PISA. Because many countries did not meet sampling requirements for the end-of-secondary population, drawing valid comparisons among countries has proved difficult.

Despite this, the end-of-secondary school results have been of great interest to policy makers, and many countries used the data nationally, as can be seen in profiles from Austria and New Zealand.

7 Several caveats with regard to Austria's end-of-secondary data are described in the appendix to this chapter.

8 The outcomes of the IMST study described in this profile are based on data delivered by Dr Günter Haider of the Austrian IEA Research Centre at the University of Salzburg. The calculations of percentages of correct answers were not tested for statistical significance.

9 In New Zealand years 4 and 5 correspond to TIMSS 1995 population 1 (third- and fourth-grade students), years 8 and 9 correspond to population 2 (eighth- and ninth-grade students) and years 12 and 13 correspond to population 3 (end of secondary school).

10 The National Education Monitoring Project (NEMP) forms part of the National Assessment Framework of New Zealand. The project commenced in 1993 with the task of assessing and reporting on the achievement of year 4 and year 8 students in a representative sample of New Zealand schools. Different curriculum areas and skills are assessed each year over a four-year cycle.

11 The twelve anchor items were used to assure that the two groups of students answering multiple-choice and open-ended items were comparable in achievement and, if necessary, to calibrate for different levels of performance. However, the summarised p values for the anchor items in mathematics and science were nearly identical across the four groups (i.e. females and males answering multiple-choice items, females and males answering open-ended items), meaning that the groups could be regarded as equal with respect to mathematics and science performance, and consequently no calibration was necessary.

12 This profile, however, focuses mainly on the results for mathematics and science.

References

Summary

Martin M.O., Mullis I.V.S, Gonzalez E.J., Gregory K.D., Smith T.A., Chrostowski S.J., Garden R.A. and O'Connor K.M., 2000. *TIMSS 1999 International Mathematics Report* (Chesnut Hill MA: International Study Center, Lynch School of Education, Boston College).

Mullis I.V.S., Martin M.O., Fierros E.G., Goldberg E.L. and Stemler S.E., 2000. *Gender Differences in Achievement* (Chesnut Hill MA: International Study Center, Lynch School of Education, Boston College).

Mullis I.V.S, Martin M.O., Gonzalez E.J., Gregory K.D., Garden R.A., O'Connor K.M., Chrostowski S.J. and Smith T.A., 2000. *TIMSS 1999 International Science Report* (Chesnut Hill MA: International Study Center, Lynch School of Education, Boston College).

OECD, 1998. *Education at a Glance* (Paris: OECD).

OECD, 2000. *Education at a Glance* (Paris: OECD).

OECD, 2003. *Education at a Glance* (Paris: OECD).

Austria

Baumert J., Klieme E. and Watermann R., 1998. Jenseits von Gesamttest- und Untertestwerten. Analyse differentieller Itemfunktionen am Beispiel des mathematischen Grundbildungstests der Dritten Internationalen Mathematik- und Naturwissenschaftsstudie der IEA (TIMSS). In Herber and Hoffmann (eds),

Schulpädagogik und Lehrerbildung (Innsbruck and Wein: Österreichischer Studien Verlag), pp. 301–24.

BMUK and Österreichischen Statistischen Zentralamt, 1998. *Österreichische Schulstatistik 97/98* XLVII (Wein: BMUK).

IFF, 1999. Zwischenbericht zum Projekt IMST (Innovations in mathematics and science teaching. In BMUK (ed.) *Auftrag des Bundesministeriums für Unterricht und kulturelle Angelegenheiten* (Klagenfurt: IFF).

Mullis I.V.S., Martin M.O., Beaton A., Gonzalez E.J., Kelly, D.L. and Smith D. (eds), 1998. *Mathematics and Science Achievement in the Final Year of Secondary School. IEA's Third International Mathematics and Science Study* (TIMSS) (Chestnut Hill MA: International Study Center, Lynch School of Education, Boston College).

New Zealand

Education Review Office, 1999. The achievement of boys. *Education Evaluation Reports* 3 (Wellington: Education Review Office).

Garden R.A. (ed.), 1996a. *Mathematics Performance of New Zealand Form 2 and Form 3 Student. National Results from New Zealand's Participation in the Third International Mathematics and Science Study* (Wellington: Research and International Section, Ministry of Education).

Garden R.A. (ed.), 1996b. *Science Performance of New Zealand Form 2 and Form 3 Students. National Results from New Zealand's Participation in the Third International Mathematics and Science Study* (Wellington: Research and International Section, Ministry of Education).

Garden R.A. (ed.), 1997. *Mathematics and Science Performance in Middle Primary School. Results from New Zealand's Participation in the Third International Mathematics and Science Study* (Wellington: Research and International Section, Ministry of Education).

Ministry of Education, 1992. *Mathematics in the New Zealand Curriculum* (Wellington: Learning Media).

Ministry of Education, 1993a. *National Education Framework. Te Anga Matauranga o Aotearoa* (Wellington: Learning Media).

Ministry of Education, 1993b. *Science in the New Zealand Curriclum* (Wellington: Learning Media).

Praat A., 1999. *Gender Differences in Achievement and Participation in the Compulsory Education Sector. A Review of Information held by the Ministry of Education 1986–1997* (Wellington: Research Division, Ministry of Education).

Netherlands

De Bruijn I., 1997. 'Het studiehuis en het gebruik van computer ondersteund onderwijs' (The Studyhouse and the Use of Computer-assisted Instruction), mimeo.

De Bruijn I., 2001, Natuurkunde in de Tweede Fase, uitkomsten van een enquete (Science in upper secondary education). *NVOX, Tijdschrift voor natuurwetenschap op school*, 26, 10.

De Goei E. and van den Heuvel-Panhuizen M., 2002. *Praktijkproject voor reken-coördinatoren* (Utrecht: Freudenthal Instituut).

Inspectorate of Education, 1999. *Werk aan de basis, evaluatie van de basisvorming* (Basic work, evaluation of basic secondary education) (Utrecht: Inspectie van het Onderwijs).

Ministry of Education, Culture and Science, 2002. *Kerncijfers 2003* (Facts and Figures 2003) (Zoetermeer: Ministry of Education Culture and Science).

OECD, 2002. *Education at a Glance 2002* (Paris: OECD).

Van den Heuvel-Panhuizen M. and Vermeer H.J., 1999. *Verschillen tussen jongens en meisjes bij het vak rekenen-wiskunde op de basisschool* (Gender differences at mathematics in primary school) (Utrecht: Centrum voor B-didactiek).

Sweden

Bell R.C. and Hay, J.A., 1987. Differences and biases in English language examination formats. *British Journal of Educational Psychology*, 57, 212–20.

Ben-Shakar G. and Sinai Y., 1991. Gender differences in multiple-choice tests: the role of differential guessing tendencies. *Journal of Educational Measurement*, 28, 23–35.

Bolger N. and Kellaghan T., 1990. Method of measurement and gender differences in scholastic aptitude test. *Journal of Educational Measurement*, 27, 165–74.

Hellekant J., 1994. Are multiple-choice tests unfair to girls? *System*, 22 (3), 349–52.

Jovanovic J., Solano-Flores G. and Shavelson R., 1994. Performance-based assessments: will gender differences in science achievement be eliminated? *Education and Urban Society*, 26 (4), 352–66.

Murphy R.J.L., 1982. Sex differences in objective test performance. *British Journal of Educational Psychology*, 52, 213–19.

Canada

CMEC, Council of Ministers of Education, 1999. SAIP *Report on Reading and Writing 1998* (Toronto: CMEC).

McEwen N., 1998. 'Selected Findings and Policy Implications of Large-scale Assessments'. Presented at the Invitational Conference on Measurement and Evaluation, Banff, Alberta.

Chapter 8

Comparing results from different countries, subjects and grade levels

Kimmo Leimu

> We go through the world, carrying on the two functions abreast, discovering differences in the like, and likenesses in the different.
>
> Likeness and difference are ultimate relations perceived . . . no two sensations, no two objects of all those we know, are in scientific rigor identical . . . any theory which would base likeness on identity, and not rather identity on likeness, must fail.
>
> (William James, 1891)

The general task of education to provide for national survival and development may be regarded as common to all nations. This never happens in isolation, and in today's world of cross-national contacts and interdependence several common interests have arisen concerning the quality and quantity of the products of education systems. Among these are problems of yield and comparative quality of education system products, implications of student and workforce mobility across borders, accountability interests related to large-scale educational reforms and, in general, the need for valid and generalisable (i.e. genuinely scientific) information on education (Bloom 1969; Husén 1979; Purves 1987; OECD 1992; Tuijnman and Postlethwaite 1994).

A case in point is comparative studies in education, particularly those of educational achievement, where a variety of physical, economic and cultural environments set the stage for interesting comparisons on issues related to rather universal goals of education. Intercultural variety can be considered a source not only of problems but also of richness and explanatory potential. In Husén's words (e.g. 1973, 1974, 1979), education may be perceived as a 'global laboratory' where similar human and societal goals are set in terms of different environments and pursued through different means and educational solutions. In this endeavour, quality becomes a national concern. Such issues were clearly recognised in the early stages of multinational co-operative studies (conducted by the IEA), and, in fact, constituted much of its driving force. Learning from the experiences of other nations was seen as a way of developing the necessary understanding of education and its socio-political implications (e.g. Purves 1989).

The challenges of what has been called the 'world education crisis' (Coombs 1968) are also to be recognised, because they exceed purely national interests. These challenges include substantial global increments in the demand for education, as well as education's rising cost yet relative inefficiency, which affects both well established education systems and those in developing countries. One may also include in this list of challenges problems relating to how to use comparative information, which are difficult to overcome without organised efforts and serious involvement by responsible parties (Alkin 1975). These challenges are legitimate concerns in any scientific work, and in the ensuing solutions lies the professional justification for comparative work on national education systems. Although the context provided by the different natural, economic and socio-cultural environments is apt to create problems of consensus and commensurability, these at the same time are thought to provide the means to respond and produce insight on a more fundamental level.

There is no denying that comparative studies are challenged by the complex nature of education systems themselves, involving their particular histories, established practices and delicate interaction at several levels of operation. Typical of social organisations, their multilevel structures, changing policies and local contextual fluctuations may be seen as inherent difficulties of dealing with any human action. Such differences tend to bring about problems in conducting cross-national studies, including their common target units, questions, contents and choices of instruments and analytical methods, as well as the timing and dissemination of results. In a field that involves a variety of cultural contexts, programmes and subject domains, the lack of compatibility and commensurability can severely affect the results and lead to erroneous conclusions. At the same time, the problems of approach and circumstances are by no means confined to comparative studies but are of concern to all studies in education. Different results because of specific education and research aims, target populations, conceptualisations, instruments and technical and analytical solutions have resulted in subsequent quests for new and synthetic approaches, such as meta-analyses (Glass *et al.* 1981). On this view, multinational replications conducted with a uniform research approach may be considered 'active meta-studies'. As such they represent steps towards improving comparability among the diversity of education studies available at large.

Some further scientific benefits of the comparative approach also may be recognised. Being able to capture existing variance across several national applications, and thus more widely and unequivocally than any isolated national studies would ever do, these studies may well be regarded as one form of basic research in education. In fact Farrell (1979) suggests that 'comparative research is not only a tool of technical elaboration and control, but also the only way of demonstrating the ethnocentric nature of many gener-alisations' (p. 203). Nevertheless, inevitable difficulties remain in claiming comparability across cross-national studies and their results. Ensuring comparability and making meaning of cross-national studies require continuous alertness to and openness with the problems involved. This is the subject of the subsequent sections.

The nature of comparisons

Comparisons constitute a cornerstone of all evaluation work, which, in general, pursues judgements based on the quality or quantity of some characteristics to be appraised. Evaluative judgements regarding empirical indices are related to more or less explicit criteria related to the aims of the assessment. Typically, one may compare the quality of certain external conditions, work activities or behavioural outcomes (knowledge and skills), which are regarded as 'comparable' in some respect, among persons or groups. In these cases, the criteria are relative to the set of participants involved in the comparison. In other cases, the criteria are more 'absolute' and quality expectations are based on pre-established goals, norms, contents and objectives of education, irrespective of the relative status or performance of the actors (cf. Stake 1967; Stufflebeam 1976). In either case, the nature and trustworthiness of the reference measures become important ethical and practical considerations. At the same time, the rationales and definitions of the evaluation criteria constitute equally important elements as the results (observables) themselves and affect the conclusions and use-fulness of assessment. Comparative studies typically have relied on comparative judgements on the state and quality of the educational environment and its outcomes.

The public appeal of international comparisons

In education, evaluation has been traditionally oriented to assessing the quality of work and learning of individual students. Various grading and reporting practices are typical examples of these (although there are other goals and approaches to student assessment). Because students in 'regular' classes tend to have rather homogeneous backgrounds (because of their local origin and age-based grouping) and because the assigned resources are reasonably similar, the relative criteria and direct comparisons used in grading practices have been considered fair and natural (cf. Dreeben 1968). In so doing, however, a number of delicate but influential background factors tend to be overlooked, although these may affect an individual's capacity for attaining the goals set for learning. Because every human being is edu-cated through a 'life curriculum' different from his or her peers, comparisons involving knowledge, conceptual structures or world views could be regarded unfair and thus undesirable. If taken literally, however, such a stand would make it impossible to have a common understanding of a book or lecture or to enjoy a witty debate with others on the grounds that their meaning structures are unique. In education surrendering to such purist ideas would make it questionable, for example, to design common curricula or courses of studies, on the grounds that individuals' backgrounds and personalities vary so greatly that they prevent learning experiences conducive to common understanding of the concepts and relationships involved. Extending such reasoning to different education systems would complicate the issue even further.

On the other hand, a good deal of the human experience may be considered shared, enough to make the categorical claim of the uniqueness of the individual experience of less concern for comparisons. Not denying the existence of significant differences, there is practical evidence of sufficient commonality in meanings to allow distinct disciplines of knowledge or common programmes of learning to emerge even across borders. As a token of such possibilities, international comparisons have become increasingly attractive to the public, although they are often noted without further consideration of the goals and means. Because the task of educating citizens for the future is an important challenge for every society, assessments of the quality in education can certainly be conceived of as serious enough to raise general interest. Although considerable tolerance is accepted in normal coexistence and information exchange, the following question arises: on what conditions would cross-national comparisons of entire social systems become legitimate? Although one may accept certain general commonalities in school learning (e.g. 'the international curriculum') as prerequisites for system comparisons, underlying issues of relevance and fairness, based on complex cultural phenomena and educational provisions, including intricate issues of expectations and environments, may warrant a closer look.

The nature of comparative studies

Discussion of comparative education as a discipline has traditionally been dominated by concerns for methodology and model paradigms, of which the classical analysis of Bereday (1964) provides good examples (Altbach 1991). Quite naturally, the particular research interests, propositions to be examined and means available determine both the information content and methods of a study. Cross-national assessments of student learning may be seen as a special field within comparative education, with their main focus being on the ultimate outcomes of education systems rather than on descriptive accounts of education contexts. In so doing, assessments can be identified broadly as evaluation studies, which may have either administrative (decision-making or accountability) functions or more scientific orientations (cf. Cronbach and Suppes 1969).

Regarding the overall purposes of comparative research, Noah (1973) distinguishes between the search for universal, general principles and those dependences and interactions that change as a function of school system characteristics. According to Noah, comparative research 'proper' will be at issue when an education phenomenon changes its character according to some contextual factors. Stated differently, comparative education as a field of study can be understood as research that is concerned with the relations between education's intra-system phenomena and those system characteristics and contextual factors that may affect changes in those relations (Leimu 1981). Pursuit of such contingencies thus constitutes the essence of the comparative experience. Mere juxtaposing of single-level data from different education systems, therefore, does not qualify it as comparative study in a deeper sense. So conceived, on the other hand, comparative studies are possible also within one single system (e.g. education in Finland, changes in American education) over time and stages of development, provided that relevant background information is available. Such contextual control means not only accounting for a number of extrinsic variables in the theoretical model, but controlling for various sources of bias – fundamentally enhancing the validity of its conceptual approximations and affecting the stability of each observed variable in the database. This embeddedness in a complex network of histories, intentions, practices and effects is apt to make comparative studies an ambitious and difficult field, where several different needs have to be reconciled. Comparative research is therefore hardly conceivable without organised teamwork and multiple expertises, nor without compromise solutions.

Technical and analytic potential has grown considerably since Bereday (1964) introduced his 'total analysis' principles (i.e. description, interpretation, juxtaposition and comparison proper) or since Noah espoused the necessity for both explanation and prediction. The latter presumes structural modelling and proceeds from careful conceptual intra-system analyses toward discriminations on the basis of effective between-system differences. Inevitably, multi-level analyses both within and between systems become necessary (see Chapter 9). Broadfoot (1977) stated the case concisely: 'The comparative study of education is not a discipline: it is a context. It allows for the interaction of perspectives arising out of a number of social science disciplines.' Thus to claim that simple and direct comparisons of single system characteristics are comparative study at all becomes questionable because such a claim would presume relatively comprehensive (conceptual-theoretical and statistical) controls in the essential analyses. As far as the author is aware, such a level of refinement in comparative work is rarely achieved.

Because of the phenomena characterising system-level assessments, therefore, comparative research is ideally and fundamentally not only multi- and cross-disciplinary but open and transparent, rather than being a closed territory with fixed canons (Altbach 1991). For example, in international education indicators work, where the focus is on general societal and policy needs, the main interest lies in systemic data. These data may be of great variety, typically including the structure, functions, economy and products of formal education. The work on indicators draws its strengths from explicit inclination towards policy-relevant content orientation, with high value placed on reliability, transparency and timely delivery. By pointing out such orientations, the indicator movement associates itself with systemic administrative and accountability interests and seeks to make use of limited sets of empirical data, rather than undertaking extensive explorations on contextual effects. The latter would perhaps more appropriately belong to the territory of educational research per se, where the choice of perspective is likely to be even wider. The common ambition in both policy- and research-oriented activities is high standards of conceptualisation and data quality, with the pursuit of careful control of all important phases of fieldwork, data management, analysis and interpretation.

Comparison versus comparability

Comparability is a problem not only in international assessments but also in all kinds of research, be it based on official statistics, case studies or isolated pieces of information. The challenges of international assessments have brought the problems of commensurability and comparability more clearly into the open by insisting upon increasingly stringent technical standards and paying attention to the sampling of both individuals and study contents. At the same time, concerns for yet other kinds of quality have arisen, bringing about a demand for improved cultural and 'ecological' controls, such as common meanings of terminology, translation quality and the place of functionally equivalent institutions and practices in the system. Because of their increasing prominence, international assessments are wise to respect such concerns as prerequisites of serious comparisons.

Issues of equivalence

The statements by William James that open this chapter succinctly state the case of comparison. Perceived similarity on one hand, and the demonstration of differences on the other, constitute the essence of comparative attempts. Raivola (1985) starts with a definition of the word 'difference' in the *Oxford English Dictionary*: 'a discrimination or distinction viewed as conceived by the subject rather than as existing in the objects'. According to Farrell (1979, pp. 208–14):

> Similarity is a relationship between an observer and the data, one that depends on the observer's system of concepts. Similarity is not something that is an inherently inseparable part of an empirical observation. . . . The researcher cannot set about collecting a body of material in the hope that some comparison dimension will automatically emerge from it, inductively. A working hypothesis to tell one what to look for is necessary.

Both these viewpoints highlight the basic understanding of comparison being in 'the eyes of the beholder', in the sense of representing a relationship between the observer and the data and depending ultimately on the observer's system of concepts. In Raivola's terms (1985):

> hypotheses are formed not by relating facts (observations, variables), but by relating concepts, making comparisons on the basis of analogies in the observations misleading. [Further,] depending on the culture, the same concepts can be operationalised by different combinations of facts. In this case, the same relationship of concepts can be found in different cultures, even though not a single identical indicator of the concepts is used in the statistical testing of the hypothesis.

On the other hand, identical indicators do not necessarily stand as proof of the same representation. Because similarity and difference are thus identified as part of a meaning-making process, 'the mere availability of empirical data as such will not lead to new comparative knowledge nor to the formation of theory' (Raivola 1985) – or of policy, one might add.

Nowak (1977, pp. 41–5) discusses problems of comparison rather extensively, accepting something less than complete identity:

> When the researcher is using the notion of 'equivalence' rather than of 'identity' he usually wants to stress that the relationally identical phenomena are not identical with respect to their absolute properties, and this is the only way in which the notion of equivalence should be understood at the level of concept formation.

Because several aspects of context, inputs, processes and outcomes may constitute the substance of comparison, this question may be asked: what are the factors affecting our inferences and introducing bias in comparisons? Nowak's (1977) types of relational equivalence are illustrative because they specify the different kinds of relation involved. Raivola (1985, pp. 366–9) considers them as demonstrations of the basic multi-dimensionality of the comparability concept, instead of providing a simple continuum of similarity. These are described in Box 8.1.

Box 8.1 Defining equivalence

- *Cultural equivalence* is achieved when the objects or phenomena are perceived or evaluated in a similar way in different cultures. Regarding the case of common achievement measurements, one might perhaps note that 'cultures' and 'sub-cultures' are also within nations, even between schools, and that some deep and often intangible aspects of their harmony, such as established practices, communication modes or critical quality expectations, are at issue.

- *Contextual equivalence* is achieved when objects (i.e. individuals, institutions, communities) belong to higher-level aggregations or systems previously classified as being similar with regard to their general properties. In multinational comparisons, one might consider the comparison of neighbouring nations as more reasonable and interesting than the comparison of systems with very different physical, social or economic contexts. One might also be concerned about the equivalence of some particular issues, such as the role and position of teachers or the quality and functions of written learning materials.

- *Structural equivalence* is at issue when objects occupy the same relative position within structural systems that have previously been defined as similar with respect to other properties. In multinational studies, one might compare different educational paths and programmes, although the particular branches might differ in terms of their timing or attractiveness. Likewise, particular school types (e.g. public versus private) could take on analogous roles in different systems, although their particular character might differ in absolute terms. Errors of inference loom large, however, and it is advisable to be careful in making too straightforward conclusions about structural equivalence.

- The concept of *functional equivalence* is similar to the previous concept, implying that the objects compared play the same role in the functioning of the systems concerned. Sometimes different institutions may be responsible for the same functions, whereas sometimes similarly structured institutions may carry out different tasks. Examples include specialisation and selection effects, although the degree and nature of specialisation may differ among the participants. Likewise, concepts such as parents' SES, 'disadvantaged groups', or 'special education arrangements' are likely to be functionally rather than absolutely equivalent. In comparative work, these potential differences impose special responsibilities for the precision and validity of the concepts used, which is not merely a question of adequate translation but which implies deeper knowledge of the system.

- *Correlative equivalence* is achieved if the phenomena being studied are correlated in a similar way with a criterion variable or if they are related across systems on the basis of previous research. This represents an empirical-operational method of demonstrating equivalence. The possibility of spurious correlations necessitates special care in accepting such evidence. Exploring structural-theoretical models statistically is, therefore, necessary for establishing this type of equivalence, which is closely related to the traditional notion of construct validity.

- Phenomena are *genetically equivalent* if they are defined as coming from a similar source of influence, such as a common intention or value base. This also is the case if their causes reside in phenomena that were previously defined as belonging to the same conceptual category. For example, in different countries different education arrangements may be undertaken to counteract various sources of inequality. The existence and value base of these arrangements may be seen as genetically equivalent, but the concrete means of implementation may represent different aspects of contextual, structural or functional equivalence.

- Cultural and contextual equivalence together might be called *ecological equivalence*, especially when considering a phenomenon from an individual's point of view, and, if sufficient empirical evidence exists, correlative equivalence may also be demonstrated.

Perhaps the main lesson from the exhibit is the realisation of the multi-dimensionality and, hence, complexity of comparisons across systems with different economic, socio-cultural or educational environments. This realisation led Raivola (1985, pp. 368–71) to introduce serious questions concerning the acceptance of various equivalence considerations involved in a study – in short, to request reasonable validity for the measurements. The equivalence notion is indeed close to the concept of validity in comparisons, which has received less conscious attention than reliability issues in cross-national work and in evaluation in general (cf. House 1980, pp. 85–93).

Issues of expectations

Comparative studies and international indicators tend to bring along a multitude of expectations. In an earlier article, the author (1992b) explored some of the interests in comparative assessment studies, obtaining researchers' views on expected contributions of such studies. The range of potential criteria turned out to be quite extensive, providing several implications concerning validity. These are interests and expectations are elaborated in Box 8.2. Some of these expectations go beyond the usual mandate adopted in planning comparative studies, opening a field with far more complexity than one might be prepared to accept as reasonable. Nevertheless, the potential scope of interests in and utilisation of these studies are useful to know. At the same time, considering the variety of interests and questions, validity issues become a challenge for international assessments. Furthermore, openly declared ambitions related to quick delivery, controls for national peculiarities and new developments, together with demands for advanced analyses and other enhancements in quality standards, add to the challenge. The following question arises: to what extent is approaching such complex research issues in a cross-national context in a unified way possible?

Box 8.2 Why comparative international studies are undertaken

Examples of education system and policy-level interests and questions

- *Cultural.* What is the status and role of formal education in different cultures and at different levels of societal development (e.g. in terms of economic structure or modernisation)? How can the structures, processes and outcomes of education be understood in the frames of their own values, aims, resources and practices?
- *Historical.* What have been the changes in the education system?
- *International comparative.* How is our own education faring among other nations and systems? What are our particular strengths and weaknesses? How can our national system be characterised within a general international framework?
- *Contents.* What is the quality of learning in different disciplines of knowledge (typically reading, mathematics and science)? What attitudes are developed? Can they support the continuity and development of cultural values, scientific potential and the economy (e.g. national identity and ability to compete in international markets)?
- *Economic.* Is our system of education efficient, productive and cost-effective? What is its external effectiveness (i.e. how does it function in terms of expectations, or how do its outputs respond to immediate economic and cultural needs)?
- *Prospective.* How well can our stock of educated people be expected to meet the nation's survival and development needs in terms of general welfare and quality of life, as well as cultural offerings? What are the prospects of securing an educated labour force in various fields?

- *Policy*. What specific insight could be derived from the results concerning the effects of particular education or societal policies – relating to issues such as equity or yield? What impulses for further policy needs or national research and development strategies can be derived from the research?
- *Administrative*. How does the education system function as a multi-level organisation involving planning, implementation management and accountability? How does the education system function as a multi-level organisation involving problems of implementation, leadership and management?

Examples of scientific (conceptual-professional) interests and questions

- *Conceptual-theoretical perspective – comparative education*. How can education be understood theoretically as a multi-level, multi-sector activity? What concepts are used to describe its characteristics and processes? What causal relationships are postulated and observed? What relationships are found to be consistent across several systems?
- *Structural perspective*. What are the effects of particular contextual factors and structural system features in explaining education phenomena, especially the quality of student learning? What importance do general societal conditions, administrative practices, curriculum and teacher or school and home characteristics have for the quality and variability in educational means, processes and outcomes?
- *Curriculum perspective*. What can the research contribute to problems encountered in setting, implementing and assessing general curricular aims, such as general liberal education pursuits versus specialisation? How are specific curricular contents, objectives and outcomes mapped and accounted for? How are issues of curricular intentions and actualities observed and resolved?
- *Sociological perspective*. What societal functions can be identified in education, immediately and in the long run? What consequences do different attainments and achievements have for the life of an individual, in terms of issues such as urbanisation, industrialisation or (im)migration?
- *Psychological perspective*. What and how does one learn in kindergarten, school, community and home? What is the prevalent conception of 'knowledge' or 'learning' as a process? What learning experiences do schools offer? What are the human costs

of failure or learning to a certain level (e.g. what kind of attitudes and human relations are fostered)?

- *Techno-methodological perspective*. Are state-of-the-art concepts and methods well known to the researchers? What research paradigm is used, and why is it being used? How does one secure validity, reliability and comparability? How large are error margins in sampling students? How is research information obtained and analysed? What generalisations or comparisons are safe to make?

Examples of practical (administrative-technical) interests and questions

- *Time and timing*. At what time in the school year are the data collected? How much time is required from participating students, teachers and school heads? When are results made available, *vis-à-vis* their potential use? What is the length of time taken from the beginning of a study to the final reporting and dissemination?
- *Resources*. What are the annual and total accumulative costs of the project? How and from what sources is the work funded? What alternative projects become thereby overlooked? What synergy benefits are gained in conducting the study? What are the estimated research contributions (information value or conclusions/decisions enabled) when set against costs? What training and competence-building effects can be derived from active participation?
- *Managing*. How are the international and national study activities distributed, roles assigned? How are decisions made? What individuals and institutions are represented in the planning, implementing and reporting the study? How are development work, fieldwork, data analyses, reporting and dissemination organised? How is the study organised and managed locally, e.g. how is the co-operation of schools, teachers and students secured? What excuses were used by schools and accepted for non-participation? What kinds of additional expertise are necessary?
- *Accountability*. What consequences do the study results have for the participating schools, teachers and students? What consequences do they have at the system level, as feedback or in support of decision making? How are the research data archived for future use (such as longitudinal and secondary analyses)? What rights and responsibilities do the researchers involved have regarding the results and the database? Who is entitled to use the data now and in the future?
- *Reporting*. What national contributions to international reports are envisaged? Are national reports expected? For what audiences?

Do these need different types of reporting? How wide is the publicity for each? Who is involved in the reporting process? What are the expectations concerning secondary analyses and other use?

- *Utilising*. What organised use will the research results and data be put to? What are their expected consequences? What are the main purposes, strategies and institutions involved? How is it made active for accountability and decision purposes?

Sources of bias in comparisons

The multiple expectations of international comparison should not lead to solutions where quality is sacrificed for quantity. It is crucial to the future of comparative assessments that their cornerstones are solid, so that inferences and decisions from them are based on tenable grounds. This necessity takes us further into issues of the general trustworthiness of results – their validity and stability – and, in many ways, back to the basics of empirical study.

Much attention and several safeguards have already been established in assessment work for ensuring the quality of data – some of which are described in the first and subsequent chapters of this volume. Every organised proposal, every professional discussion among colleagues and every national comment on results and their interpretations represent attempts to improve the general trustworthiness of a study. In fact, the co-operative approach that incorporates national expertise is apt to enhance such validity. At the same time, in most attempts to secure quality, technical considerations and procedures have figured foremost, as indicated by the relative abundance of publications on technical standards (e.g. AERA/APA/NCME 1985, Hambleton 1994, OECD 1999, Schleicher 1994a, b, Selden 1992 and others). While it is certainly important for the field to agree on important technicalities and controls that seek to ensure structural and procedural uniformity as bases of reliability of comparability, the problems involved are not only technical, but certainly more profound and problematic. Fundamentally, therefore, it becomes necessary to touch upon aspects of validity (as was begun in the previous section) to face openly the problems of genuine comparison.

In early empirical work relying on national replications (notably by the IEA), the underlying ideals were scientific and contextualised, rather than competitive. At the pioneering stages of comparative assessment, substantial interest and approval could be received merely by virtue of using common assessment measures in a number of countries and looking at the differences with an eye to feasibility and certain commonalities. Basic comparability issues were also taken seriously early on, although not visible in the headlines (Foshay 1962; Degenhart 1990; IEA 1998). With the main validity concerns being with the fairness of the measures, the principal remedies introduced at that time dealt with sampling procedures and certain curriculum controls, notably underlying curriculum analyses and opportunity-to-learn ratings (Husén 1974). Since this early work there has been considerable progress on various fronts (as many contributors to this volume have already noted), notably in conceptual modelling and methods of analysis, but also regarding official information needs and public interest. With the growing sophistication of the data users, as well as the accumulating experience of the implementers, quality expectations likewise have grown. Modern comparative work as *bona fide* research may, therefore, be expected to have high ambitions and quality standards.

With PISA as an intergovernmental activity with enhanced financial and human resources, further opportunities have arisen for developing the content and procedures of international assessments of student achievement. Although the interests of PISA are on both academic and cross-curricular outcomes, with standards of design and implementation that are becoming ever stricter, validity issues in all their comprehensiveness still remain a serious challenge. In fact the widening publicity and circle of users are rendering such concerns increasingly meaningful.

Aspects of validity

Problems of validity are profound and perennial – in fact classical (e.g. Campbell and Fiske 1959; Cronbach 1961; Adams 1965; House 1980). Yet discussion of their implications for particular studies systematically and comprehensively is not very common. Although simple standards or straightforward solutions can hardly be expected, reasonable attempts to demonstrate awareness of the problems involved may be necessary for the interested user. Thus even limited attempts at discussing validity issues may be considered welcome.

Vahervuo (1958, pp. 172–6) succinctly presented the main qualities that determine the overall trustworthiness of psychometric measures, such as educational tests. Their results may be biased in either of two ways – by being open to chance effects or by measuring something other than what was intended. Chance effects, the first of the potential biases, are related to reliability and constancy, which together constitute aspects of instrument stability. The second of the potential biases represents validity, or relevance of the method or instrument for capturing the defined target characteristics. More practically this second bias may be defined as the value of the data for making correct judgements and inferences (Adams 1965, p. 103). (Both reliability and validity are abstract concepts to the extent that their existence cannot be directly measured. Indirect methods of estimation, therefore, have to be used.)

In this reasoning, reliability represents the stability of the instrument or, more generally, the method used for producing 'clean' and consistent results.

As such, reliability is related to the presence or absence of random error, which is typically estimated by measures of internal criteria (i.e. test homogeneity, based on item intercorrelations). Constancy refers, instead, to the stability of the subject's characteristics in question, or the random fluctuation in observations because of the instability of the target characteristics from one measurement to another. Constancy is typically estimated by using test–retest measures. Constancy is also expected across different student samples (as used in cross-national replication studies), which are thought to represent the relevant characteristics in a stable way. By way of illustration, the trustworthiness construct can be pictured as in Figure 8.1 (Vahervuo 1958, p. 174).

Estimates of validity are obtained by relating the results of measurement (usually indirect indices) to some external criterion which is thought to represent a more authentic, if not direct, indication of the target characteristics (e.g. success in further studies, or in some other current or future tasks). Such criterion evidence is not necessarily easy to obtain because it is open to intervening effects (such as the subsequent selection and rejection of certain sub-groups in question). Instrument validation, therefore, tends to become a long and tedious process where the quality of both the instrument and the criterion are at stake. While approved measures for estimating reliability are more feasible and even routine, validity estimates tend to be less common because of the difficulty of obtaining acceptable proofs. Relying on professional judgement based on experience and supported by field test data is perhaps most common.

Many of the validity concerns are likely to arise in interpreting results. Perhaps too often the potential caveats are left to the reader to account for. This situation is problematic because lack of validity may be quite devastating to the entire measurement. The case may be highlighted by claiming that deficiencies in reliability represent random error while deficiencies in

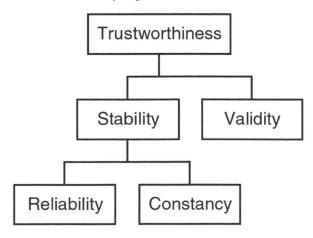

Figure 8.1 Measures of trustworthiness.

validity may be seen as systematic bias. In group studies, the former tend to cancel themselves out or to be estimated through relatively straightforward technical methods. The latter can accumulate and distort the results. Securing validity therefore tends to claim every bit of substantive-professional expertise available for a study and interpreting its results. There is, thus, ample reason to consider validity as requiring serious attention.

When the aim of a study is to arrive at generalisations and conclusions for a particular system or population – as is typically the case with comparative educational assessments – acceptable proofs of trustworthiness are necessary. Instrument stability and validity characteristics must then be supplemented by considering sample quality. This is a problem related to the representativeness of the population by samples of subjects (e.g. students or teachers) and also to the content and situations in which the subjects demonstrate their learning. These problems are related to the various types of validity that are commonly discussed in the literature (e.g. Campbell and Fiske 1959; Cronbach 1961; Gulliksen 1962; Adams 1965). Essential issues regarding validity in terms of representativeness are those of generalising from a sample to a population or (conceptually) from manifest variables to latent (theoretical) variables. Because this chapter is intended to 'preach rather than teach', the traditional types of validity will not be discussed in detail, save for a short listing. Their implications will be touched when discussing issues related to the sources of bias affecting validity in comparisons and to the possibilities for counteracting such effects.

The usual validity definitions are based on the kinds of judgements one wishes to make. The first two kinds of validity in Box 8.3 are defined on the basis of their inference characteristics in terms of timing – content validity on its concurrent power to establish fairness and serve as a basis for generalisations and construct validity for generating hypotheses and providing explanations of outcomes in a more timeless manner. The other types, less classical, are related to embeddedness in a socio-cultural context or the subjectively felt relevance and adequacy of the critical situation, instruments and behaviour expectations, as experienced by the subject and the data user (i.e. ecological and face validity).

Box 8.3 Types of validity

- *Concurrent validity* is implied when inferences are concerned with the present status or performance of the subjects in a given universe of situations of which the assessment is a sample. It has to do with educational influences impinging upon the subjects (usually students) under their current circumstances of life and learning. The basic question becomes how closely test scores are correlated with the prevailing criterion status or behaviour.

Concurrent validity is thus most important for establishing a sound database on present circumstances. Examples of ways to improve concurrent validity may include procedures such as curriculum analyses for preparing test blueprints to secure proper content coverage, for using results in classroom testing for diagnostic or for grading purposes or soliciting special expertise for issues on terminology or prevailing practices.

- *Predictive validity* is pursued for predicting future performance in similar or related tasks and situations. Selection purposes are often involved, whereby an individual's future success (e.g. in further education or working life) will be predicted on the basis of current performance on the assessment. In systemic assessment, predictive validity may be at stake if current results of student learning are supposed to precipitate the quality of future labour force and perhaps ultimately the economic capacity of the nation. The predictive power of a test battery or theoretical model elements might be explored with the purpose of finding sets of measures (indicators) to explain such future expectations. Longitudinal follow-up studies to serve such practical long-term interests then become necessary for confirming more intuitive claims.

- *Content validity* may be considered a more extensive concept, by virtue of involving educational influences over an extended period in time. As with concurrent validity, content validity is related to the sampling and representativeness of the contents and circumstances to be covered in the assessment itself. However, these may represent not only concurrent events, but also something that has happened in the past, such as earlier learning in terms of various curricular programmes. The multi-level and multi-sector nature of education provision is likely to render this aspect of validation both a theoretical and practical problem. Curriculum validity is of particular interest in cross-national studies of education, where fairness of comparisons is an important premise. A good deal of effort has indeed been devoted in these studies to securing comparability in achievement tests and student samples, whereby curriculum analyses underlying instrumentation have received attention (e.g. Husén 1974). Whereas student sampling is nowadays considered a routine and well established operation, further work would seem necessary regarding the curriculum concept, notably actual learning opportunities, which tend to produce perplexing results. Despite the difficulties encountered, overlooking the implications of curriculum validity would be tantamount to abandoning an important logic in all education: that of exposure to contents and active engagement in goal-oriented learning processes.

- *Construct validity* has to do with the conceptual-theoretical underpinnings of a study, especially in terms of capturing the hypothesised 'latent variables' it claims to measure (e.g. Noonan and Wold 1983). There are two practical sides to this coin: how well do the 'manifest variables' (actual observations) represent the proclaimed latent constructs, and how well does the measure differentiate among groups that are expected to differ with respect to the said characteristics? Establishing construct validity requires theory-oriented empirical work, starting with model building and exploring the contingencies through multi-level structural analyses (Goldstein 1995). As such, it requires extensive and consistent scientific work.

To supplement these traditional types of validity, one is inclined to add two more rarely acknowledged aspects of validity which are noteworthy in cross-cultural studies.

- *Ecological validity* can be taken as the cultural relevance of (especially external) assessments, including their contents and procedures in general. Ecological validity can be understood as the degree of familiarity of the subjects with the particular research approach and environment established in the study, including the instructions and operations involved. The prevailing modes of conduct and conventional practices in the school, vis-à-vis the particular type of questioning employed, are at issue. Thus, for instance, local assessment practices (e.g. essay or multiple-choice testing techniques) will determine the facility with which the students and teachers set themselves to doing what is required in the comparison. Ecological validity can be understood as the grand total of such psychological effects, including the general atmosphere in which the testing is received and conducted in the school, the approach adopted in test administration and supervision, the contents dealt with, and the response format. As an example, the somewhat authoritative – if not authoritarian – approach necessitated by certain standardisation (equivalence) needs may be felt unnatural and oppressive by teachers and students. Such situations are likely to affect testing morale and may turn a serious situation into a joke or rebellion. Similar effects may be expected not only because of the formal setting and procedures but also because of content choices and language code.
- *Face validity* may be considered an element of ecological validity. Face validity represents the impressionistic perception of the

quality and appropriateness of the task assigned, as felt by the participants in the measurement situation. Inappropriate instructions, test items or even minor faults in language conventions may demonstrate lack of professional touch with the realities of the contents or education context, rendering the testing situation awkward and even suspect and thus lowering testing morale and eventual validity of the results. Such pitfalls are particularly likely in international ventures, where tests and questionnaires are translated from material in a foreign language. On the other hand, stringent procedures and reasonably relevant test items with valid terminology are apt to improve the situation and participant effort, diminishing disturbing chance effects. Not only validity, but also test stability, will thus be positively affected.

Attempt at a synthesis

There might be interest in reconciling the two approaches – the traditional one in Box 8.3 and that based on (Nowak's) equivalence considerations in Box 8.2 – to validity issues. The virtues in doing so are to gain a better understanding of the purpose for which particular types of validity are identified.

Correlative equivalence in simple form could be related to two traditional kinds of validation purposes, concurrent and predictive validity. Correlative equivalence in complex form could be related to demonstrations of construct validity.

The next set of concepts is less tangible, and thus their validation is less straightforward. Genetic equivalence could perhaps most naturally be related to content validity, because the reasoning concerning content inclusion and coverage is not far removed from their origins. One needs only to think about the complex roots of curricula as multi-level and multidisciplinary 'reservoirs of educational goals and contents' with their particular histories. Cultural (distal and general) equivalence could be related to the idea of ecological validity. Contextual (proximal and specific) equivalence would be more closely related to face validity.

In either set of categories, construct validity emerges as a concept crucial for comparative studies, to which several important equivalence considerations would seem to apply. Structural equivalence carries meanings that would typically establish similarity among structurally defined and inert systemic elements. Here the pitfalls hide in the apparent homology of corresponding structures, which may have different functions and powers in different systems, depending on the nature of their decentralisation. Functional equivalence is a generally more dynamic aspect of theoretical constructs, dealing with corresponding institutional roles and functions. As implied above, one should not assume functional equivalence on the basis of structural equivalence of systems. Rather, intimate knowledge on system operation is required for attaining validity in this regard.

Correlative equivalence could also be brought to bear because of the role of complex statistical methods in testing structural models through the use of quantitative data (Noonan and Wold 1983; Goldstein 1995). The point to emphasise is the necessity of a theoretical structural model, which organises the research expectations and helps to safeguard against spurious relationships. Correlations as such are no proof of a sound research logic, and some of them could render the results unintelligible (cf. Farrell 1979; Raivola 1985). Communicative equivalence, or commonality of meanings, although not mentioned by Nowak, deserves special recognition in international assessments. Conceptual relevance together with the proper form of presentation is an important and inherent part of valid instrumentation. When materials are translated, the original intentions and meaning structures need to be carefully retained and appropriate conventions applied. Mere linguistic translation is not enough in this process, where some intricate qualities of construct validity in terms of functional, substantial and practical relevance will come into play.

Possibilities of controlling bias in comparisons

What have been referred to in this chapter as problems of reliability and validity are often discussed as item or test bias. Although the concept remains somewhat vague, it is commonly regarded as 'differential item functioning' and distinctions between external and internal bias can be made. (See Adams 1992 for a useful discussion.) External bias refers to contextual factors, viewed as antecedents to testing, while internal bias is concerned with the technical and psychometric properties of the actual assessment and its individual items. Parallels to earlier discussions are easy to see. Those aspects of instrumentation that have to do with construct, content and predictive validity or socio-cultural fairness may be regarded as external sources of bias, which are open to stimulus-analytical procedures. Internal bias is thought to arise primarily from the technical-procedural aspects of assessment and can be subjected to reaction-analytical strategies, which relate to the validity of conclusions. Much work has been done to overcome the latter effects and ensure that instruments demonstrate proper empirical 'behaviour', particularly to prevent significant sub-group differences arising from the administration procedures or other technical qualities of testing. Ideally, this is done proactively, for example with the help of careful field testing (implying alternating reaction-analytical and stimulus-analytical phases).

In general terms, stimulus-analytical procedures are involved at stages of developing instruments and conducting fieldwork when the process has not yet produced any respondent data. They are, therefore, necessarily based on certain plans and preconceptions of both the ends and the means of the assessment (Pitkänen 1967). Response-analytical procedures become possible after data have been collected and are ready for analyses. While the data constitute the usual basis of indicators, many of the validity-enhancing actions have to be taken and problems resolved prior to analysing responses because the hour would then be too late for further quality precautions.

Stimulus-analytical bias control procedures

In the stimulus-analytical category are conceptual controls for construct validity, curriculum controls for content validity and translation controls for communicative quality.

Conceptual controls for construct validity

Conceptual controls for construct validity imply procedures for pursuing and reaching consensus in definitions, terminology and shared meanings of content to be assessed. This work is most appropriately undertaken in the early stages of a project, as has indeed been the practice in IEA studies and PISA. Yet there is always room for increased clarity, because conceptual difficulties tend to haunt the fundamental validity of any piece of comparative work, even if it is in experienced hands or the concepts implemented in the work are commonplace.

For example, the concepts of what is a school, a teacher or a student may present problems, especially in non-formal and adult education. More than ever, education is becoming a set of activities and services that are not tightly bound in time, place or authority. However, even in traditional settings, specifying the extent to which physical versus functional characteristics determine the classifications is important. A school may be a physical or an administrative unit; a teacher may be a person (present or not) or a program rather than a person. Likewise, the links between a student and a teacher or school may be more or less loose and transient. Agreements on these key terms will be needed.

The concepts of curriculum, instruction, type of schooling and education level are closely related to the previous ones and are likewise controversial. Other important concepts concerning specialisation/differentiation or qualification for further studies are often brought to bear on such problems in search of structural and functional equivalence. Fundamental conceptual issues related to construct validity are involved. Similarly, further considerations may arise regarding concepts considered self-evident, and these problems are inflated when constructing indicators. One example is the student-to-teacher ratio, where complications arise on account of the conceptual dilemmas mentioned above. How does one calculate such a ratio if the basic elements are controversial? There can be no acceptable solutions unless fair agreements on the basics are reached.

The concept of a target population is always crucial. Essential considerations are manifold. Should it be an age- or grade-based sample? What structural or functional system characteristics should be complied with? Which stages of education are actually desired to study? What constitutes acceptable exclusions? The achievement measures themselves, with their underlying aims, contents and methods, also involve important decisions on the basic principles for securing the relevance of the assessment overall. These have traditionally received major attention in international assessments, where considerable advances in curriculum analyses and test construction have been witnessed.

Curriculum controls for content validity

Another strategy to control external bias is to implement curriculum controls for content validity. Content sampling decisions in international comparative work are among the most fundamental. They are intimately related to the basic curricular aims and purposes of cross-national comparisons. The curriculum concept itself has received due attention in various IEA studies, especially in SIMS and TIMSS. Although the different levels and realities of curricula complicate the picture, inescapable is the question of whether or not it is possible or acceptable to compare, generalise and explain results if the test instrument is not well aligned with the curriculum of one or several participants. Answering questions such as these requires conceptual and practical work for valid solutions. Errors of omission and commission loom large. The test validity indices that were introduced in SIMS (IEA 1988) to address this included the curriculum relevance index, describing the extent to which the international test covered the national curriculum; the test relevance index, indicating the extent to which the items in the test were appropriate to the national curriculum; and the curriculum coverage index, indicating the extent to which the total national curriculum covered the curriculum of all countries.

The findings suggested that curriculum relevance was less than complete in most participating countries. However, looking across countries, there was a relatively narrow distribution of scores on the indices, indicating that there was indeed 'equal unfairness for all', as the aim has been described. At the same time, the excluded parts may vary a good deal across countries, reducing the commonality of actual substance.

Although these first experiences were not entirely satisfying, further work on such validity indices seems necessary. Future development could include improving the actual ways of posing the critical questions or enhancing the conceptual base of the programme raters. Practical difficulties because of the decentralisation of matters of curriculum are perhaps more difficult to overcome, unless all ratings are obtained post hoc at the classroom level. The methodologies for analysis deserve attention as well (cf. Leimu 1992a).

Although the measurement orientation and instrument quality are important, they are not simple and straightforward content coverage issues because there is a need to agree upon the fundamental orientations in assessment. Among these is the question of curriculum orientation versus more universal criterion orientation in testing. Further questions arise on the inclusion of core competences or traditional contents or for provisions for a more extensive scope (e.g. identifying an 'international curriculum' based on what should be learned), enabling measures that go beyond common curricular expectations and strictly national constraints. At the same time, the challenges of the curriculum concept in all its complexity will unavoidably be met. This was the case in PISA, where many participating countries still examined the fit of the assessment content to their local curriculum to help understand and interpret results.

A related consideration is whether expecting identical programmes and performance standards from students of the same age across the world is reasonable. In other words, how valid is 'the international curriculum' as a basis of passing judgement on the quality of education in particular systems? This may be an issue of values and priorities or programme organisation rather than a question of educational quality as such. It may be pertinent to ask how appropriate is age-based sampling of students if they start schooling at different ages or reach policy-relevant stages in their education at different times across countries.

Translation controls for communicative quality

Once the contents and instrumentation of the assessment have been developed, the task of communicating equivalent meanings across languages and cultures remains. How translations are handled represent another set of procedures that can assist in controlling bias. It is commonly held that back-translations are a necessity, and they were indeed the prevailing practice during the 1990s. However, they could be seen as an example of reliability considerations taking precedence over validity interests. The translation of instruments, items and concepts is not only a linguistic operation but also a more profound task of transforming one 'cultural version' to becoming applicable in another. Such a transformation requires familiarity with the conventions of terminology and practical realities in the subject domain and in the classroom, an understanding of the measurement ideas (e.g. the underlying goals at the item level or the reasoning underlying particular response alternatives) and skill in avoiding the use of inappropriate clues or too obvious or peculiar expressions.

Such considerations render the 'translation' process a creative one, presuming profound understanding of the measurement aims and instrument.

The minimum necessary expertise involves the languages concerned, but more ideally would also include subject domain competence and considerable acquaintance with the concepts in curriculum documents and textbooks, as well as insight into assessment practices within schools.

Reaction-analytical bias control procedures

Analytical methodology is of central importance in comparative work, including as it relates to controlling possible test bias, and, therefore, has received much attention in international studies (Keeves 1992; Teune 1977). The problems are not restricted to the particular statistical method chosen, but represent broader issues in the choice of the analytical approach. One basic requirement for fairness of comparisons in assessment studies would be sufficient accounting for antecedent conditions, including various contextual and input characteristics. (The importance of contextual background and issues relating to analysis of such are addressed in the next section.) Although direct between-school comparisons in the form of simple rank ordering and without deeper analyses would nowadays be considered unfair by any reasonably enlightened researcher, this condition generally is not so strictly observed when public discussions of entire education systems take place. Yet one may suggest that any one-point comparisons that do not observe and account for other circumstances would lead to unacceptable labelling. In the classical form of comparative education studies, even the simple 'travellers' tales' included some acquaintance with contextual features in the systems under study (cf. Bereday 1964). Ignoring such necessities in modern empirical work would represent a step backwards. Therefore, for any comparisons to be regarded as fair, their analytical ambitions should represent some multivariate approach – such as is described in the next chapters. Sophisticated methods and programmes are already available for this purpose (Keeves 1992; Goldstein 1995), and in the pursuit of fair comparisons and educated guesses about realities these approaches are also used.

Activities related to data management also are pertinent to this discussion of reaction-analytical procedures. The data originally obtained from empirical fieldwork may be said to be in 'raw' form and often need considerable work to become more amenable to 'trustworthy' analyses. After a number of checks to ensure basic technical quality, a variety of research variables can be generated out of the original items. In this process, various recodings and computations are needed to work out variables and indicators that have better conceptual relevance or are technically more feasible for use in multivariate analyses (e.g. subtotals, percentages, ratios). Some variables may have to be excluded altogether. Together with weighting procedures, this operation will produce 'working data files', whose validity, reliability, usefulness and even legitimacy may be considerably enhanced from the raw version.

Adams (1992) discusses several methods as checks on data quality, most of which are used routinely and in good faith in the international arena. Related to the nature of bias, the core interest is in differential performance by different sub-groups of subjects taking the test. In international assessments, nationality forms an almost self-evident basis. However, there are almost endless possibilities of other relevant groupings, which depend on the research or policy questions or needs for controlling particular types of bias. Gender, age, ethnic origin, general ability or curriculum choices are potential bases of such groupings. The indices usually include item difficulty and various indexes of discrimination, where the usual criteria are sought from total scores in the same test. In effect the main emphasis is on quality in terms of reliability and, particularly, of internal consistency. Both traditional item analyses and some newer developments may be based on assumptions and solutions whose tenability may be viewed critically and, therefore, leave room for further developments. As an example, at the formative stage of instrumentation, when the criterion composite includes a wide variety of proposed items, several iterations are necessary in the 'purification' process, which is apt to become long and tedious and remain less than complete. Latent trait models and logarithmic methods have gained prominence in recent years because they can most effectively capture the item-by-group interactions in question.

Importance of context and other bias control strategies

The significance of general contextual circumstances (of society and its systemic educational provisions, as well as individual learning environments) has become evident in both national and international assessments. Husén (1977) maintains that even a glance at the purely descriptive statistics suffices to convince observers that schooling is not the sole source of education; it operates within a larger socio-economic structure. Boyer (1983, as cited in Noah 1984) put the case in equally strong terms by stating that a report card on public education is a report card on the nation. Schools can rise no higher than the communities that support them. Because student competence can only to a limited extent be attributed to purely scholastic factors, the IEA in its pioneering studies deliberately tended to play down the conceptions of its projects as a kind of intellectual Olympics. This downplaying was related to the deeply felt need for adequate contextual information as background for learning outcome data. According to such research ambitions, attempts have been made by the IEA not only to collect background information but also to analyse it in terms of structural models. Similarly, the EAG publication series by the OECD provides a rich source of such information related to national educational indicators. However, model building on the basis of indicators has so far been more limited.

Contextualisation in comparisons of student achievement may represent either case-oriented or variable-oriented approaches, both of which are present in international assessments. The latter approach is typical of research interests, where conceptual modelling and statistical controls are an essential part of the discourse. The main ambitions are related to finding universally valid circumstances under which learning outcomes may be expected to vary. In this approach, national cases are associated with characteristics (variables), which may indeed be related to the quality of criterion results (typically student learning outcomes). Case orientation rather is more clearly geared towards understanding national circumstances. In this approach, contextual information is sought from a wider set of data, which ideally is acceptable for comparative purposes. Such acceptance is possible when respectable educational indicators or trustworthy authoritative accounts are available. Particular system characteristics may then be juxtaposed with similar information on other systems. Neither the characteristics nor the systems compared are necessarily similar from one comparison to another. However, since the choice of contextual features is at the discretion of users, their choice may remain more piecemeal and, at any rate, open to various political considerations (cf. Leimu 1992b). Here the dangers of limited scope of comparison and even simple league tables are obvious. At the same time, however, such comparisons are likely to stimulate relevant discussions and recommendations concerning particular system needs

The implications of contextualisation are evident at both the planning and the interpretation stages. Despite their prominence, socio-economic and cultural context features are not clearly enough brought to bear on deeper interpretations of achievement outcomes. They may be recognised and mentioned, but it is often left to the readers to make their own impressionistic interpretations. The consequence is certain 'isolation' of effects in the search for universals in variable-oriented comparisons, where in Nowak's words (1977, p. 9) 'a given nation is important only because it represents a given value (or a set of values) of universally defined variables. Our interest foci are on assessment of the range of variation of these values, or of the pattern of relationships between the corresponding variables.' Policy-relevance may be regarded as the capacity to enable conclusions regarding patterns among concrete cases – in one's own country in particular. It may well be that the methodology of accounting for the effects of general contextual factors is still lacking under this approach or that the problem has not been taken seriously. Better comprehension of national contexts in international comparisons is needed, and a more visible role given to such orientation is called for. A first step could be providing context information a more prominent place in conceptual modelling and giving it an organised role in interpretations.

Attempts to avoid effects arising from contextual (cultural) bias lead to an interesting question of principle: should only very similar systems and phenomena be compared? For instance, will the historical, political and economic similarity of countries (often involving competition) be an important prerequisite of reasonable comparisons? Or should one try to use the wide international variance to improve on understanding education more generally? The answer obviously depends on the perspective adopted and the problems posed in comparative work. It is safer and fairer to present direct comparisons among cases with similar contextual features. On the other hand, attempts to understand reasons and consequences more generally would benefit from a wider variance. Such considerations actually differentiate between the 'research-oriented' and 'policy-oriented'.

Some principles of strategy that Noah and Allardt discussed should be considered. Although Allardt (1990) proposes a general approach for comparative studies whereby qualitative studies should follow – and not precede – quantitative ones, Noah (1973), with a more quantitative research orientation, suggests adding the name of particular countries last in the equation. (The 'name' represents other, hitherto unattended factors, or residual variance after all other sources of information have been exhausted.) Here again are two compatible views from somewhat different traditions. As far as comparative research is concerned, the entire world may well be regarded as the 'educational laboratory', which has been the perception for decades (Husén 1974, 1979). The universal principles would then remain valid from the perspective of research, producing sets of indicators and testing models that constitute one form of basic research in education. Regarding policy interests, a 'strategic' model could perhaps be suggested in which some core international data on system universals would be sought and refined into comparative indicators. The problems identified would then guide further work at the national or regional level, with supplementary data collection. Here analyses would be more focused, while better familiarity with the more proximal circumstances would enable deeper and more pertinent interpretations of results.

General issues related to international assessments

Organisational issues

A key tactic for coping with validity concerns in comparative studies and indicator work has been to adopt a co-operative approach whereby national experts are actively involved in the studies, from conceptualisation to interpretation, reporting and dissemination. Through the regular use of national committees, together with international experts, the professional base can be (and has been) broadened significantly. This approach may be considered highly effective, as ostensibly external studies are rendered factually internal. The critical review of all proposals by local experts throughout the planning process is secured and has become an important element guiding preparatory work. Its role in enhancing the validity of instruments and adequate local understanding in the interpretations is also evident. The approach is not without its dangers, however. Pertinent viewpoints and suggestions may sometimes be left at the mercy of debating skills and demonstrations of intellectual or other hegemony, combined with the care involved in preparatory work. This leaves some room for further improvements.

Several strategies are suggested as remedies to problems of implementation. First, allowing and requesting national viewpoints on international reports and presentations would moderate otherwise purely external interpretations and make them more adequate. There might be some argument for organised case studies at the level of participating nations – perhaps based on additional national context information and reasoning. The solicitation of national feedback on international reports is now more common across the major studies.

Second, where the range of national contexts is wide (as in the recent IEA studies) or when the study's aims are exploratory, more flexibility is necessary in what is studied. This can be achieved either with international options, in case aspects of the general design cannot receive overall consensus, or with national options, where the needs are even more specific and comparisons are constrained even further. These options may be regarded as enrichments or further validation of the study according to national needs. At the same time, common analyses will be limited by the actual choices made and groups emerging among the participating systems. Questions arise on the extent to which such needs reflect deficiencies in the original design versus esoteric peculiarities among the systems involved.

Third, relating new data to existing data is important. One step to this end could be to present direct references to relevant contextual indicators, for example, cross-referencing across EAG. The problem lies in making convincing demonstrations of actual contingencies, which requires basic research work. As an intermediate step, one might suggest (1) conducting secondary (in-depth) analyses on existing data, in order to explore such contingencies and reveal issues that have not been dealt with in the international publications or (2) organising analytic discussions at the cross-national level around specific problem issues. Again, these are strategies that are beginning to be pursued in the major assessment programs.

Practical issues

Broad issues of strategy arise in accommodating national and international studies into a coherent data strategy or in reconciling research and policy interests into sustained and multilevel indicator work. One may well consider the stepwise approach to assessment studies with different aims and methods, as Allardt (1990) does when discussing the profitable sequence of large-scale quantitative studies versus intensive qualitative ones. With the recognition of the different paradigms as complementary rather than mutually exclusive, conceiving such rational strategic approaches is possible.

With the increasing national and international (plus local and regional) assessment activities, the need for comprehensive approaches in the field of educational evaluation is definitely rising. In seeking solutions (1) mapping the natural domains of interest, expertise and responsibility both at the levels of national educational policy and implementation and (2) considering the relevant ways and means of collecting, organising and using information for a variety of purposes will become necessary. These are likely to include political, administrative, practical and theoretical interests. Also included would be the needs of international work on educational indicators. Among the benefits would be more systematic and articulated coverage of multi-level information needs, economy in avoiding duplicate work and distribution of the total assessment burden.

The latter consideration brings us to the effects of school and pupil overload in test taking. Although net test time per pupil is fixed ahead of time, particularly large-scale assessments presume lengthy and careful preparation, as well as substantial control procedures. The programme easily becomes a relatively demanding project for participating schools, involving considerable organisational tasks requiring firm leadership and teacher resources. Together with other external requests on schools and students (which is not so unusual), participation also may bring about a certain exhaustion and test-weariness among pupils. Although routines may be quickly learned, they may also result in respondent burden, which has been demonstrated to have adverse effects on the quality of data (Sirotnik 1987; Frankel and Sharp 1980). The issue may also be seen as one of student motivation and (more or less favourable) testing morale. One may safely suggest that there are vast differences between schools and countries in the test-taking attitudes of their students. Considering the extensive data and the sophisticated multivariate analyses sensitive to missing or inconsistent responses, such effects may have serious consequences on the stability of measures and the possibility of adequately analysing and interpreting the study results. As remedies, matrix sampling and computer-aided on-line data recording have been introduced (Sirotnik 1987).

Issues of utilisation

Finally, it is not insignificant as to how and for what purpose data on education systems are disseminated and how the resulting discourse is conducted. The ways in which assessment results are disseminated and used have received more attention in recent years than ever before. In fact, House (1980, pp. 249–57) and Messick (1994) expand the entire validity concept to include the criterion of consequences, with the former expounding three domains of utility in a decision process: personal, interpersonal and public. In House's terms, assessment results (in the form of indicators) must first be true. At the personal level this has not only technical but also deep moral implications, such as regarding fairness. In the inter-personal context, reported results also have to be credible and trustworthy. The third level, by virtue of its public nature, brings in yet another requirement, normative correctness (cf. also Clayton's 1972 discussion on the sources of assessment criteria). Such viewpoints take into account not only measure-oriented validity but also user-oriented validation of measures, conclusions and meaningfulness. International assessment studies, as multi-level enterprises, are examples in which comprehensive and responsible deliberation clearly becomes necessary.

In the article mentioned previously (Leimu 1992b) some general research interests and questions were explored. Not only are the contents and communication style important, but so also are the combination of this style with and the intended use of the information. Expectations of comparative assessments are abundant. The communication style may range from 'formal and shiny', but distant, reporting to more interactive research and development work for addressing specific questions or to a personal approach with co-operative sharing of responsibilities. Certain kinds of information and particular purposes are differentially amenable to various strategies of dissemination and utilisation. Although the circle of interest in international assessment has grown enormously since the earliest comparative results were published, the scientific sophistication of the users has grown as well. Policy makers, planners and administrators at different levels, as well as teachers and even students, are willing and able to digest whatever information is relevant for them in the findings. Because much interpretation is often left for the user to consider and account for, more effort should perhaps be devoted to educating the user by suggesting justified conclusions and presenting critical considerations that might complicate the issues. Such a dialogue would also educate the researcher.

Another way to proceed would be related to the discussion on the strategic approach mentioned earlier. According to Bryk and Hermanson (1994; cf. Allardt 1990, Leimu et al. 2001), information needs and its production are considered a multi-level 'pyramid', with cross-national indicators constituting the most general signals at the top. Such gross findings should mainly guide further, more intensive research on issues requiring deeper clarification. This research should ideally be both qualitative and quantitative. The main point would be to get across useful and valid information for serious users at every level of the education enterprise.

The answers hinge on our ability to formulate the underlying purposes of assessment not only in a manner that is policy-relevant but also in a manner that would lead to meaningful interpretations based on adequate understanding of relevant contingencies and that would be conducive to active discourse on education and school learning. International comparisons and the indicator movement can and should be prime movers in developing evaluation culture, rather than a cult of evaluation. Comparisons can do so by producing valid data reliably measured and properly analysed and presented in ways that generate open and critical discussion. Continuous and intensive international co-operation with an open mind is necessary for achieving such goals.

The second statement of William James at the opening of this chapter indicates that in an enterprise dealing with human beings and their social organisations a good deal of tolerance is required. Much depends on the criteria of quality and preciseness adopted in endeavours to understand education and its multi-level processes. Demands for absolute identity are unreasonable in humanistic ventures, however objective and rationalistic they may be. Doing the work in conformity with high-level professional ethics and arriving at conclusions for which credibility can be defended by reasoned argumentation, international comparisons can help to establish results and produce indicators that are as meaningful as they are influential. These comparisons will gradually build up the kind of understanding and evaluation culture that our education systems, teachers and – above all – our children deserve.

References

Adams S., 1965. *Measurement and Evaluation in Education, Psychology, and Guidance* (New York: Holt Rinehart & Winston).

Adams R.J., 1992. Item bias. In Keeves (ed.) *Methodology and Measurement in International Educational Surveys* (The Hague: IEA), pp. 177–88.

AERA/APA/NCME, 1985. *Standards for Educational and Psychological Testing* (Washington DC: American Psychological Association).

Alkin M., 1975. Evaluation: who needs it? Who cares? *Studies in Educational Evaluation*, 1 (3), 201–12.

Allardt E., 1990. Challenges for comparative social research. *Acta Sociologica*, 33 (3), 183–93.

Altbach P. G., 1991. Trends in comparative education. *Comparative Education Review*, 35 (3), 491–507.

Bereday G.Z.F., 1964. *Comparative Methods in Education* (London: Holt Rinehart & Winston).

Bloom B.S., 1969. *Taxonomy of Educational Objectives* (New York: McKay).

Broadfoot T., 1977. The comparative contribution: a research perspective. *Comparative Education Review*, 13 June, pp. 133–7.

Bryk A. and Hermanson K., 1994. Observations on the structure, interpretation and use of education indicator system. In *Making Education Count. Developing and Using International Indicators* (Paris: OECD), pp. 37–53.

Campbell D.T. and Fiske D.W., 1959. Convergent and discriminant validation by the multitrait–multimethod matrix. *Psychological Bulletin*, 56 (2), 81–105.

Clayton A.S., 1972. Valuation in comparative education. *Comparative Education Review*, 16 (3), 412–23.

Coombs P. H., 1968. *The World Education Crisis. A System Analysis* (New York: Oxford University Press).

Cronbach L.J., 1961. *Essentials of Psychological Testing* (New York: Harper).

Cronbach L.J. and Suppes P. (eds), 1969. *Research for Tomorrow's Schools. Disciplined Inquiry for Education*. National Academy of Education (London: Collier Macmillan).

Degenhart R.E., 1990. *Thirty Years of International Research. An Annotated Bibliography of IEA publications 1960–1990* (The Hague: IEA).

Dreeben R., 1968. *On What is Learned in School* (Reading MA: Addison Wesley).

Farrell J.P., 1979. The necessity of comparisons in the study of education: the salience of science and the problem of comparability. *Comparative Education Review*, 23 (1).

Foshay A.W. (ed.), 1962. *Educational Achievements of Thirteen-year-olds in Twelve Countries* (Hamburg: UNESCO Institute of Education).

Frankel J. and Sharp L.M., 1980. *Measurement of Respondent Burden* (Washington DC: Bureau of Social Science Research).

Glass G.V., McGaw B. and Smith M.L., 1981. *Meta-analysis in Social Research* (London: Sage).

Goldstein H., 1995. *Interpreting International Comparisons of Student Achievement* (Paris: UNESCO).

Gulliksen H., 1962. *Theory of Mental Tests* (4th edn, New York: Wiley).

Hambleton R.K., 1994. Translating achievement tests for use in cross-national studies. *European Journal of Psychological Assessment*.

House E.R., 1980. *Evaluating with Validity* (London: Sage).

Husén T., 1973. Foreword. In Comber and Keeves, *Science Education in Nineteen Countries*. International Studies in Evaluation I (Stockholm: Almquist & Wiksell), pp. 9–16.

Husén T., 1974. Multinational evaluations of school systems: purposes, methodology, and some preliminary findings. *Scandinavian Journal of Educational Research*, 18 (1), 13–39.

Husén T., 1977. Policy implications of cross-national education surveys. *Studies in Educational Evaluation*, 3 (2).

Husén T., 1979. An international research venture in retrospect: the IEA surveys. *Comparative Education Review*, 23 (3), 386–407.

IEA, 1988. *Science Achievement in Seventeen Countries. A Preliminary Report* (Oxford: Pergamon Press).

IEA, 1998. *IEA Guidebook 1998. Activities, Institutions and People* (Amsterdam: IEA).

James W., 1891. *The Principles of Psychology* (London: Macmillan).

Keeves J.P. (ed.), 1992. 'Methodology and Measurement in International Educational Surveys', MS (The Hague: IEA).

Leimu K., 1981. Kansainvälisen ja vertailevan koulutustutkimuksen luonteesta (On the nature of international and comparative research in education). *Institute of Educational Research Bulletin* 184 (Jyväskylä, Finland: University of Jyväskylä). In Finnish, with English summary.

Leimu K., 1992a. Explorations in opportunity-to-learn: Finnish national analyses of IEA/SISS data. *International Journal of Educational Research*, 17 (3–4), 291–317.

Leimu K., 1992b. Interests and modes in research utilization: the Finnish IEA experience. *Prospects* (84), XXII (4), 425–33.

Leimu K., Linnakylä P. and Välijärvi J., 2001. *Merging National and International Interests in Educational System Evaluation* (Jyväskylä, Finland: Institute of Educational Research, University of Jyväskylä).

Messick S., 1994. The interplay of evidence and consequences in the validation of performance assessments. *Educational Researcher*, 23 (2), 13–23.

Noah H.J., 1973. Defining comparative education: conceptions. In Edwards, Holmes and Van de Graaff (eds) *Relevant Methods in Comparative Education. Report of a Meeting of International Experts*. International Studies in Education 33 (Hamburg: UNESCO Institute of Education), pp. 109–17.

Noah H.J., 1984. Use and abuse of comparative education. *Comparative Education Review*, 28 (4), 550–62.

Noonan R. and Wold H., 1983. Evaluating school systems using partial least squares. *Evaluation in Education. An International Review Series*, 7 (3).

Nowak S., 1977. The strategy of cross-national survey research for the development of social theory. In Szalai and Petrella (eds) *Cross-national Comparative Survey Research.Theory and Practice* (Oxford: Pergamon Press), pp. 3–47.

OECD, 1992. *The OECD International Education Indicators. A Framework for Analysis* (Paris: OECD).

OECD, 1999. *Measuring Student Knowledge and Skills. A New Framework for Assessment* (Paris: OECD).

Pitkänen P., 1967. On the congruence and coincidence between stimulus analytical and response analytical actor results. *Jyväskylä Studies in Education, Psychology and Social Research*, 13 (Jyväskylä, Finland: University of Jyväskylä).

Purves A.C., 1987. The evolution of the IEA: a memoir. *Comparative Education Review*, 31 (1), 10–28.

Purves A.C. (ed.), 1989. *International Comparisons and Educational Reform* (Alexandria VA: Association for Supervision and Curriculum Development).

Raivola R., 1985. What is comparison? Methodological and philosophical considerations. *Comparative Education Review*, 29 (3).

Schleicher A., 1994a. *Standards for the Design and Operations in IEA Studies* (The Hague: IEA).

Schleicher A., 1994b. International standards for educational comparisons. In Tuijnman and Postlethwaite (eds): *Monitoring the Standards of Education. Papers in Honor of John P. Keeves* (Oxford: Elsevier), pp. 229–47.

Selden R., 1992. Standardizing data in decentralized educational data systems. In *The OECD International Education Indicators. A Framework for Analysis* (Paris: OECD), pp. 107–13.

Sirotnik K.A., 1987. The information side of evaluation for local school improvement. *International Journal of Educational Research*, 11 (1), 77–90.

Stake R.E., 1967. The countenance of educational evaluation. *Teachers' College Record*, 68 (7), 523–40.

Stufflebeam D.L., 1976. 'Evaluating the Context, Input, Process and Product of Education'. Presented at the International Congress on the Evaluation of Physical Education, University of Jyväskylä, Finland.

Teune H., 1977. Analysis and interpretation in cross-national survey research. In Szalaiand and Petrella (eds) *Cross-national Comparative Survey Research. Theory and Practice* (Oxford: Pergamon Press), pp. 95–128.

Tuijnman A.C. and Postlethwaite T.N., 1994. *Monitoring the Standards of Education. Papers in Honor of John P. Keeves* (Oxford: Elsevier).

Vahervuo T., 1958. *Psykometriikan metodeja* I. *Tilastolliset peruskäsitteet* (2nd edn, Porvoo: WSOY).

Chapter 9

Moving beyond bivariate indicators

The role of multi-level modelling in international comparisons

Roel J. Bosker and Tom A.B. Snijders

Like almost all social systems, education is structured hierarchically. Grouping, thus, is a key feature, which in itself may be important to study, but which can also be somewhat troublesome for researchers attempting to study the impacts of education. Two pupils from one class will look more alike than two pupils from different classes because they share the same teacher, the same instructional group and probably many more things such as the same neighbourhood. Conventional statistical models like multiple linear regression, however, assume that observations (or, more precisely, residuals in the model) are sampled independently. Constructing education indicators (possibly with margins of errors attached to these) therefore should be based on models that represent this multi-level nature adequately. This chapter briefly introduces the multi-level statistical model and illustrates how it can be put to use in education research endeavours, such as the calculation of indicators of the performance of education systems using international assessment data.

The basic multi-level model

The multi-level model is an adequate means to handle the 'noise' caused by employing a multi-stage sampling design. Box 9.1 provides an example of how a multi-stage sampling design was used in the OECD/INES Project. The sampling scheme employed in the example violates the simple random sampling design and causes observations (namely those done in the same neighbourhood) to be dependent. Handbooks on sampling (e.g. Cochran 1977) show how corrections can be made to prevent a deflated estimate of the standard error of the mean. Basically, the two-stage sample might be reweighed to its simple random equivalent. However, to achieve this, one needs to have an estimate of the intra-class correlation, a measure expressing the alikeness of two observations from the same cluster. A basic multi-level model can be applied in this situation both to estimate the intra-class correlation and to provide a proper (unbiased, efficient) estimate of the population mean and its standard error.

Box 9.1 Public confidence in the schools

For the 1995 edition of EAG, INES Network D surveyed the public in twelve OECD countries on their attitudes and expectations about secondary education. Several modes of data collection were allowed. Some countries completed and mailed in self-report questionnaires; other countries conducted telephone interviews. In both these cases, simple random sampling was feasible. In some countries, however, costly face-to-face interviewing was preferred, for a variety of reasons. In order to reduce the costs, these countries used a two-stage sampling design in which first neighbourhoods were sampled randomly, and then within each sampled neighbourhood two or more respondents were selected randomly. The probability of being selected in the second stage depended on the outcomes of the first stage. That is, for respondents living in neighbourhoods not selected in the first stage the probability of being selected in the second stage was zero, whereas for other people it was not. (See indicator C23 in EAG, OECD 1995.)

$$\text{Attitude}_{\text{respondent neighbourhood}} = \beta_{0,\ \text{neighbourhood}} + R_{\text{respondent neighbourhood}}$$

$$(9.1a)$$

$$\beta_{0,\ \text{neighbourhood}} = \gamma_{0\ 0} + U_{0,\ \text{neighbourhood}} \tag{9.1b}$$

For convenience, full names (respondent, neighbourhood), rather than a standard subscript notation, are used to indicate units. Equation 9.1a states that the measurement of the attitude of a respondent in a neighbourhood can be modelled as a function of a neighbourhood characteristic $\beta_{0,\ \text{neighbourhood}}$, which is the mean attitude towards education in a neighbourhood, and some residual term indicating that a respondent's opinion may deviate from the average of the neighbourhood he or she is living in, $R_{\text{respondent, neighbourhood}}$. Equation 9.1b then states that this average neighbourhood attitude can be modelled as a population average for this attitude measurement $(\gamma_{0\ 0})$ and a residual term indicating that the neighbourhood's average attitude deviates from this population average, $U_{0,\ \text{neighbourhood}}$. A standard assumption is that the residuals are normally distributed with a mean of zero and some unknown variance, and, moreover, the residuals at either level are uncorrelated. Because a two-stage sampling design is used, the observations are elements from a population and, therefore, sampling-error variation is present in the data.

The multi-level statistical model is suited to help in separating two sources of between-neighbourhood variability: sampling-error variation (caused by randomly sampling respondents within each neighbourhood) and 'true' between-neighbourhood variation. These two sources total up to the observed between-neighbourhood variation, yet it is, of course, only the 'true' between-neighbourhood variation that is of interest. This variation is denoted by τ^2, and the variation between respondents within neighbourhoods is denoted by σ^2. A measure of the alikeness (or 'dependence') of respondents 'caused' by the neighbourhoods they live in is then the intra-class correlation coefficient $\rho = \tau^2 \,/\, (\tau^2 + \sigma^2)$. If the two-stage sample is reweighed to its simple random equivalent, then the following formula 9.2 might be applied for estimating the design effect, in which we use n as the average sample size of respondents within each neighbourhood:

$$\text{Design effect} = 1 + (n - 1) \times \rho \qquad (9.2)$$

If N denotes the number of neighbourhoods, then the effective sample size (i.e. the simple random sample size equivalent to the two-stage sample) can be calculated in equation 9.3 as:

$$N_{\text{effective}} = (N \times n) \,/\, \text{design effect} \qquad (9.3)$$

In estimating the standard error of the mean, this $N_{\text{effective}}$, rather than $N \times n$, should be used. If five respondents are sampled per neighbourhood, and the intra-class correlation is estimated to be 0.10, then the design effect is 1.4, meaning that the effective sample size is only 71 per cent of the total two-stage sample size. Stated otherwise, without reweighing the sample, the standard error of the mean would have been underestimated by a factor of $1\sqrt{1.4} = 0.85$. This, of course, is rather serious when comparing the means of two countries in which the two confidence intervals almost overlap.

The intra-class correlation as an indicator of equity of schools

The straightforward application of multi-level modelling has been in use since the 1993 edition of EAG (OECD) (see Box 9.2). In this case, the 'noise' that is caused by employing a two-stage sampling strategy is not of concern, but instead intra-class correlation is viewed as an interesting indicator in itself. The intra-class correlation coefficient is a kind of measure of equity of schools. The multi-level model equations 9.1a–b indicate residuals both at the student level and at the school level, reflecting that there is variance within and across schools. The variation across schools might be more readily interpreted as variation in the schools' average achievement levels. The intra-class correlation coefficient is simply a standardised measure (ranging from 0 to 1) to express this amount of variation. An education system where the intra-class correlation is near 0 is egalitarian (at the institutional level) – that is, it does not matter for a student's achievement level which school he or she attends because the school average

---

Box 9.2 School differences in science achievement

For the 1993 edition of EAG, INES Network A produced an indicator called 'school differences in science achievement', which was based on outcomes of the second IAEP study of science achievement of 13-year-old students. As an indicator the intra-class correlation coefficient (times 100) was used. (See indicator R3 in EAG, OECD 1993.)

---

achievement levels are the same. Alternatively, if this indicator is almost 1, all the achievement differences between students within a country can be 'explained' by the schools they attend, which points to a highly segregated system, and, conversely, the achievement differences between students within a school are – on average – negligible.

The multi-level statistical model helps in providing a proper estimate of the intra-class correlation. If the two sources of between-school variability, namely sampling-error variation and 'true' between-school variation are not separated, this coefficient would be erroneously overestimated. For example, for a 'true' intra-class correlation coefficient of 0.20, having sampled twenty-five students per school, the 'wrong' estimate – in which the two sources of between-school variation are not separated – would be 0.23.

Two statistical issues regarding the equity of schools indicator described in the example need to be addressed. First, the value of this indicator is estimated with error (because a sample was used). Donner (1996) gives a formula to estimate standard errors for the intra-class correlation coefficient (see also Snijders and Bosker 1999, p. 21). For example, suppose within each country 100 schools are sampled and within each school twenty-five students are sampled. If the intra-class correlation is 0.20 for a certain country (as was the case for the United States in the indicator referenced in Box 9.2), then the standard error of this intra-class correlation is 0.027. The 90 per cent confidence interval for this intra-class correlation then runs from 0.156 to 0.244. The boundaries for an intra-class correlation of 0.10 (e.g. Italy in the same example) would have been 0.071 and 0.129. The use of the confidence intervals is, of course, suggested to prevent one from mistakenly judging one education system as being more egalitarian than another whereas, in fact, the differences may stem from sampling-error variation. In general, these margins of error are smaller if the size of the sample of students within each school is larger and/or if the size of the sample of schools is larger. The size of the sample of schools, however, is far more important in achieving high levels of precision of such an estimate than the size of the sample of students within each school.

The second issue has to do with the number of levels in the education hierarchy. In the example given, a two-stage sample was assumed, but instead there might have been a three-stage sample: schools, classes and students.

What happens if such an intermediate level in the design is ignored? In some countries, especially those with a complete categorical secondary education system (e.g. Germany, Belgium, the Netherlands), schools will differ quite a lot. Whereas in countries with a horizontal, integrated system (e.g. the United States) much of the variation may lie between classes within schools, which may especially be true if some form of ability grouping is used. If the intermediate level of the classroom is not acknowledged, that is, if a two-level model is used instead of a proper three-level model, the between-school variance will be overestimated and, consequently, the between-students within-school variance will be underestimated. Once again, an example indicates what is occurring. In SIMS the variation in science achievement within Sweden was 0.00 between schools, 0.45 between classes within schools and 0.55 between students within classes (Scheerens et al. 1989). Ignoring the classroom level, and assuming that students were sampled from four classes per school, one would erroneously have come up with the following estimates: 0.11 between schools and 0.89 between students within schools (the intra-class correlation being 0.11 as well). This gives the wrong message to policy makers – they may think that there are patterns of inequity pertaining to schools, whereas in fact these patterns probably have to do with curricular tracking and homogeneous ability grouping within schools. The application of a three-level statistical model, mirroring the true nature of the education hierarchy, would have shown what is really happening.

Value-added indicators for equity of schools

The equity of schools indicator just discussed is based on a rather crude measure of achievement differences across schools. It describes perfectly the differences present, but it does not explain whether these differences were already present when the students entered the secondary system or whether they came into existence during secondary education as a consequence of differences in the quality of education provisions across schools. Thus examining four different definitions of school effects is essential before choosing one that may be of particular interest for in the OECD/INES context:

*   *Gross school effects.* The first operational definition uses the mean (uncorrected) achievement score of pupils in a certain school as the measure of school effect. The value of this definition lies in its use within a criterion-referenced framework: if a standard is set (or if a growth continuum is specified) *a priori* this gross school outcome measure provides the information to judge whether the school, on average, performs above, at or below the standard. It does not, however, imply that all pupils within that school meet the standard. This definition can be labelled as the 'gross' school effect. In operational terms, it is the mean achievement – that is, it is averaged over the pupils within a

school with a correction for sampling error. This definition was implicitly used in the previous paragraph.

- *School effects based on unpredicted student achievement.* The second operational definition starts from unpredicted achievement. In this case a prediction equation is estimated from the data, where achievement is predicted from aptitude, SES, age, gender, ethnicity and other student variables. The reasoning behind this approach is that schools differ widely in their pupil populations and that, because the previously mentioned variables have a strong relationship with achievement, their effects on achievement should be partialled out. Most of these variables are static and not subject to (much) change, though the aptitude of a child may be. For this reason, the aptitude assessment should (ideally) take place before or at school entrance.

- *School effects based on learning gain.* The third operational definition can be seen as a specific case of the second one: achievement is predicted from prior achievement. Once again, the same argument applies as in the case of the aptitude assessment. If prior achievement is assessed at a later point in time than school entry, the school effect transforms into the effect of a school on its pupils within a certain time interval.

- *School effects based on unpredicted learning gain.* The last, and seemingly strictest, definition combines the previous two, and unpredicted learning gain forms the basis. Using a post-test score corrected for a pre-test score, the resulting score is, in turn, corrected for aptitude, SES, age, gender, ethnicity and other student variables, because these are related to the learning progress that pupils make. In this case, prior achievement as well as aptitude should (ideally) be assessed at school entrance.

In the literature on school effectiveness (e.g. Scheerens and Bosker 1997) school effects are mostly referred to as value-added measures (i.e. some kind of intake adjustment is applied). However, there are at least three different sets of value-added-based school effects. In the INES and PISA contexts, with cross-sectional assessments, school effects based on unpredicted student achievement are the best approximation available for a value-added conceptualisation of the equity of schools indicator. Socio-economic status, gender, ethnicity and age can be seen as proxies for prior achievement.

The multi-level model can then be extended by including one or more of these covariates. Because a three-level model is preferred, a more complicated model that is a rather straightforward extension of 9.1a and 9.1b is being used. For simplicity, the case of one covariate will be addressed:

$$\text{Achiev}_{\text{pupil, class, school}} = \beta_{0,\text{class, school}} + \beta_1 \text{SES}_{\text{pupil, class, school}} + R_{\text{pupil, class, school}}$$

$$(9.4a)$$

$$\beta_{0, \text{ class, school}} = \delta_{0\,0, \text{ school}} + U_{0, \text{ class, school}} \tag{9.4b}$$

$$\delta_{0\,0, \text{ school}} = \gamma_{0\,0\,0} + V_{0, \text{ school}} \tag{9.4c}$$

Interesting estimates of variability to be obtained are the residual within classes – between-student variance (9.4a), the residual between classes – within-schools variance (9.4b), and the residual between-schools variance (9.4c). In all cases, 'residual variance' is used because the effects of SES on achievement are partialled out. The value-added indicator for equity of schools is now simply the size of the between-school variance relative to the total variance: the smaller this residual intra-class correlation the more equity at the school level. A second indicator might be constructed in which one looks at the between-class variance relative to the variance between classes and between schools: the smaller this residual intra-class correlation is, the more differences there are between classes within schools. A telling picture, conveying all the information at once, might look like Figure 9.1. Country A has a selective school system with relatively large value-added differences between schools, whereas in country B such differences show up between classes within schools.

Slopes as outcomes

Up to this point a rather simple multi-level model that is similar to the random-effects ANOVA model or, in case some kind of covariate is employed, the random-effects ANCOVA model have been used. The next step is towards a random coefficient model, in which the effect of some covariate may vary across groups (e.g. schools). Burstein (1980) used to call this type of model the 'slopes as outcomes' approach; it is also sometimes referred to as gradients measuring patterns of inequity.

Using this model, and assuming that both the achievement and the SES variable are standardised, the coefficient for the regression of achievement on SES (β_1) that is obtained for each country can be compared. The picture might look like Figure 9.2, which uses data from TIMSS 1995 and in which coefficients for the regression of mathematics proficiency of 14-year-olds on SES for eleven countries are estimated. Each line in the figure represents the

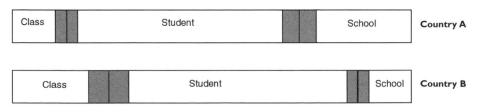

Figure 9.1 Value-added-based achievement differences among schools, classes and students

regression of mathematics on SES for a country. The lines show that, in all the countries involved, high-SES students show higher mathematics levels than low-SES students. However, the gap between these groups is relatively small in Belgium (Flemish community) and the Netherlands and relatively large in Scotland. The rest of the picture is rather blurred. Extending the previous unfolded ideas of constructing margins of errors around each indicator, Figure 9.3 tells the same story with a bit more detail.

Belgium (Flemish community), the Netherlands and Germany have an association between SES and achievement that is statistically significantly below the average, whereas in Sweden, Canada and Scotland the association is stronger than average. The error bars are 80 per cent confidence intervals. For pair-wise comparisons this would be almost equal to performing a t test with a significance level of 10 per cent (see Goldstein and Healy 1995 for details).

If the multivariate character of the information is too technical for a policy-maker audience, a simple solution may be to predict, within each country, the achievement for a low-SES student (e.g. two standard deviations below average SES) and a high-SES student (e.g. two standard deviations above average SES) on the basis of the estimates found for the multi-level model equations 9.4a–c. One then can compare the achievement levels of low-SES students across countries, as well as those of high-SES students. Moreover, one can compare the gaps across countries.

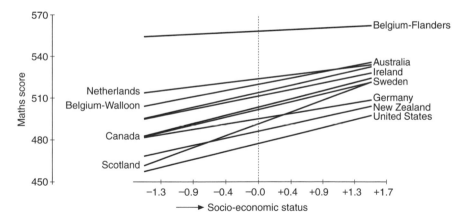

Figure 9.2 The relationship between mathematics proficiency and SES in eleven countries.

Source: IEA, TIMSS 1995

Box 9.3 Inequalities in educational achievement pertaining to SES differences

PISA 2000 assessed achievement levels with respect to reading, mathematical and scientific literacy of 15-year-old students. In addition to producing measures of countries' mean literacy in these domains, a specific aim also was to produce indicators of achievement differences that were related to pupils' SES. The indicator constructed represents the gap between a low-SES student and a high-SES student. One way to construct this indicator is to run a separate multi-level analysis for each country involved, with achievement as a dependent variable and socio-economic status as a predictor. If both variables are standardised, the coefficient for the regression of achievement on socio-economic status is the parameter value for this equity indicator.

This 'slopes as outcomes' example, in which a regression equation was estimated for each country separately, is not really what is meant in the context of multi-level modelling. A question that is related to what is to be demonstrated would be the following: are countries different in the amount of between-school variability in the gaps between their low- and high-SES students? To address this question, a random coefficient model,

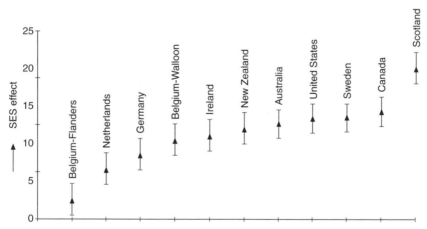

Figure 9.3 The relationship between mathematics proficiency and SES in eleven countries.

Source: IEA, TIMSS 1995

a model where the effect of SES varies across schools within a country (Longford 1993), is needed. The model might look like the following equations, in which, instead of the full subscripts, p is for pupil, c is for class and s for school:

$$\text{Achiev}_{pcs} = \beta_{0,cs} + \beta_{1,cs}\,\text{SES}_{pcs} + R_{pcs} \qquad (9.5a)$$

$$\beta_{0,cs} = \delta_{00,s} + U_{0,cs} \qquad (9.5b')$$

$$\beta_{1,cs} = \delta_{10,s} + U_{1,cs} \qquad (9.5b'')$$

$$d_{00,s} = \gamma_{000} + V_{0,s} \qquad (9.5c')$$

$$d_{10,s} = \gamma_{100} + V_{1,s} \qquad (9.5c'')$$

The model looks somewhat awkward now, but it is quite simple. It indicates that the effect of SES on achievement varies across classes within schools (9.5b'') as well as across schools (9.5c''). As Raudenbush and Bryk (1986) showed when reanalysing US *High School and Beyond* data, one should look at between-school variation in achievement, in particular as related to SES. The statistical 'nitty-gritty' stems from the need to treat the slopes as a sample from a population of slopes (thus ridden with sampling-error variation). By obtaining estimates of the variances (including the variance of the regression parameter β_1 across schools and classes) and covariances (at each level, but not across levels, the residuals may be correlated) separate estimates can be provided for the intra-class correlation coefficient for low-SES students and for high-SES students.

Further extensions

The logic of multi-level modelling can be used for a variety of purposes, and thus for a variety of education indicators. First, the models can be extended by including a school-level predictor variable, such as school size. Its effect on (or, better, its 'association with') achievement or value added to achievement within each country could be estimated. The idea is that of conventional regression; the only 'new' thing is that this effect and its accompanying standard error are estimated properly when using multi-level statistical models acknowledging the hierarchical nature of the data. Another extension is to try to sort out whether in some countries cross-level interaction effects show up: does school size 'explain' the width of the gap between low and high-SES students?

Straightforward extensions, of course, concern other dependent variables (e.g. instead of achievement, years of schooling may be used), other predictors, other equity issues (e.g. gender equity) and other combinations of these. The generalised multi-level model allows for estimating models for hierarchically structured data with other than normal error distributions. Models have been developed (and implemented in software) for ordinal outcome measures (e.g. number of science subjects chosen for examination), for dichotomous outcome measures (e.g. graduated or not, dropped out or not) and for polytomous (unordered) outcome measures (e.g. labour market segment chosen by the student). Each example given might have been related to such outcome measures as well.

Description or causal inference?

As shown, the multi-level statistical model can be put to use in calculating indicators for education systems in OECD countries. It is a misunderstanding, as Goldstein and Blatchford (1997) show, that only randomised controlled trials ('true experiments') can help in sorting out cause-and-effect questions. They clearly show that, at least in education, where young people receive their instruction in institutions over a relatively long period, the generalisability of the results obtained from such experiments is questionable because of problems pertaining to ecological validity and population definition.

In all the examples, causal attribution (i.e. showing that schools cause the effect) is difficult to achieve. Raudenbush and Willms (1995), following Rosenbaum and Rubin, argue that, because randomisation cannot be achieved, assignment of students and schools to treatments should be 'strongly ignorable'. This qualification expresses that the different treatment outcomes for a student and a school 'are conditionally independent of treatment assignment given a set of covariates' (Raudenbush and Willms 1995, p. 312), which implies that value-added measures should be preferred. The covariates available in INES studies (such as PISA) are only proxies of differences between students at school entry, and, thus, assignment of students to treatments (i.e. schools with specific organisational characteristics) is not 'strongly ignorable'. School effects based on unpredicted achievement are only substitutes for value-added measures. From a scientific point of view, to reach causal inference a better set of covariates, including prior achievement, is necessary.

But, on the other hand, it is possible that value-added-based school effects underestimate true school effects. When 'privileged' students are more likely to choose 'good practice' schools, controlling for students' SES, for instance, results in over-adjustment. To complicate things further, in compensatory systems, school effects may appear only after adjustments for covariates are made. In compensatory systems, unfavourable scores on the covariates are compensated by (and thus correlated with) good education practices. Moreover, these school effects can disappear again when context variables, which are negatively associated with good education practices for the same reason, have been considered. For these reasons, one should always provide gross (uncorrected) measures next to net (corrected) measures. Causal attribution, however, pertaining to effects of variables, such as school size or class size, is impossible in the kind of INES studies currently being conducted. Estimates of associations should be treated with caution and may be used to explore issues of common concern in education systems around the world.

Finally, the issue of committing type I and type II errors needs to be briefly addressed. In all cases, if information is needed on student achievement, on the functioning of schools or on the relation between both, it is optimal with a given total sample size to have a large sample of schools with relatively few students per school.

References

Burstein L., 1980. The analysis of multilevel data in educational research and evaluation. *Review of Research in Education*, 8, 158–233.

Cochran W.G., 1977. *Sampling techniques* (New York: Wiley).

Donner A., 1996. A review of inference procedures for the intraclass correlation coefficient in the one-way random effects model. *International Statistical Review*, 54, 67–82.

Goldstein H. and Blatchford P., 1997. *Class Size and Educational Achievement. A Methodological Review* (London: University of London Institute of Education).

Goldstein H. and Healy M.J.R., 1995. The graphical presentation of a collection of means. *Journal of the Royal Statistical Society*, Series A, 158, 175–7.

Longford N.T., 1993. *Random Coefficient Models* (New York: Oxford University Press).

OECD, 1993. *Education at a Glance* (Paris: OECD).

OECD, 1995. *Education at a Glance* (Paris: OECD).

Raudenbush S.W. and Bryk A.S., 1986. A hierarchical model for studying school effects. *Sociology of Education*, 59, 1–17.

Raudenbush S.W. and Willms J.D., 1995. The estimation of school effects. *Journal of Educational and Behavioral Statistics*, 20 (4), 307–35.

Scheerens J. and Bosker R.J., 1997. *The Foundations of Educational Effectiveness* (Oxford: Elsevier Pergamon).

Scheerens J., Vermeulen C.J.A.J. and Pelgrum W.J., 1989. Generalisability of instructional and school effectiveness indicators across nations. *International Journal of Educational Research*, 13, 789–800.

Snijders T.A.B. and Bosker R.J., 1999. *Multilevel Analysis. An Introduction to Basic and Advanced Multilevel Modelling* (Newbury Park CA: Sage).

Chapter 10

The methods used for international assessments of educational competences

Fabrice Murat and Thierry Rocher
Translated by Jason Tarsh

Since the end of the 1950s numerous studies have sought to compare the attainments of pupils in various countries in subject areas such as mathematics, reading and science. The IEA has played a major role in conducting the majority of these international assessments. In the words of the founder of IEA, it is a matter of 'treating the world as a laboratory' in order to better understand the operation of education systems, to identify problems that are not very apparent at the national level, and to find high-performing educational approaches. Recently the OECD has also developed such a study in order to assess more closely the effectiveness of systems in relation to the resources (input) and pupil outcomes (output).

International assessments are often very instructive, whether as fundamental research or for educational policy making. Nevertheless, these assessments are often only turned into league tables, which rank countries on an attainment scale according to the scores that they have obtained.[1] But, for the test designers, the chief aim is ensuring the construction of a league table that is as fair as possible, that is, which does not favour one country over another in what is sometimes seen as a competition. This preoccupation with comparison of scores, which strongly influences the method used by such studies, thus limits the question of the comparability of the results to that of the robustness of the league table.

The purpose of this chapter is not to present the results obtained from these assessments but to identify the problems raised by or associated with using methods that compare the attainment of pupils from different countries on a common test. The various international assessment programmes, though they differ in their objectives or in their subject areas, rest on a common method which is developed and refined from one study to another. This chapter first describes this method, discussing various issues to do with comparability; then it demonstrates how, in spite of efforts to make instruments universally valid, many biases related to national cultural characteristics remain and weaken the reliability of the final league table. However, far from invalidating the results of international assessments, these biases often bring interesting insights into the attainments compared among pupils that national assessments would not have revealed. Finally, beyond the comparability of the results obtained in terms of ranking, the chapter addresses comparability from the point of view of the dispersion. Comparison of inequalities in attainment indeed raises other problems, particularly when adapting the test to countries or when the choice of the modelling can influence the results. This chapter is based primarily on PISA 2000 results and, to a lesser degree, on the TIMSS results (see Box 10.1).

Box 10.1 Overview of PISA and TIMSS

Thirty-two countries took part, under the aegis of the OECD, in PISA 2000, which evaluated pupil attainment in reading literacy, mathematical literacy and scientific literacy. The full study will take place over three points in time. In 2000 the key part of the assessment was on reading literacy, and mathematical and scientific literacy came in only as a lesser component. In 2003 mathematical literacy is the primary area evaluated. Finally, in 2006 the focus will be scientific literacy. This system should thus allow tracking of trends in the results.

The PISA programme is much more concerned with students' ability in applying knowledge than in knowledge itself. In the three domains tested by PISA, priority is given to the ability to apply various fundamental processes in diverse situations, generally different from academic situations, in drawing on broad understanding of key concepts rather than on the accumulation of specific knowledge. First results from PISA 2000 were published by OECD (2001).

In 1995 forty-five countries took part in the IEA's TIMSS. Five grades from the primary schools to the upper secondary schools were involved in this study. Forty-one countries took part in TIMSS 1999, which was the same assessment for the eighth grade. This assessment allows countries to analyse the variations of their students' proficiencies from 1995 to 1999.

The TIMSS tasks are very close to those tasks that students are involved with at school. The aim is to examine the results in comparison with the curricula. TIMSS 1995 results can be found in Beaton ... Smith (1996) for science and in Beaton ... Smith and Kelly (1996) for mathematics. As for TIMSS 1999 results, they can be found in Mullis *at al.* (2000).

Issues of comparability

International assessments are undertaken with the aim of measuring the attainment of pupils on a common scale for all countries. A fundamental assumption of international assessments is thus the existence and the universal nature of the competence that they seek to measure. It is therefore assumed that the target of the measurement is independent of cultural and linguistic contexts. The issue of comparability then transfers into processes and the measuring instrument: on the one hand, there has to be assurance that the conditions of the test ('observations') are identical among countries; on the other hand, the test instrument has to be adapted to each context.

International assessments proceed by observation and, as in all studies, the operation of the test instrument can influence the result of the test itself. This is the reason the procedures for gathering the information (organisation, sampling, transfer, etc.) are standardised as much as possible to guarantee identical conditions of observation. These methods have been refined at the level of international comparisons so as now to constitute a robust whole.[2] These different aspects will not be addressed but Adams and Wu (2002) fully describe these procedures for PISA.

Construction of the test instruments

What is of interest here relates more particularly to the development of the competence scale. The choice of test content, the construction of the items, the process of translation and then the calculation of the scores raise important questions on the comparability of the test measure.

The content of the assessment

In contrast to other international assessments, the competences addressed in PISA are not directly linked with the content of the curriculum. PISA draws on the concept of literacy (as other chapters also describe) and seeks to assess 'the ability of young people to apply their knowledge and their skills to deal with the challenges of real life rather than examining how far pupils have acquired specific subject matter from a school curriculum' (cf. OECD 2001). PISA is defined broadly as an assessment of general competences which do not depend on specific curricular knowledge and which are supposed to be useful to 15-year-olds in their future lives, seeking employment, continuing their education or being good citizens. This choice of content orientation, which stems above all from a policy desire to evaluate the 'pay-off' of educational systems, also requires better comparability of results. Indeed, it is assumed that, whatever their country of origin, 15-year-olds will be faced with similar situations requiring the application of these competences which are *a priori* assumed to be independent of different cultural contexts. In the view of those devising PISA, the universal nature of these competences justifies the construction of a common unidimensional scale.[3]

The construction of the test items

At a national level, the measurement of attainments is already a sensitive and debated topic. The construction of test items measuring well defined operations, which can be categorised and subsequently put in a hierarchy, raises many theoretical and empirical questions. How can one assure, beyond the validity of the measure, the construction of a test instrument that is valid from one language to another, from one culture to another?

In each of the three domains assessed by PISA, an expert group developed a framework whose broad outlines were defined by the participating countries. This framework specified the competences to be evaluated, the types of text to be used, the variety of situations and the distribution of item formats. With this base, the institutes in the consortium implementing PISA proposed items, and countries were invited to contribute to the production of the items.[4] The items proposed were then reviewed, modified and adapted by the expert group in relation to the set aims.

The development of the test instrument thus is presented as a collaborative process, supposedly restraining any resulting linguistic or cultural domination in the initial development of the test.[5] In PISA 2000, for reading literacy, in spite of this apparent collaborative effort, proposals for material and items from only nine countries were used, after adaptations and modifications, which represents about 45 per cent of the total of 129 items. The rest of the items came from the consortium (38 per cent) and the IALS study (17 per cent).[6] The weight of countries in the process of development of the test is thus not very high. From a linguistic balance point of view, again for reading literacy, of the thirty-seven items tested, twenty-two are from documents drafted in English, which represent about two-thirds of the items.

The procedures for translation

International assessments are based on a common test translated into all the languages represented by the participating countries. One of the fundamental hypotheses of such assessments is that the translation of an item does not change its nature: the competence is the same whatever the language – reading it in Japanese or in French does not change the nature of the task to be accomplished – and the level of difficulty remains the same after translation. In fact, it is primarily the latter point that most concerns the test designers, because they are concerned with the construction of a reliable scale and are thus more interested in performance than in competence. In terms of rigour, it is of little importance that reading in Japanese does not imply the same intellectual processes as reading in French; the key aim is comparing the performance of pupils when they are called upon to read the same test material (airline timetables, for example). From this point of view, it is essential that the translation maintains the same level of difficulty of the task.[7]

Following the problems identified in the translation in previous international assessments,[8] rigorous procedures are used in PISA to ensure equivalence between the different translations or adaptations. First, starting with the items chosen for the assessment, the international experts produced two versions of the test, one in English and the other in French. These two source versions of the test are supposed to be 'equivalent' from the point of view of the translation. Anglophone and francophone countries used the corresponding source version direct, with some adaptations. The other countries were responsible, in the first round of the translation process, for independently translating the two source versions into their language. In a second round, a third translator compared the two versions, reconciled any differences and produced the final version. These translations were then verified in part at the international level by a team of translators. The technical report for PISA 2000 (Adams and Wu 2002) details these procedures and compares the methods.

These strict procedures are necessary but do not guarantee the equivalence of the translations. In terms of difficulty, terms that are more or less exact, repetitions or certain expressions, all can help students in understanding. The relative length of the texts according to the language can also have an influence on the equivalence of the translations. One study undertaken by the international experts on a sample of the PISA test instruments shows that, in relation to their English versions, the French texts have on average 12 per cent more words and 19 per cent more characters (Adams and Wu 2002). It would furthermore seem that the very operation of translation means a lengthening of the texts because the texts drafted in French lengthen slightly when translated into English. Does this finding have an effect on the comparative success of French and English-speaking pupils? In light of the results of this study, the more the test material lengthens when it is translated from English to French, the more difficult are the items for French-speaking pupils relative to their English-speaking counterparts.

The construction of the scores

The reliability of the test instrument is affected not only by translation problems. More generally, the adaptability of the test to each of the cultural contexts will condition the robustness of the scale. To better capture this variability and to come up with a score continuum across all countries, most recent international assessments, such as PISA and TIMSS, draw on specific psychometric models based on IRT.

Item response models

These models assume that the probability of a pupil succeeding on an item depends on both the pupil's level of attainment and the level of difficulty of the item. The aim of these models is to separate the two concepts. The capability of a pupil is defined independently of the difficulty of the assessment or the test, and conversely the difficulty of the items is not a function of the attainment level of the pupils.[9] In addition, the competence levels of the pupils and the parameters of difficulty of the items are set on the same scale that is on the same latent variable, often called the 'latent trait'. This specific feature allows the straightforward prediction of the probability of success of a pupil having a given level of competence on a test item of a given level of difficulty. Other parameters concerning the item can subsequently be added: the two-parameter model incorporates the power of discrimination of the items, that is, their level of correlation with the attribute evaluated; the three-parameter model also adds a parameter called the 'pseudo-chance', used when the items (e.g. multiple-choice questions) can be answered correctly by chance. To learn more the reader can refer to introductory texts like Hambleton *et al.* (1991).

The advantage of these models for international assessments is clear: if the characteristics of the test can be seen as absolutes, the results from different countries can be directly compared.

The unidimensional hypothesis

These models rest on the hypothesis of unidimensionality, that is, that success on the items, given their level of difficulty, is conditioned by a single, common factor: the pupil's level of attainment. To put it another way, pupils' performances on the assessment are explained by the degree of mastery of a single common competence, independently of the linguistic and cultural contexts. In practice, this hypothesis is obviously not fully satisfied, given the complexity of the mental processes leading to success on the items and problems related to translation and the inevitable cultural specificity of the items. In addition, there is no perfect method of validating this hypothesis because the dimensionality of a group of items is a difficult concept to measure (Nandakumar 1994).

Unidimensionality is thus a simplifying hypothesis that allows a better summary of the results in a synthetic variable, supposedly measuring the competence of pupils in the subject area considered. In reality, many contradictions can appear. In particular, with respect to the curriculum, the unidimensional character of the measured competence rarely satisfies the experts and the teachers, who are more inclined to see in each subject many competences and areas of knowledge to acquire. This diversity also occurs at the international level: each subject does not have exactly the same significance in all countries, some aspects are tackled at different points in a school career in individual countries, cultural attitudes can condition pupils' replies, the test can be unidimensional in one country but not in a neighbouring one,[10] etc. Finally, careful analysis of the differences or similarities in success, item by item, between countries is in contradiction with the search for a single, overall dimension, common to all countries where the items are distinguished only by their level of estimated difficulty. Indeed, the items have to function as indicators of the same variable.[11] Therefore 'it can be inconsistent to claim to use a unidimensional scale and at the same time present results which relate to separate elements' (Goldstein 1995, p. 25).[12]

Be that as it may, the contribution of these models is not limited to the simple production of test scores and item parameters on a robust scale, all the more because these estimates are often similar to what is seen in a descriptive manner.[13] The aim of modelling is first to confront the statistics with the hypotheses on which they rest. From the experimental phase, these models provide important elements for detecting items whose successful answering depends on a factor other than just the level of attainment of pupils, notably the fact of coming from a particular country or speaking this or that language.[14]

Therefore, for a given country, an item is 'biased' if, for the same level of attainment, the pupils perform either better or worse on it than do the pupils of other countries.[15] In that case another factor, apart from that of the single competence being assessed, has played a part in the performance on the item for the pupils of that country. This may be because of technical problems (translation errors, printing typos, etc.), in which case the item is then modified or eliminated. But, more generally, there are items showing what is known as cultural bias. (The following section describes a variety of reasons that can explain a bias.) Once the biased items are identified and subsequently removed so as to ensure the most unidimensional scale possible, pupils in the different countries take the final test, and the scores are calculated by item response models.

From the conception of the tests to the statistical analysis of the results, the prime concern thus remains the construction of a single scale of competence, invariant according to the contexts in which pupils of different countries could be classified in a reliable manner. Furthermore, the theoretical foundations of item response models clearly illustrate this particular vision of international comparisons. Nevertheless, the scale derived is obviously not perfectly unidimensional. Biases remain, and they do not inevitably add to the errors in the measure but very often reflect 'cultural' differences among countries.

Unidimensionality and the measure of biases

Rather than looking at results on a unidimensional scale devised *a posteriori*, it is interesting to examine the differences observed in relation to the modelling. Recall that an item is termed biased in relation to a group of pupils (e.g. boys versus girls, France versus Italy) when there are seen, at the set level of competence, different performances by pupil group. Two statistics are mainly used to detect item bias. The Mantel–Haenszel measure, seen in terms of distance, is the difference between the rates of success of two groups, having determined that they have the same level of competence. The statistic known as the statistical index of bias (SIB) relates to the gap between the difficulty parameters of the items when they are separately estimated for each group (see Box 10.2).[16]

Box 10.2 Two indicators of bias

The Mantel–Haenszel statistic

Considering two groups (for example boys and girls) and making J clusters of 'same' level of proficiency. The table below presents the sizes of cells for the level j:

	Item answer		
Group	*Correct*	*Incorrect*	*Total*
1	A_j	B_j	n_{1j}
2	C_j	D_i	n_{2j}
Total	m_{1j}	m_{2j}	T_j

The Mantel–Haenszel statistic is:

$$\text{MH} = \frac{\left(\left| \sum_{j-1}^{J} (A_j - E(A_j)) \right| - \frac{1}{2} \right)^2}{\sum_{j-1}^{J} \text{Var}(A_j)} \tag{10.1}$$

where:

$$E(A_j) = \frac{n_{1j} m_{1j}}{T_j}$$

and:

$$\text{Var}(A_j) = \frac{n_{1j} n_{2j} m_{1j} m_{2j}}{T_j^2 (T_j - 1)} \tag{10.2}$$

Undo the hypothesis $H_0 : A/B = C/D$ (the item success does not depend on the group) and we have $MH \sim X_1^2$. (At 5 per cent risk the value is 3.84; at 1 per cent it is 6.63.)

The statistical index of bias (SIB)

Another way to proceed is using the following index, proposed by Lord:

$$d_j = \frac{\Delta b_j}{\sqrt{S_{j,1}^2 + S_{j,2}^2}}$$

where $\Delta b_j = b_{j,1} - b_{j,2}$ is the difference between the estimates of item j difficulty for the countries 1 and 2. $S_{j,k}$ is the standard error of $b_{j,k}$ estimate. *A priori*, the two populations have different average scores. To eliminate this effect we force the b_j mean to be 0 for each of the two groups. One tests hypothesis $H_0 : d = 0$ against $H_1 : d \neq 0$. Undo H_0, $d \sim N(0, 1)$. So, at 5 per cent risk, if $|d| > 1.96$, the item presents a statistically significant differential functioning. (At 1 per cent risk the value is 2.57.)

France versus the United States

Drawing on the PISA results in reading literacy and TIMSS mathematics, a study compares bias in two countries, France and the United States. In PISA these countries get comparable overall scores in reading literacy and are at the average of the participating countries. In contrast, French pupils, on average, achieve better results than American pupils in mathematics in TIMSS.

Detecting biases

Of the 129 items for reading literacy in PISA, the average success rate is 62.3 per cent for France and 60.8 per cent for the United States. Nearly fifty items (of 129) show a difference of over 10 per cent in favour of one country or the other. But the simple comparison of success rates does not allow the determination for sure whether the item is biased. Indeed, for equal success rates across all pupils, there are seen to be significant differences in success for some levels of competence and not for others. This is why the two indicators of bias have been calculated for each item (see Box 10.2).

To illustrate the results obtained, Table 10.1 shows three examples of biased items. For each of the items, the observed rates of success for the five groups

Table 10.1 Three examples of items that are biased when comparing France and the United States (percentage of correct responses)

Quintile	Item R111Q02		Item R104Q06		Item R220Q04	
	France	USA	France	USA	France	USA
First	3.5	7.2	61.6	71.5	42.0	16.8
Second	10.6	33.9	77.6	80.8	64.3	35.2
Third	23.1	43.7	89.9	88.8	77.9	49.4
Fourth	34.7	54.4	95.5	93.5	89.4	65.3
Fifth	58.2	73.5	95.1	95.1	95.5	84.3
Total	23.1	43.3	85.1	86.3	74.7	50.4
Mantel–Haenszel	172.6		10.5		167.9	
SIB	−14.6		−4.4		12.4	

Source: PISA 2000.

of pupils in terms of comparable competence level are reported, as well as the two bias statistics described in the exhibit.[17]. For the first item, R111Q02, whichever competence group is considered, apart from the first quintile, the success rate of US pupils is about 20 per cent higher than that of French pupils. This is one of the most biased items as measured by the two statistics presented above. In contrast, item R222Q04 is clearly biased in favour of French pupils, 75 per cent of whom succeeded with it whereas only 50 per cent of US pupils managed it. Item R104Q06 is interesting in that the rates of success seen in France and the United States are similar, although this item is slightly biased in favour of US pupils, principally at the low levels of attainment.

In sum, even if the statistical tests are sensitive to the sample sizes, it is striking to see that eighty-four items out of 129 are biased in relation to both of the two statistics, at the 1 per cent confidence level.[18] But, beyond this audit,[19] it is interesting to ponder the many reasons that could explain these differences in difficulty by country. It is not necessary to revisit the possible problems stemming from translation: in PISA and TIMSS very few errors arose as gross as those identified in IALS (cf. Carey *et al.* 2000). The differential outcomes often have many other causes, more complex than simple technical shortcomings. Moreover, these outcomes enable a more refined and illuminated analysis of pupil results than would than a simple comparison of overall scores.

Cultural biases

Cultural bias is when some categories of individuals gain an advantage by their prior knowledge of the test instrument. For example, familiarity with the test material on which the questions are based can be one cause of bias. The performances seen are then also a reflection of 'cultural' closeness[20] and not only of the latent competence of the individuals.

In this sense, the study of biased items in relation to French and US pupils in PISA shows an effect linked with the test material. French pupils get excellent results on an extract from a play by Anouilh, test material that France had submitted. In contrast, US pupils scored badly on this text whereas on test material of the 'work-related' type (e.g. advice to office workers in a firm on being vaccinated against flu) US pupils got markedly better results than French pupils, who did very poorly on these questions.[21] The two examples show clearly that pupils 'specialise' according to that which is culturally familiar. Furthermore, on the eighteen items drafted originally in French, fourteen are biased,[22] thirteen of them in France's favour. However, the same phenomenon is not seen for the items drafted originally in English: of the sixty-six items concerned, thirty-seven are biased, twenty favouring the United States and seventeen favouring France. These items do not, it seems, raise problems of translation but have a strong cultural dimension.

A cultural bias can bring together very different ideas. In the previous examples, the influence of the content of the curriculum can be seen: US pupils are more often faced with materials from the world of work than are French pupils. But the extract from the Anouilh play is culturally closer to French pupils. The familiarity that pupils may have with different test material refers, across teaching approaches, to objectives of different educational systems. To study them rather than to see them as indicators or measurement error is quite interesting.

The question format

The question format can also be a source of bias. In the case of multiple-choice questions explicitly requiring at the start of the assessment a reply with only one of the alternatives offered, French pupils frequently ticked several replies to the same question. By way of example, in PISA several multiple-choice items ask pupils what is the main purpose of a text (or of an extract from a text) and offer four possibilities. Often, one alternative is quite close to the correct reply, without being correct. French pupils are more likely to tick the two replies which seem to them the most plausible, while US pupils tick only one. In France, up to 13 per cent of 'double replies' are seen on some questions, while this rate rarely exceeds 1 per cent in the United States. For the most part, these items are biased in favour of US pupils, who are perhaps more familiar with this type of question.

Along the same lines, the items biased in favour of the United States are more often questions needing a written, constructed response. Indeed, for this type of question French pupils tend to abstain from answering where they are unsure while US pupils always reply, even if they may answer wrongly. We even see instances where although the item is not biased the French pupils more often do not answer. For example, an item requiring significant writing to justify a point of view is handled as well in the United

States as in France. But, for this item, 18.2 per cent of French pupils declined to answer, compared with barely 5.5 per cent of US pupils who did not answer (see Ministère de l'education nationale 2003). Finally, French pupils are more at ease with open-ended questions that call for a short and precise answer. The problems encountered with multiple-choice questions are not present here, and the reply does not need much writing. This is, moreover, a type of question that is familiar in French education.

School curricula

In the case of assessment aligned closely with school practices, one of the most important sources of 'bias' is the influence of the curricula of the different countries. To put the point simply, if in one country particular emphasis is put on a certain part of the subject area assessed, there is a risk of finding that all the items relating to this domain are biased in favour of the country, whereas many other items will be biased in the other direction. It moreover appeared in the examination that many items 'favouring' France in TIMSS related to geometry, while the algebra items were relatively more difficult in France than they were in the United States. It is precisely that geometry had a privileged place in France compared to the United States.

Sometimes the difficulty of the question is transformed by a small modification which can appear harmless but which refers to differing uses. So, in TIMSS, 68 per cent of US pupils can find the equivalent of y^3 among five options, when the correct answer is given as $y \times y \times y$. In the French test question the preference was to replace the correct answer with another equivalent expression $(y.y.y)$, with significant effects: only 32 per cent of French pupils recognised the identity, half as many as in the United States. By way of comparison, a question on the identity $m + m + m + m = 4m$ was answered correctly by 60 per cent of French pupils, as against 43 per cent of those in the United States. It might thus be thought that it was the use of a more 'scientific' and less familiar formula which worried French youngsters.

Generalising to several countries

Similarity of performance and cultural profiles

We can now look to generalise this type of analysis based on a comparison of two countries. To do so, it would be of interest to calculate, for each pair of countries and each item, a bias statistic, and then aggregate the results. A simpler way of proceeding is to study countries' performance profiles, that is, for each country, the hierarchy of items by the proportion of correct answers. If the unidimensionality hypothesis is valid, all countries should have the same performance profile, corresponding to the hierarchy of items in terms of their difficulty parameters, with random errors unrelated to the countries.

To test this, a hierarchical classification of countries according to their performance profiles on reading literacy items in the PISA study has been created. The method is taken from a similar analysis undertaken on the IALS results (Guérin-Pace and Blum 1999) and repeated on those from TIMSS (D'Hautefoeuille *et al*. 2002). For each country, we attribute to each item its rank in the performance hierarchy and we proceed to a hierarchically ascending classification of countries according to these profiles.[23] This leads to the same finding as for the two previous studies: the similarity of the performance profiles of countries generally coincides with their similarity in terms of geography, culture or language.

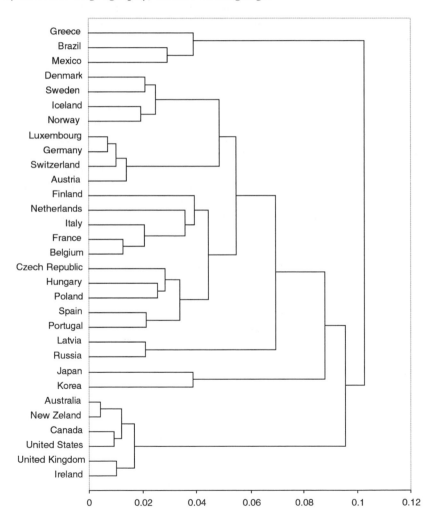

Figure 10.1 Classification of countries according to their performance profiles in PISA reading literacy.

Looking at the tree diagram that results, we do indeed see the clustering of countries broadly according to three criteria (Figure 10.1). Anglophone countries make up a homogeneous group, as do the Nordic countries and the German-speaking countries. Greece, Brazil and Mexico stand out from the other countries for their very good scores on certain difficult items whereas they rank bottom of the overall test. Eastern European countries split into two groups, Russia and Latvia on the one hand, the Czech Republic, Hungary and Poland on the other. Japan and Korea have profiles that are similar, Spain and Portugal likewise. Finally, one group brings together such diverse countries as Finland, the Netherlands, Italy, Belgium and France.[24]

To illustrate the tree diagram, we have shown graphically the scatter plot of the percentages of correct replies for Great Britain and the United States on the one hand and Great Britain and Japan on the other. Each point represents one item for which the x axis is the percentage of correct answers in Great Britain and the y axis is the percentage of correct answers for the United States (Figure 10.2a) or Japan (Figure 10.2b). These displays show that the performance profile of Great Britain is very close to that of the United States but quite distant from that of Japan. Furthermore, the correlation of the rankings reaches 0.92 in the former case, as against 0.72 in the latter.

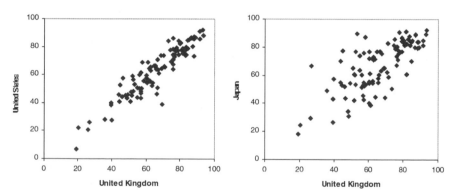

Figure 10.2 Comparison of performance profiles in reading literacy, (a) United Kingdom and United States, (b) United Kingdom and Japan. *Note* Points are items in reading literacy and axes are percentages of correct answers

Areas of strength and weakness for the country groups

According the above classification, countries are split into seven groups. For each one of these groups the most characteristic items have been determined, that is, the items that are answered particularly well or poorly by the populations. For example, it seems that the anglophone countries are 'specialists' in materials of a professional nature (job application, forms, etc.). They also stand out on open questions needing a written, constructed reply. On the other hand, they are less good at documents based on maps or charts.

It would thus be possible to describe in a precise way the strengths and weaknesses of each group of countries, that is, the items that contributed to the clustering of the groups.[25] There would certainly be errors in the translation but, more generally, as in the case of the France/United States comparison, 'informative biases' emerge from the analysis. Beyond the linguistic difficulty which such a study means, it is not always possible to explain the reasons for a bias. Thus Greece, Brazil and Mexico have excellent results on an item which makes a major contribution to the creation of that cluster. The item relates to a text by a journalist on the problems of pollution of beaches. What can we conclude? This particular item was in fact kept for the calculation of the scores, the experts having been unable to find any explicit reasons for the appearance of such a bias.

The country league table changes markedly depending on whether the calculation is based on the weaknesses or strengths of a particular group. Moreover it was already possible to notice in descriptive terms this fragility of the league table: in PISA, for twenty-nine items out of 129, France ranks in the top five countries while it is among the bottom ten for another twenty-nine items.[26] There are thus questions to be asked about the robustness of the rankings published by OECD.[27]

Finally, the performance profiles have shown that they are very different depending on the sub-groups of items considered and that this instability is due not to simple errors of measurement but to cultural factors. It is fairly significant, from this viewpoint, that the test which disadvantages the United States is also one which disadvantages Australia and Great Britain. In spite of the methods which can be used to reduce cultural biases, the problem is more general and relates to the essential differences between countries, whether they are particular cultural ways of functioning or different educational objectives. One could henceforth be satisfied to establish a league table, inevitably broader-brush, of some ten well chosen items and devote the rest of the analysis and reporting to highlighting the specific features of countries by means of tests that are better adapted for this. Apart from the difficulty of accepting the credibility of a league table based on a limited number of items, this type of approach, firmly multidimensional, is technically feasible (cf. Vrignaud and Bonora 1998).

Furthermore, even supposing that we succeed in constructing a test that perfectly measures a single common dimension for all countries, we are far from having solved all the problems. A test can be bad not only because it is liable to cultural bias which systematically works against some countries but also because it inevitably is not as well adapted to each one, that is, it does not allow a proper distinction between individuals according to their level of attainment. For example, if a very easy test is put to a very able group of people, all the individuals will succeed and they will be all seen as very capable. As a result, the differences between them as individuals will be misperceived. The next section shows that this phenomenon weakens the measure of the dispersion of the results.

The measurement of the dispersion of scores

Assuming that, with the help of a 'smoothing out' of the results, the construction of an international scale common to all countries has been successful, it is then possible to rank the countries from the best to the least good by their average score. However, this information quickly appears inadequate to study issues such as equality of opportunity, the existence of a proportion of the population facing serious difficulties or, at the other extreme, the absence of an elite group. For this, we have to make a finer analysis of the distribution of the results. Such analyses can reflect various aspects: analysis of the quantiles (scores of the best 10 per cent and the lowest 10 per cent), broad indicators of dispersion (the standard deviation or interquartile range), differences in averages between groups chosen *a priori* (differences between children from working-class and managerial and professional families, for example). Here we will focus particularly on the broad indicators of dispersion, in particular the standard deviation, but all the ideas developed are more or less transferable to other indicators of dispersion.

As a preface, it is useful to distinguish two concepts: (1) differences in attainment (it is a matter then of actual inequalities existing in the population but not directly observable) and (2) the dispersion of performance measured by a statistical indicator (typically the standard deviation) in a given test (a matter of giving a measure of the range of results between pupils seen in the tests). If these two concepts are inevitably correlated, a third factor related to the proposed test – quality – has to be considered. The dispersion of performances admittedly depends not only on the existing inequalities in attainment but also on the quality with which they are measured. As a counter-example, a test could be imagined whose questions would be so badly phrased that pupils would reply at random: the dispersion of results would be low not because the inequalities of attainment are such but because they are badly measured.

Dispersion of the results and adaptation of the test

The aim of an assessment is to highlight groups in very marked contrast to one another, to distinguish the best from the least good. To understand the point better, the situation of a professor in his class can be thought of: a university professor is not going to give all his students ten out of ten because they know how to count. Conversely, a primary school teacher will avoid asking his pupils about quantum mechanics. The professor adapts his demands so as to distinguish pupils according to their level of competence.

He will thus devise a test of average difficulty, with easy questions to identify pupils in severe difficulty and hard questions to separate out the best ones.

An apparent conflictof objectives is thus highlighted: if one of the principal aims of a good education policy is to keep the differences in attainment between individuals as low as possible, that of the designer of assessments is to find the best test possible, one which best distinguishes the better from the less good, the high and low-performing countries. They thus aim for the greatest possible dispersion in order to be able to explain the differences more easily. In this sense, finding a high standard deviation can be the outcome of a test well adapted to a diverse population.

An illustration of the link between the dispersion of results and the adaptation of the test to the target population is simply the level of difficulty of the test. It would be difficult to imagine recruiting young elite engineers on the basis of a test consisting of a hundred addition sums. Similarly, if a test is proposed on quadratic equations to pupils in year 4 of primary school and it is found that their scores vary between 0 and 10 per cent of the items answered correctly, it would still be misguided to conclude that mathematics competences at that level are weak and little dispersed. Such caricature examples recur in international comparisons of dispersions: does the low standard deviation for Brazil in reading literacy genuinely reflect a greater uniformity in the attainment levels of pupils or does it stem from the fact that the test was not adapted to Brazilian pupils, who are at the bottom of the international league table? This question is very difficult to reach a decision on because no entirely satisfactory indicator of relative dispersion exists.[28]

Apart from the difficulty of the test, which can complicate the interpretation of the dispersions, the adaptation of the test is linked with the discrimination of the items. Empirically, it is seen that the discriminatory power of an item can vary considerably between countries. Many factors can account for these variations: the style of the questions or familiarity with this or that test material, which are likely to affect the better pupils in one country and more sharply distinguish, by their level of competence, the pupils of another country. Furthermore, as with the performance profiles, the discrimination profiles seem also to carry a cultural dimension. Stated another way, an item that discriminates well in one country will tend to work similarly in another culturally close country. It is moreover possible to construct sub-tests, better adapted to a given country, which has the effect of noticeably increasing the dispersion of the results in that country. The same population of pupils is thus rendered 'diverse' simply by choosing a more closely adapted test.

Therefore, great prudence in regard to interpreting the dispersions is required. Do they then shed light more on the degree of adaptation of each test to the population than the actual differences in attainment? Expressed another way, finding a low standard deviation in one country relative to others may signify that the test works 'poorly', that it has difficulty in distinguishing the better from the less good in that country. The result may also be interpreted in the sense that the inequalities in attainment are actually less significant than elsewhere.

The impact of the modelling: identical data, different outcomes

Beyond the problems of interpretation, which the indicators of dispersion raise, the choice of statistical model has an impact. Various publications of the TIMSS results offer proof of this.

In 1995 about forty countries took part in TIMSS, undertaken by the IEA (see Box 10.1). Twenty-six countries repeated this activity for the eighth-graders in 1999 with the TIMSS-Repeat study. This repeat assessment thus allows an examination of the variations in performance of countries over four years (Mullis *et al.* 2000 and the 2001 edition of the annual OECD publication *Education at a Glance*, 1995–2000). But what is of interest here is not the comparison of the results of the two studies but just the results of TIMSS 1995, which change between publications.

Indeed, in 1995 the scaling and the calculation of the TIMSS scores were confined to the researchers at the Australian Council for Educational Research (ACER) according to a method based on the Rasch model, that is the one-parameter item response model (Martin and Kelly 1996). The analysis of the data from TIMSS 1996 was carried out by ETS, who used two- and three-parameter item response models (Martin *et al.* 2000).[29] For the new team of psychometricians responsible for the analysis of the data it was a matter not only of producing scales for TIMSS 1999 but also of making the comparison with TIMSS 1995. As their methods differed from those of the ACER researchers, the TIMSS 1995 data were completely rescaled according to the ETS method.

For the same data, from TIMSS 1995, the ranking of the country averages remains the same on both procedures although the values are different (see Figure 10.3a). On the other hand, the standard deviations vary markedly (see Figure 10.3b). For example, the results for Japan and the United States can be compared. In 1995 Japanese pupils, on average, got much better results than their US schoolfellows in mathematics at the eighth grade. That remains true with both statistical procedures. What about the dispersion of the results? As a result of the first procedure, by ACER, the dispersion is much greater in Japan than in the United States (standard deviation of 102 as against 91). The attainment level of Japanese pupils is thus very good but inequalities are higher. In the United States, on the other hand, though the pupils are on average less good at mathematics, they are a more homogeneous group. The second procedure on the data – that of ETS – gives the opposite results: Japanese pupils are slightly more homogeneous than US pupils (the standard deviation is 79 for Japan and 85 for

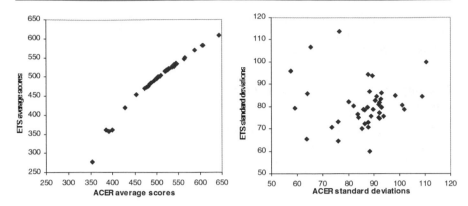

Figure 10.3 Comparison of average scores and standard deviations. *Note* Points are countries and axes are (a) average scores or (b) standard deviations according to ACER scaling or ETS scaling.

the United States). It could be concluded, in this case, that Japan succeeds in getting its pupils up to a very good average level while keeping inequalities in attainment at a level that is reasonable, indeed low.

How is it possible to see such differences, starting from the same data? The third parameter of the item response model means that, below a certain level of attainment, the probability of correctly answering a multiple-choice question is non-zero and quasi-constant. Even if the pupil is very low-attaining, he or she can answer the item correctly by chance. In addition, this parameter varies between items; it is not fixed at 25 per cent for a multiple-choice question with four possible answers, for example. Indeed, distractors varying in attractiveness are likely to cause the probability of answering the item correctly by chance to vary. In TIMSS, most of the items are multiple-choice, offering four choices, and some have a chance parameter above 0.4: whatever the attainment level of the pupil, he or she has a 40 per cent chance of answering the item correctly by chance. In that case, the correct reply is too obvious and the distractors are not fulfilling their purpose.

Looking at the data, the variation in standard deviation from one procedure to another seems to depend strongly on the average score obtained: countries that score poorly see their standard deviation rise under the second procedure while that of high-performing countries diminishes (Figure 10.4). One possibility is that the introduction of the third parameter tends to increase the variability of the scores estimated over the lowest-attaining pupils. Certainly, the act of introducing a parameter increases, as a matter of fact, the variability of the scores.[30] Nevertheless, the third parameter particularly affects the low attainment levels, since below a certain threshold the model predicts a probability of answering correctly that is non-zero and quasi-constant and, starting from some threshold, this becomes the two-parameter model. This hypothesis deserves to be tested, for example by

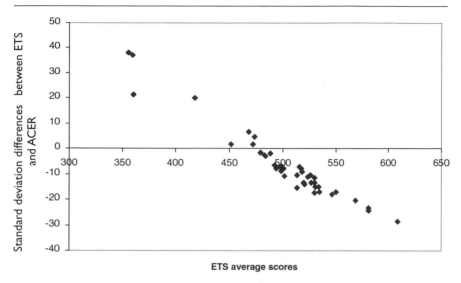

Figure 10.4 The link between average scores and differences between the two standard deviations.

applying a two-parameter model to the data which have just been presented. But it might be thought that, beyond the simple introduction of the third parameter, there are different estimation procedures which, taken together, lead to these results.[31]

Whatever the case, there has been no debate on these points as to the choice of the method to use for an international assessment. The reliance on this or that model and the statistical procedures that follow constitute a 'black box' for most of the participants in these international assessments. Yet these choices are not neutral and can perceptibly change the policy interpretation of the results, as has been seen above on the example of the relative dispersions in Japan and the United States.

Conclusion

The framework of methods described here is shared by most international assessments of attainment. It is a rich inheritance of which PISA is the culmination. Many technical aspects, such as the translation procedures or the methods of collecting the data are now well understood. However, the chief preoccupation of this type of test remains the production of a robust ranking of countries on a single scale of competence. Whether designing the test or using item response models, the method is guided entirely by the desire to produce reliable league tables. Yet, in spite of the efforts undertaken, it turns out that biases remain to weaken the validity of the rankings obtained. Very often, these biases do not stem from simple technical shortcomings. They refer rather to cultural differences as well as to the objectives of educational systems. In showing the strengths and weaknesses of each, they make up, from this point of view, a source of interesting information for the participating countries.

However, international assessments are constructed in such a way that the biases are reduced to the minimum. Would it not be more worthwhile to show the specific features of each country than to seek to erase them? One might, for example, think of using assessments adapted to different contexts, keeping a limited common foundation. One would thus genuinely take account of the specifics of countries without making statistical selections to satisfy *a priori* hypotheses. It would still be possible to establish a summary ranking, as an overview, while additionally developing analyses differentiated by country.

This multidimensional approach would certainly not solve the problems related to the measurement of the dispersion of attainment, which remains a little explored area in international assessments. Indeed, the comparability of the dispersions is a delicate question which relates as much to the adaptability of the test as to the choice of model. This subject certainly deserves to be looked at in depth because the study of inequalities constitutes an important part of international assessments.

Whatever the case, the results of these assessments are undeniably a rich mine of information – if this information is taken beyond simple league tables and is supplemented with detailed analyses of the similarities and differences between countries – that is, if the information is used comparatively.

Notes

1 Following the appearance of the PISA results, the press headlines focused on the country league table: 'France an average pupil in the OECD class' (*Le Monde*, 4 December 2001); 'UK pupils move close to the top of world class, survey shows' (*Guardian*, 4 December 2001); 'Students in Finland, Japan, Korea at top of class' (*New York Times*, 4 December 2001), etc. The presentation of the results, in itself, implied this focus on league tables (see Bonnet 2002).

2 In spite of all this, as soon as one uses a sample the results are subject to random error: for example, in reading literacy, of the thirty-two countries taking part in PISA, using a 95 per cent confidence interval, France comes between the eleventh and sixteenth positions and Japan between third and tenth place (based on the estimated standard errors in the sampling framework described in Adams and Wu 2002). Furthermore, from one survey to another, some results seem surprising. (For a critical comparison of the British pupils' results from several surveys in mathematics see Prais 2003.)

3 TIMSS adopted a different approach: it was concerned with assessing competences clearly linked with school curricula. The results show that countries have weaknesses in some subject areas and strengths in others. The French, thus, are better at geometry than at algebra, compared with other countries. Most of the time this type of difference is the result of educational policies. France has emphasised geometry, which is not the case in, for example, the United States. As a result, the ranking of countries on an overall scale loses its meaning.

4 The institutes responsible for PISA having provided the items are the Australian Council for Educational Research (ACER) and the Netherlands National Institute for Educational Measurement (CITO).

5 This step is distinct from that adopted in TIMSS, where all the items were devised by the experts in the consortium responsible for the study.

6 The IALS study took place in 1994 and covered adults' competence in reading and understanding of texts taken from everyday life (cf. OECD and Statistics Canada 1995).

7 Another approach, developed in a European framework, consists of comparing pupil performance on 'native' tests not translated but drawn from a common frame of reference. The results of a first experiment with this will be found in Bonnet et al. (2001).

8 As regards the critical assessment of the IALS study, in particular on the problems with translation (see Carey et al. 2000 and Guérin-Pace and Blum 1999).

9 In theory, this leads to the assumption that a question relating to logarithms is just as difficult for university students as for primary school pupils and that if the latter perform less well it is because they are less competent.

10 On this suggestion, reference can be made to an assessment in mathematics which took place in Scotland and the United States in 1997. Though in either country the test is practically one-dimensional, it is not possible to construct a common scale for both, as the items operate in a different way in each country (Wijnstra et al. 1998). Whether reading in French and reading in Japanese can be put on the same scale and show the same competence needs to be considered.

11 As Geoff Masters unambiguously says, speaking on behalf of the IEA, 'From the test designers' point of view, the items are of relatively small importance taken in isolation. What is of interest is the variable which they are trying to measure' (see Goldstein 1995, p. 36).

12 In IALS a similar contradiction consists of producing sub-scales, aggregated afterwards into a single scale (cf. Dickes and Flieller 1997).

13 The simple one-parameter item response model shows that there is a functional relationship between the scores from the one-parameter item response model and the simple percentages of items answered correctly (D'Hautefoeuille et al. 2002). In PISA's case the modelling is a little more complex: it uses a multinomial one-parameter model, taking account of partially correct replies. It is seen, nevertheless, that the correlation between the scores coming from these models and the simple percentages of correct answers is 0.96.

14 To test the reliability of the translations and of the procedures put in place, a field test for PISA took place in 1999 to prepare the full assessment in 2000. In the major domain of reading literacy, over 350 items were field tested and around 140 were retained.

15 When speaking of the bias of the item, specialists prefer to use the more neutral term 'differential functioning of the item'. We stick with the term 'bias' here for convenience.

16 Note that the competence levels came from the aggregate results of the test. In the case where all the items were biased, these two statistics have no information value. It might be imagined that a radically different conception of the subject area assessed affects the pupil results from a given country and does so in a uniform way across all the items. But in this hypothetical case is difficult to detect and obviously lies outside the framework of the modelling.

17 To calculate the Mantel-Haenszel statistic, pupils were divided into five homogeneous competence groups based on the percentage of items correctly answered in reading literacy. This division into quintiles was used because of sample size. Thus, pupils did not do all the items (the 129 items are divided into different booklets, using the method known as 'rotating booklets'). Thus in France, for example, an item was done by only 1,000 to 1,500 pupils out of the 4,673 in the sample.

18 The calculation of the SIB, whether starting from the one- or two-parameter model, gives very similar results: around ninety items are biased at the 1 per cent confidence level. The Mantel-Haenszel statistic is barely more tolerant: at the 1 per cent confidence level, 89 per cent of items are biased according to this measure. Of the eighty-nine items, eighty-four also operate differentially according to the one parameter SIB and seventy-eight on the two-parameter SIB.

19 It seems more interesting to study what these biases signify rather than their impact on the results. First, if the performances are calculated only on the items that are not biased, the ranges of the results are unchanged (65.1 per cent for France and 63.1 per cent for the United States). A compensating effect applies, and the biases identified do not invalidate the general results of the study. In addition, the model used here (one-parameter item response model) is little different from that used in PISA (a model generalised to allow for partial credit in the case, as it turns out, of sixteen items). In the end, those in charge of the study were led to eliminate some items in certain countries. (In total, about twenty items were excluded from the calculation of national scores.) They did not undertake a systematic elimination of the biased items but, rather, looked to determine the causes of the biases before deciding on inclusion in the calculation of the scores, even if it meant keeping items that were patently biased for certain countries.

20 The adjective 'cultural' is to be understood in its broad sense when speaking of cultural bias: it can affect groups in society, differences between boys and girls, etc.

21 On another test material, this time a literary text proposed by the United Sates, it is also via the marking instructions that cultural specificity can operate. See Robin (2002) for an analysis of the open-ended questions relating to this text and which are biased in favour of the United States.

22 As determined by the two bias measures presented earlier, at the 1 per cent confidence level.

23 Ideally, rather than the percentages of correct answers, it would be preferable to use the difficulty parameters stemming from the modelling used by PISA (i.e. an item response model allowing for partially correct answers). It would be necessary to apply this modelling to each country separately, and then to compare the results with the aggregate of all countries. This refinement seems, however, unnecessary, given that a correlation of 0.99 is observed between the difficulty parameters estimated in PISA and the simple rates of correct answers.

24 Note that practically the same groupings are found in mathematical or scientific literacy.

25 Technically, starting with the results of the classification, one can, for example, use factor analysis to identify the items which contribute to the differentiation of the country groups.

26 The strengths of French pupils come out particularly in reading graphs and culturally familiar test materials (an extract from a French theatre play, for example). In contrast, they encountered more difficulty with test materials of a technical sort or on questions calling for a personal opinion (cf. Robin and Rocher 2002).

27 On this point, another approach has been developed by McGaw (2002), head of the Education Directorate at the OECD. Prior to the study, each country undertook a 'marking' of the items according to their relevance. This study indicates that there is little significant variation in the league tables observed if they are calculated only on the most relevant items for each country. This result tends at least to prove that country 'preferences' do not match the tasks they subsequently do best on. This approach is based on an *a priori* judgement of the items. We have preferred to use statistical results and to proceed to an *a posteriori* analysis, which we judge more appropriate to study the variability of the results according to country.

28 Note that the use of the coefficient of variation is not allowed for scores obtained in some assessments because they are not on a common scale. In addition, the link between an average score and its standard deviation is not linear but quadratic, that is, the standard deviation will tend to be lower for an average score close to zero or 100 per cent, if a percentage of correct replies is considered, for example, and could be greater for an average score close to 50 per cent.

29 These two bodies correspond to two different 'schools' of psychometricians which developed around item response models.

30 The functional relationship which links the one-parameter item response models and the percentages correctly answered (cf. D'Hautefoeuille *et al.* 1999) is no longer valid when the second parameter is added. The variability of the two-parameter item repsonse model

scores is therefore greater than that of the simple percentages correctly answered that is observed.

31 The same phenomenon is not seen if the three modelling methods applied to multiple-choice questions in PISA are compared: the standard deviations of sub-groups of pupils (grade repeaters/non-grade repeaters, etc.) are stable, whichever model is considered.

References

Adams R. and Wu M. (eds), 2002. *PISA 2000 Technical Report* (Paris: OECD).

Beaton A.E., Martin M.O., Mullis I.V.S., Gonzalez E.J., Kelly D.L. and Smith T.A., 1996. *Science Achievement in the Middle School Years. IEA's Third International Mathematics and Science Study* (TIMSS) (Chestnut Hill MA: International Study Center, Lynch School of Education, Boston College).

Beaton A.E., Martin M.O., Mullis I.V.S., Gonzalez E.J., Smith T.A. and Kelly D.L., 1996. *Mathematics Achievement in the Middle School Years. IEA's Third International Mathematics and Science Study* (TIMSS) (Chestnut Hill MA: International Study Center, Lynch School of Education, Boston College).

Bonnet, G. (2002). Reflections in a critical eye: on the pitfalls of international assessment. *Assessment in Education. Principles, Policy and Practice*, 8 (3), 387–99.

Bonnet G., Braxmeyer N., Horner S., Lappalainen H-P., Levasseur J., Nardi E., Remond M., Vrignaud P. and White J., 2001. *The Use of National Reading Tests for International Comparisons. Ways of Overcoming Cultural Bias* (Brussels: European Commission).

Carey S., Bridgwood A., Thomas M. and Avila P., 2000. *Measuring Adult Literacy. The International Adult Literacy Survey in the European context* (London: Office for National Statistics).

D'Hautefoeuille X., Murat F. and Rocher T., 2002. La mesure des compétences : les logiques contradictoires des évaluations internationales. *Actes des Journées de méthodologie statistique 2000* (Paris: INSEE).

Dickes P. and Flieller A., 1997. *Analyses secondaires des données françaises de la première Enquête Internationale sur l'Alphabétisation des Adultes (enquête IALS)* (Nancy: Université Nancy II).

Goldstein H., 1995. Interpreting international comparisons of student achievement, *Educational Studies and Documents*, 63 (Paris: UNESCO).

Guérin-Pace F. and Blum A., 1999. L'illusion comparative : les logiques d'élaboration et d'utilisation d'une enquête internationale sur l'illettrisme (The illusion of comparing: the logic behind the way an international literacy survey is devised and used), *Population*, 54 (2), 271–302.

Hambleton R.K. Swaminathan H. and Rogers H.J., 1991, *Fundamentals of Item Response Theory* (Newbury Park CA: Sage).

Martin M.O. and Kelly D.L. (eds), 1996. *TIMSS Technical Report* I–II (Chestnut Hill MA: International Study Center, Lynch School of Education, Boston College).

Martin M.O., Gregory K.D. and Stemler, S.E. (eds), 2000. *TIMSS 1999 Technical Report* (Chestnut Hill MA: International Study Center, Lynch School of Education, Boston College).

McGaw B., 2002. Assessing policy lessons from PISA 2000. OECD PISA Symposium, Berlin, 18–20 November.

Ministère de l'éducation nationale, 2003. Les compétences des élèves français à l'épreuve d'une évaluation internationale : premiers résultats de l'enquête PISA 2000 (Initial results from an international survey of pupils' achievement), *Les Dossiers* 137 (Paris: MEN–DEP).

Mullis I.V.S., Martin M.O., Gonzalez E.J., Gregory K.D., Garden R.A., O'Connor K.M., Chrostowski S.J. and Smith T.A., 2000. *TIMSS 1999 International Mathematics Report. Findings from IEA's Repeat of the Third International and Science Study at the Eight Grade* (Chestnut Hill MA: International Study Center, Lynch School of Education, Boston College).

Nandakumar R., 1994. Assessing dimensionality of a set of item responses : comparison of different approaches. *Journal of Educational Measurement*, 31, 17–35.

OECD, 1995–2002. *Education at a Glance* (Paris: OECD).

OECD, 2001. *Knowledge and Skills for Life. First Results from PISA 2000* (Paris: OECD).

OECD and Statistics Canada, 1995. *Literacy, Economy and Society. Results of the First International Adult Literacy Survey* (Paris: OECD).

Prais S.J., 2003. Cautions on OECD'S recent educational survey (PISA), *Oxford Review of Education*, 29 (2).

Robin I., 2002. L'enquête PISA sur les compétences en lecture des élèves de cinquante ans : trois biais en question (The PISA survey on the reading competence of fifteen-year-old pupils: three biases in question), *VEI enjeux-migrants-formation* (Paris: CNDP). pp. 65–87.

Robin I. and Rocher T., 2002. *Reading Literacy among Fifteen-year-olds. An International Comparative Study*, Données sociales (Paris: INSEE).

Vrignaud P. and Bonora D., 1998. Literacy assessment and international comparisons. In Wagner (ed.) *Literacy Assessment for Out-of-school Youth and Adults* (Philadelphia PA: UNESCO/International Literacy Institute).

Wijnstra J., Eggen T., Semple B. and McArthur J., 1998. *Scottish–Dutch Collaboration in Assessment of Mathematics Achievement at the End of Primary School. The Pitfall of Differential Item Functioning in International Comparisons*, CITO (Arnhem: National Institute of Educational Measurement) and Scottish Office internal document.

Acknowledgements

In large part this chapter is a translation of T. Rocher (forthcoming), 'La méthodologie des évaluations internationales' (The methodology of international assessments) in *Psychologie et psychométrie*, Editions et Applications Psychométrique.

Afterword

Eugene H. Owen

The idea for this volume was actually born several years ago at a meeting of INES Network A in Salzburg, Austria. It was Uri Peter Trier, the Swiss delegate at the time, who, while contemplating a review of the various indicators that had been prepared over the years and discussing with other members the impending implementation of the Network's data strategy (PISA), remarked on how much progress had been made in the field of the comparative study of learning outcomes and the abundance of data becoming available. There was wide agreement around this observation, and the Network set about to review this progress from their unique perspective of being involved in thinking through the policy implications of assessment designs and how resulting information from assessments can be used to impact education policy.

First and foremost this volume demonstrates that there are numerous efforts under way to better measure the outcomes of learning; more clearly define the domains in which knowledge, skills and abilities are assessed; make more rigorous the scientific and other standards by which cross-national comparative studies are conducted; and render more meaningful (in terms of usefulness for policy) the information that is produced. Each of these efforts is built on the foundation of forty years of progress, which began with the early IEA studies and the pioneering work of researchers like C. Arnold Anderson, Benjamin Bloom and Torsten Husén.

Despite this progress, challenges remain, and these challenges range along the full continuum of the assessment endeavour. At one end, there is the most basic issue of identifying those domains that within a few years will be most relevant to measuring and monitoring, in particular in the context of the new, complex and changing demands facing society. On what knowledge, skills and abilities – on what competencies – do policy makers need information? We have generally limited ourselves to what we have learned how to measure well (i.e. achievement or literacy in key subject areas such as mathematics or reading). The high costs, in both human and financial terms, make this scenario quite reasonable and, indeed, inevitable. While there are many talented and innovative professionals in this field, and while there have been many advances and useful experimentations with respect to both the content and the methods of assessment, development work in new areas must necessarily proceed incrementally, building on small-scale experiments, national experiences and finally field testing in cross-national settings. The experiences with the new international measures for selected cross-curricular competencies, as described by Peschar and Klieme in Chapters 4 and 5, make this apparent.

In some ways, the development work for an assessment of ICT literacy is especially novel – as it is attempting to build a cross-national assessment essentially from scratch where no large-scale national examples exist. However, the INES and PISA stakeholders in OECD agreed: they could not afford not to take the risk with this development work, given the importance of technology for everyday life and its widely perceived, if not well understood, role in individuals' potential learning opportunities and experiences. The assessment framework that has been developed has received wide support from the countries involved but the next challenge already looms: financing the effort, which is projected at several million dollars in international costs.

In terms of specifying domains, the results of the Swiss-led OECD project DeSeCo may provide a useful framework in which to develop future assessments. DeSeCo defined a concept of competence that is demand-oriented, demonstrated through action, and vital to successful lives and well functioning societies, and furthermore identified three categories of key competencies: acting autonomously, using tools interactively and functioning in socially heterogeneous groups. This conceptualisation of competence and three-fold categorisation of key competencies can provide a valuable basis for discussion and consensus building about which new competencies should and could be included in future international assessments.

The methodologies used in assessments – namely those that provide reliable group results – also are a constraint on what can be and is being done and represent another challenge area for the future. International assessments are used for system monitoring and benchmarking and not for the diagnosis of individuals. Although sub-national results can be obtained, there can be some difficulty in obtaining reliable results at the school level, which puts even more pressure on having well thought out sampling designs and high response rates and, in some countries, makes precarious their ability to recruit schools to participate and makes the results of the assessment seem less relevant to actual practitioners. Up until this point, international (and national) assessment programmes have justified their cost by providing the benchmarking and trend information that spark the interest and inquiry of policy makers and researchers. The challenge in the future will be to find more streamlined ways to measure these key benchmarks and maintain trends lines, but also to consider the possibility of integrating large-scale assessment with more diagnostic approaches.

Finally, at the other end of the continuum of assessment challenges is to be increasingly creative and innovative with respect to analysis in order to get the most we can out of the data that have been collected. Admittedly, because the focus is so heavily weighted toward development and operations to ensure that resulting data will be trustworthy, it is not uncommon to run out of time and money before this stage, and in-depth analyses are left for independent research that may or may not receive wide attention. In PISA in recent years there has been an attempt to support additional analyses on policy topics of interest and additional funding streams have been secured. However, we should also heed the advice given in Chapter 10, that it is not simply that we need to do more analysis but that we need to think more creatively about how to do it. Murat and Rocher offer several examples in this regard.

While the challenges for assessment are great, the demand is even greater. As many systems are moving to accountability-based practices, developing appropriate assessment technologies from the classroom level to the international level is imperative. Taking up the challenges that I have described, as well as others outlined in this volume – such as expanding the cultural and linguistic traditions from which test material is drawn, as described by Lafontaine and Murray in their respective chapters, or expanding the standard tools for analysis with multi-level modelling techniques, as described by Bosker and Snijders, or allowing the difficulties in making comparisons across countries to become the tool for deeper understanding of cross-system differences, as Leimu demonstrates – are our important next steps.

Index

Page numbers in italics denote figures, tables or boxes